Jouissance as Ānanda

Jouissance as Ānanda

Indian Philosophy, Feminist Theory, and Literature

Ashmita Khasnabish

LEXINGTON BOOKS

A division of
ROWMAN & LITTLEFIELD PUBLISHERS, INC.
Lanham • Boulder • New York • Toronto • Oxford

LEXINGTON BOOKS

A division of Rowman & Littlefield Publishers, Inc.
A wholly owned subsidary of The Rowman & Littlefield Publishing Group, Inc.
4501 Forbes Boulevard, Suite 200
Lanham, MD 20706

PO Box 317
Oxford
OX2 9RU, UK

British Library Cataloguing in Publication Information Available

The hardback edition of this book was previously cataloged by the Library of Congress
as follows:

Khasnabish, Ashmita, 1959–
    Jouissance as ānanda / consciousness / Ashmita Khasnabish.
      p. cm.
    Includes bibliographical references (p.) and index.
      1. Psychoanalysis. I. Title.

BF173.K427 2003
150.19'5—dc21   2003040094

    ISBN-13: 978-0-7391-5 (cloth : alk. paper)
    ISBN-10: 0-7391-0467-5 (cloth : alk. paper)
    ISBN-13: 978-0-7391-1673-9 (pbk. : alk. paper)
    ISBN-10: 0-7391-1673-8 (pbk. : alk. paper)

Printed in the United States of America

⊗™ The paper used in this publication meets the minimum requirements of American
National Standard for Information Sciences—Permanence of Paper for Printed Library
Materials, ANSI/NISO Z39.48-1992.

For my mother and my two daughters, Inrava and Srijesa

Contents

Acknowledgments

The ambience of The Pembroke Center for Study and Research on Women at Brown University provided the inspiration for this book. I owe special thanks to the participants of the 1996–1997 seminar and also to the 1998–1999 seminar, where the earlier versions of some of my chapters were presented. The book would not have materialized without the constant encouragement and intellectual support of Professor Paget Henry of Brown University. My greatest thanks go to him for reading both the earlier and current versions of the text. My warmest thanks go to Professor Teresa Brennan, of Florida Atlantic University, who inspired me to write a significant chapter of this book and provided impetus for completion of the book. I thank Professor Ellen Rooney of Brown University and Professor Alice A. Jardine of Harvard University for reading an earlier version of the manuscript. I warmly thank Professor Elizabeth Weed, of Brown University, who has generously offered me the affiliation with The Pembroke Center as a Visiting Scholar for the past few years.

Finally, I thank my husband and my two daughters who constantly inspired me to write. I owe special thanks to my father who blessed me for this book, my mother who sent me abroad for higher studies, and my sister for her constant encouragement.

Preface

I forgot to write a preface for the first publication of the book. Therefore, I take this chance to mend it. The book is about feminist theory, and also about love and politics. I never openly addressed in any of the chapters of the book that theory of jouissance as *ānanda* could work for not only literary theory, but maintain peace and harmony. In one of my recent interviews with one of the students at Evergreen College, I was asked this question one more time— the implication of the term jouissance. I mentioned the word "harmony," although it is not exactly the literal translation of the term. What I meant is this. Harmony means concord. Jouissance with its corporeal and spiritual aspects can help oneself to keep an inner harmony, which also helps resolve the mind-body divide. This harmony is also related to cosmic harmony. I cannot help remembering the Indian Nobel laureate Rabindranath Tagore's poem, *"Viswasāthe joge jetāya bihar, seikhāne jog tomār sāthe āmāro"* (*Rabindrarachanabali* Vol. 4) (I am connected to the supreme consciousness where it intersects with the global and cosmic harmony).

With this book I traveled to many places, to disseminate its inner message. It was most warmly embraced by the feminists at the conference on "Women and The Divine," held at the University of Liverpool, London, where I was asked to present a talk on the book by Luce Irigaray herself, whose work I still adore. Another place where the book drew attention was in India. At my book talk for my old abode, the Asiatic Society, Kolkata, India (where I worked as a research scholar before I came abroad), I was complimented on how well I connected an intellectual postmodern theory with the divine. I was also asked a very important question about the theoretical hiatus between Lacan and Irigaray. Likewise, in my book talks at various universities in the USA I was asked similar questions about the theoretical underpinning of the book—about how Luce Irigaray's theory of jouissance, Sri Aurobindo's theory of supramental consciousness, and my interpretation of *ānanda* could be used and cultivated in real life. Voilà, there you go! It is all about it. It addresses both theory and praxis. It is about attaining the supreme form of consciousness beyond the ego, cultivating Sri Aurobindo's theory of supramental consciousness through meditation on how to control one's ego or the vital energy, and how to transform the vital into psychic power. My realization is that Sri Aurobindo does not limit his *sādhanā* of supramental consciousness to the practice of yoga, but the mind control is based on one's knowledge about supreme consciousness and the urgency to attain it as well. It combines philosophy with psychoanalysis. Thus, Sri Aurobindo's theory is based on the ascent and the descent: one has to attain that supreme level of consciousness, but it has to be brought down and manifested on the earth. Likewise, Luce Irigaray constantly harps on bringing the matter and the spirit together; if the spirit is not brought onto the matter, no transformation is possible. Her theory of sexual difference and jouissance is based on bringing the spirit onto the female body to help them gain parity with men. The theory of sexual difference when properly established on the earth shall point towards the truth that the mind-body divide could be solved. Likewise, Sri Aurobindo's theory shall bring down peace and harmony on the earth proving again the material possibility of the spiritual matter.

I also want to pay special homage to the memory of Teresa Brennan whose theory of "energetic connection" and "original logic" added an extra vigor to the theories proposed in this book. The theory of original logic being connected with her theory of energy is solely devoted to decolonize the master-slave dialectic in the ego's era by retrieving the connection to nature and the mother. The book shows her to be very Oriental (Indian) by connecting her theory to the Upaniṣhadic theory of Brahman.

I hope all the theoretical chapters continue to contribute to the discourse of feminist postcolonial and postmodern theories. The chapters on literature add contributions to literary theories related to modern and postcolonial texts. This book will be able to cater to different disciplines from psychoanalysis and feminist theory to literature (modern and postcolonial) and Indian philosophy. Postcolonial literature and theory that originate through cross-cultural discussion is a very important facet of the book.

I want to end by invoking the appeal of peace and harmony in the book which I did not address explicitly. The terms "jouissance" and *ānanda* and the way I interpret the connection as the dissolution of the ego or "ego-transcendence" strives to reach a realm which is beyond chaos and cacophony. Thus, the implication of the book goes beyond theory and literature—it stands for confluence of diverse opinions—a meeting ground, which is both immanent and transcendent.

The book is also a great deal about love—love achieved through ego-transcendence, through the theory of sexual difference, and through *ānanda*. Love that makes the entire world one's own as it is said in ancient Sanskrit sloka, "*Basudhā eb kutumbakama*" (the entire world is my close relations); love that creates harmony, a cosmic harmony.

I end chanting my allegiance to Serena my publisher who made this dream come true and to Katie as well for helping the manifestation of it and to my little daughter Srijesa who thought that the author's letter is missing in the first imprint.

Part I: Theory

Chapter 1

Jouissance as Ānanda (Bliss)

Āndhādhev Khalmimāni Bhutāni Jāyante. (*Taitteriya Upaniṣad*
59)
(*Ānanda* or Bliss is the source of Existence.[1])
Rasa Bai Sah. (*Taitteriya Upaniṣad*45)
(Aesthetic pleasure is identical with Bliss or *Ānanda*.)

The book undertakes a cross-cultural analysis to configure the
meaning, underpinnings and the parameters of the Western
psychoanalytic term jouissance. The Western psychoanalysts I
focus on are Freud, Lacan and Irigaray. I dwell on Freud, critically
examine the limitation of the theory of the "ego," and introduce
Lacan as advancing Freud's theory of the ego. Nonetheless, I still
question the adequacy in Lacan's concept of the Real which almost
aspires to the transcendence of ego, but does not fully achieve it. In
this spiritual journey towards the transcendence of ego, I find Luce
Irigaray's theory of jouissance most in sync with the
Oriental/Indian theory of the conquering of ego, which is
expressed through the word, *ānanda.* The book does not stop
inquiring merely at the advancement of Irigaray's theory of
jouissance over Lacan; it also offers a rereading of Irigaray's
theory of jouissance from the Indian cross-cultural psychoanalytic
point of view. Now, the question remains why do I undertake this
study? Why is it important to bring in the cross-cultural
interpretation of the theory of jouissance as *ānanda*? My entire
book addresses this question—the importance of the translation of
the theory of jouissance as *ānanda.*

The literal meaning of *ānanda* could be translated as bliss or
joy but it is far more complex than that. It conveys not only simple
joy but transcendental joy and this transcendental happiness is

grounded in the material world and thus these empirical and transcendental worlds are closely related. The theory of *ānanda* also suggests that when the unification between the material and the transcendental world take place, the ego could be transcended. Analogous to this theory of *ānanda* Irigaray's theory of jouissance encompasses both the material and transcendental dimensions and reconfigures the Lacanian definition of jouissance as the female jouissance. But, I would like to show that in spite of certain kinds of advancements over the theory of Lacan, Irigaray's theory of jouissance still needs revision. And, it is at this juncture that the Indian philosophical concept of *ānanda* arises.

Lacan's concept of the Real underscores the truth that he believed in a transcendental dimension which might have helped balance the ego if he had had full trust in it. But, he did not attribute supreme agency to the Real because, according to Lacan symbolization and the symbolic plane override any other order. The Real is something which cannot be symbolized—and since the Real cannot be symbolized—the Real loses its status. Thus, we can conclude that the symbolic alienates the Real. If the Real could have been given full agency the ego could have been released through the meditation of the sublime. But, opposed to that, what happens is that the ego is trapped between the imaginary and the symbolic orders in the Lacanian theory of psychoanalysis. In opposition, Irigaray's theory is a great contribution because of the underlying concept of the divine in jouissance. Now it is not clear if this concept of the divine in jouissance liberates the ego and addresses the issue of transformation of society.

I valorize Irigaray's theory of jouissance because it incorporated the sublime dimension and as such advanced beyond the limitations of Western psychoanalytical theories of Freud and Lacan. Still it needs to address what happens when women are established in the symbolic plane, but it does not address to the full extent the dissolution of the ego, which I try to resolve by introducing an Indian psychoanalytical/philosophical context. Nonetheless, I attribute special significance to Irigaray's theory of jouissance and divine for opening a discursive space for a cross-cultural dialogue. Thus, the book undertakes two basic questions: if Irigaray's theory of jouissance resolves the problem of establishing women in the symbolic plane, and once established in the symbolic plane could women and men transcend the ego? In order to answer the first question, I delve into Irigaray's theory; to address the second query I probe Indian philosophy / psycho-analysis.

Jouissance as Fulfillment

The French feminist Luce Irigaray's theory of jouissance could be explained as an ethics of fulfillment (is my term)—or in Irigaray's own words as an ethics of "sexual difference." It is difficult to translate this into different cultural terminology. The moment the term "sexual difference" is uttered—one must remember the long history of French feminist theory and all the discussions related to it in which both the female body and the female mind are foregrounded. As opposed to the gender theorists, who ascribe importance only to social factors, the "sexual difference" theorists take into account psychic factors in women's lives that are necessary for a change to an egalitarian society. Without the change at the psychic level the social change is not possible. The transformation has to occur from within. Thus, Irigaray offers the ethics of "sexual difference" in her book *An Ethics of Sexual Difference*. This book is about both genders and about how the male and the female could live harmoniously—and how women's psychic status needs to be upgraded and uplifted so that women could operate at the same level with men and not marginalized. This she shows could be materialized through her theory of "female jouissance" which makes this ethics of "sexual difference" possible:

> A certain representation of feminine jouissance corresponds to this water flowing without a container. A doubling, sought after by man, of a female placelessness. She is assigned to be placed without occupying a place. Through her place would be whatever is in that she is when she contains, contains herself. "Wine," perhaps that man might spill out in sexual act? Elixir of ambrosia, and of place itself. Is there some jouissance other than that of place? Is this not the jouissance which goes from the most elementary to the most subtle? From in utero to heaven, from earth to heaven, from hell to heaven and so on. (*An Ethics of Sexual Difference* 52)

I am embarked here to enunciate the truth that Luce Irigaray's theory of jouissance is about an ethics of "Love" and about fulfillment. On the one hand it intersects with or is grounded in psychoanalysis, on the other hand, it goes beyond psychoanalysis or a rereading of psychoanalysis from a feminist perspective. From that point of view, we could define her use of psychoanalysis as being grounded in the feminist theory of "sexual difference." Her ethics of "sexual difference" thus is situated on the cusp of psychoanalysis and feminism. My argument is supported by Margaret Whitford and Teresa Brennan's remarks that it is high time to see different horizons of psychoanalytic thinking, and, going beyond that and Irigaray attempts to do that, and by using Irigaray's theory of jouissance I am attempting to do that as a postcolonial feminist gesture. However, in the first section of this chapter, I would like to limit my discussion to Irigaray's theory of jouissance.

The female jouissance has been defined in her book *Speculum*, written prior to her book *An Ethics of Sexual Difference*. But in *Ethics*, Irigaray is engaged in a more detailed enunciation of her theory of jouissance for the fulfillment in love, or as a modus operandi for the ethics of love or sexual difference to take place. The chapter called, "Place, Interval" tries to prove her theory that female jouissance has not been acknowledged so far and has been reduced to having no identity since it is actually fluid in nature. The female jouissance is subtle and it moves from utero to heaven and it is some energy or power which will actually give a place to the placelessness of women. Thus far women have been assigned a place without occupying a place and, "Her jouissance is meant to resemble the flow of whatever is in the place that she is when she contains, contains herself"(52). Instead, Irigaray tries to assign women a place of their own through female jouissance which runs from utero to heaven, or from earth to heaven and heaven to hell.

The Theory of Jouissance as Grounded in The Theory of Love
Luce Irigaray offers her own theory or her ethics of love which is based on a rereading of Western philosophers like Aristotle, Descartes, Levinas and plus the psychoanalysis of Freud. She tries to do so via her theory of jouissance. What is the connection between jouissance and love? According to Irigaray it is the female

jouissance which makes the perfect relationship between men and women or lovers of opposite sexes possible. The female jouissance which Irigaray defines as ranging from the corporeal to the spiritual needs to be understood through her theory of love, sexual difference, and sensible transcendental. Irigaray, in developing her theory of "sexual difference," uses the concept of carnal love, or carnal ethics and amorous exchange. "Carnal love" or "carnal ethics" advocates a kind of love, which acknowledges both male and female partners. It is in which their union takes place without one partner consuming the other. There is always an irreducible difference between them.

> Love is the vehicle which permits the passage between, the passage to and fro between sensible and intelligible, mortal and immortal, above and below, immanent and transcendent. Instead of an abyss, or an enclosure which defines an inside and an outside, there should be a threshold, and the possibility of permanent passage in and out, to and fro, from the highest to the lowest, and back again. Men are said to achieve this through the rhythm of the fort-da. Women too need to move freely, they need an axis which grounds them in the earth and connects them to the heavens. (Margaret Whitford 164)

The female jouissance would make that kind of love possible by ascribing to women freedom and a kind of mobility or fluidity, by virtue of which they could build a relationship with their partner in which they would be valued as both matter and spirit, as having flesh and soul, having both 'sensible' and 'transcendental' as part of their femininity. It would be possible only if women have their jouissance, own jouissance, which they could feel through different parts of their body—and then connect it to their inner heart, and undertake the upward journey necessary for their survival. This female jouissance "which would be of the order of the constant and gradual creation of a dimension ranging from the most corporeal to the most celestial," seems to be located not in women's unconscious but in the conscious mind or heart. There is another important dimension to this kind of love or jouissance—this love is independent of any child, or procreation. It takes place between the persons of two opposite sexes in which "that ecstasy of our self in us, that transcendence of the flesh of one to that of the other become our self in us, at any rate 'in me' as a woman, prior to any child." Thus, another important dimension of this jouissance is to liberate women from being tied to the role of mothers. This joy is independent of motherhood and is an emblem of a woman's existence as a woman, in which her lover looks at her for what she is.

Jouissance as both Corporeal and Spiritual
In *Irigaray Reader* edited by Margaret Whitford, Irigaray suggests:

> Female jouissance would be of the order of the constant and gradual creation of a dimension ranging from the most corporeal to the most spiritual, a dimension which is never complete and never reversible. Before, or in a different way to, any procreation of a child, woman generates through her jouissance, not, as they say or fear, a 'hole,' but a passage or a bridge between what is most earthly and what is most celestial (there are figurative examples of this: the rainbow of the goddess Isis, for example). Women's dissatisfaction, their so-called hysterical symptomatology, no doubt stems from this perpetual deferment of jouissance which is theirs, where they might find themselves, or find themselves anew, as subjects, where they would no longer wander and beg, for lack of a continuity, of a possible temporalization responsible with respect to their eroticism, their love. Does that make them superior to men? Why think in quantitative terms? They are different. And so jouissance (and not only children) is produced inside them, takes place more in their interior, in their innermost heart, whatever the complexity of its spatial trajectories. (190-91)

That jouissance ranges from corporeal to celestial dimension has been reiterated in the *Speculum* as well. In regard to corporeal jouissance one must refer to Irigaray's extensive discussion of it in the "volume-fluidity" chapter of *Speculum* in which "corporeal jouissance" has been inscribed to be represented through the multiple sexuality of the female body. But, here one must not forget the other part of Irigaray's statement that jouissance ranges from the corporeal to the celestial: means one is dependent on the other and corporeal jouissance is incomplete without its spiritual part of it. But, her main point is that male jouissance has been symbolized and female jouissance has not been symbolized yet. Therefore she insists on the term female jouissance. That does not mean that she excludes men from the ethics of "sexual difference" or the ethics of fulfillment. The change that she envisions occurring through her theory of jouissance includes men and women—one is incomplete without the other. She had already suggested that one should not think quantitatively, but rather in terms of the ultimate transformation of society.

One must not misunderstand Irigaray's theory of jouissance as overtly tilted towards women. I think she does advance the Western psychoanalytic theory a great deal by envisioning a framework which is highly transcendental and thus transcends the limitations of the binary opposition between the imaginary and the symbolic planes. Her theory envisions a neutral framework through which men and women could relate to each other through love and alliance—where neither the male nor the female partner needs to look at the other as a competitor. So, she invokes female jouissance to envision that kind of liberal ambience—which transcends the phallus—but does not undermine it, and creates a new dimension that had not yet been thought of by Western psychoanalysis. It must also be mentioned here that sometimes she uses the term jouissance and sometimes she refers to it as female jouissance, and both stand for the concept of infinity which women need to contribute to create the harmonious framework. In the section that follows, I discuss Irigaray's theory of jouissance via the concept of her fluidity, transcendence/divine, and through her concept of "wonder" as discussed in her books.

In the chapter entitled "Place, Interval" Irigaray draws our attention to the fact that women's position is divided into two categories, "on the one hand, she is habitually devalued in relation to the fluid; on the other hand, she is valued in relation to the solid" (52). Obviously, assessing her importance via child means assessing her for utilitarian purpose (my term)—a solidity which deprives her of her subtlest part. This subtlest part is diffused without being noticed and this subtlest part of her is the site of her jouissance—the jouissance of possibility which turns her lack or unconscious into consciousness or the symbolic. The problematic is that the subtlest part or the spiritual aspect of women's identity is being neglected. Irigaray wants to foreground this sublime part in women's identity which is so badly neglected in Western culture. Thus she ascribes sublimity to women's sexual identity or enriches women's sexuality through spirituality which thereby makes the passage from earth to heaven and vice versa. She locates the subtlest part of women as the place for the production of intimacy and a 'transmutation of earth into heaven.' In this regard, I consider the following observation crucial: "An alchemist of the sexual and one who tries to keep the sexual away from repetition, degradation. Attempts to keep it and sublimate it" (53). The focus is on sublimation—sublimation of sexuality by keeping it sexual at the same time.

Jouissance as Transcendence

The discussion of Luce Irigaray's theory of the "female jouissance" would further be portrayed in a more authentic way via its connection with the theme of transcendence. Irigaray is primarily engaged to foreground the element of sublimity or transcendence at the first place and then to use that element of transcendence for opening a new horizon for women. In her article "Divine Women" in her book *Sexes and Genealogies*, in *Speculum*, in *Marine Lover*, in *Ethics*, Irigaray reiterates the importance and urgency of the new horizon of transcendence for women's liberation. She dismantles the roots of not only Western philosophy, Western psychoanalysis and culture, but theology as well. She suggests, "And however many seeds may lie dormant in religious texts, invariably the mature organism grows in the direction of God the Father and not of a goddess or woman, mother and woman" (68). For fulfillment in love—the condition is the state of transcendence which will allow themselves to love themselves, "A transcendental which leaves them free to embrace the maternal while giving them back their childhood at the same time" (69). In the chapter "Love of Self" she clearly states how damaging this state of placelessness has been for women. Psychoanalysis has not thought about these categories except as pathological symptoms, "It is left in the shadow of the pre-object, and in the suffering and abandonment of the fusional state which fails to emerge as a subject" (70). She has always been a space in relation to 'man, child, housework, cooking,' and 'Not by the woman herself for herself' (70). Thus, the transcendental dimension is about exploring this inner space within women.

Irigaray further explicates this dimension of transcendence as a vertical dimension, since what is vertical is always associated with man and what is horizontal with women—but this order needs to be reconfigured since women need both horizontal and vertical dimensions. Women have been deprived of this vertical/ transcendental dimension and the bond between mother and daughter, daughter and mother has always been ripped, for the daughter to become a woman. Irigaray's comment is, "Female genealogy has to be suppressed, on behalf of the son-Father relationship, and the idealization of father and husband as patriarchs" (108). But, the important question is this new vertical/transcendental dimension needs to be explored and brought together with the horizontal dimension that has already been assigned to women, to explore their own 'symbols, laws, and gods.' So, women cannot remain satisfied with the horizontal dimension and work towards this transcendence. Her connection with this transcendence is what "female jouissance" would inspire women to achieve.

Jouissance and the Concept of "Wonder"

This section discusses how this transcendental dimension would help women to achieve fulfillment in love between partners of the opposite sexes. I see this happening through an analysis of Irigaray's four chapters "Wonder," "The Envelope: A Reading of Spinoza, Ethics," "of God," and "Fecundity of Caress" in *Ethics* in which she is rereading three philosophers: Descartes, Spinoza and Levinas. As I have argued in the previous section, the main focus is on the element of transcendence which will make the complementarity of a male-female relationship possible. One could call it the way Irigaray has expressed it at times in her text as "divine," one could call it "spiritual jouissance," one could call it "vertical dimension," or even the "horizon of accomplishment." By saying this, let me return to the chapter, "Wonder" and quote from it a very useful observation in this regard:

A birth into a transcendence, that of the other, still in the world of the senses ("sensible") still physical and carnal, and already spiritual. Wonder would be the passion of the encounter between the most material and the most metaphysical, of their possible conception and fecundation one by the other. A third dimension. An intermediary. Neither the one nor the other. Which is not to say neuter or neutral. The forgotten ground of our condition between mortal and immortal, men and gods, creatures and creators. In us and among us. (82)

Through her rereading of Descartes' theory of wonder Irigaray tries to foreground her own theory of the ethics of love according to which Descartes' theory of wonder should be extended to the sphere of love rather than being confined to the realm of art. "Wonder" does have this infinite power of "jouissance" which can create the liaison between the terrestrial and the transcendental world once it is there between lovers. "Wonder" could create that third dimension which Diotima's theory of Eros could have done if it had not been interrupted by her theory of procreation. "Wonder" the way Irigaray wants to apply it between lovers has the angelic power of making relationships of perfect love possible between lovers by making it flow from the corporeal to the transcendental.

Can Wonder Displace Slavery of the Ego?
In this section, I examine how Irigaray's theory of "female jouissance" which is a radical theory challenging the foundation of Western psychoanalysis, remains to be reread via a cross-cultural theory of *ānanda*. Why this lacunae in Irigaray's theory? The lacunae starts perhaps with the problem of articulation. Irigaray's theory of "wonder" as it is grounded in the feminist theory of "sexual difference" is very radical indeed, suggesting that the world will be a better place to live in, when women are established on the symbolic plane with men. The theory of "wonder" is a unique discovery and an excellent rereading of Descartes' theory of wonder. Perhaps through this theory of wonder Irigaray attempts to achieve a balance of the ego. When men and women admire and adore each other based on alliance and "wonder," the phallic structure dissipates, dissolving the working of the ego. The kind of relationship Irigaray invokes with God in *Speculum of the Other Woman*, she tries to replicate with lover/partner as well—in which ego is completely silenced. In "La Mysterique" (in *Speculum of the*

Other Woman) Irigaray talks about the divine love which could save women, in a way reminiscent of the Hindu religious love for the divine. In *Speculum of the Other Woman* Irigaray discusses this kind of union with God as follows: "Each becomes the other in consumption, the nothing of the other in consummation [. . .]. Thus I am to you as you are to me, mine is yours and yours mine, I know you as you know me, you take pleasure with me as with you I take pleasure in the rejoicing of this reciprocal living—and identifying-together" (196). Her ethics of sexual difference invokes this kind of love, in which one partner does not consume the other, and there is always a residue.[2] So, Irigaray's theory of "wonder" suggests a silencing of the ego. Let me finish my discussion on "wonder" and as such silencing of the ego by her observation in "Sexual Difference" in *The Irigaray Reader*:

> This has never happened between the sexes. Wonder might allow them to retain an autonomy based on their difference, and give them a space of freedom or attraction. a possibility of separation or alliance. All this would happen before becoming engaged, during their first encounter, which would confirm their difference. The interval would never be crossed. There would be no consummation. Such an idea is a delusion. One sex is never entirely consumed or consummated by another. There is always a residue. (172)

The key expression of the theory of "wonder" is that one partner does not consume the other. The emphasis is not on consummation, but on the interval based on their difference. There will always be a residue, through which they could both communicate with each other and keep each other empowered with inner strength, without completely yielding to the other person. Thus, we might argue that probably that space Irigaray configures as a zone in which both partners could strive to transcend their ego.

On Silence

However, Irigaray's latest book entitled, *To Be Two* alludes to silence, Yoga, and invokes the relationship between partners, not just based on "wonder" but "silence." In a unique way Irigaray inscribes the glory and the conquering power of silence. Irigaray thus writes in this book,

> This culture of silence can be rediscovered in two ways:
> One is that of Buddha and the yogin and yogini. It is a cultivation of silence in relationship with nature, with one's own body and sometimes with the other, but in a master-disciple relationship ultimately to be left behind in favor of a culture of silence.
> … …
> There is another way to protect silence. It can, perhaps, be faithful to and interwoven with the memory of a culture of life which we have erased. This other way is found in the respect and love between man and woman, in a practice of sexual difference which exists between the two genders.
>
> As I have already mentioned, the difference is there. It does not have to be created from nothing. We need merely be attentive to what already exists: an insuperable silence between man and woman, subjects who are irreducible to each other. (63-65)

It is quite amazing to see the way Irigaray praises silence linking it to yoga, an oriental practice. What Irigaray suggests is that through inculcating silence a harmonious relationship could be established between men and women. Irigaray proposes to use "silence" to dismantle the power relationship between men and women, as she thinks that "silence: leads to self-fulfillment and happiness." As she writes in the same book, "Only the cultivation of the breath, of the capacity to hold the breath in oneself, corresponds to the path of self-fulfillment and happiness" (64). It seems that Irigaray advances on her theory of "wonder" via her insertion of this concept of silence, which works probably better for the dissolution of "ego," although she does not explicitly state that. But, her theories of "wonder" and "silence" definitely leave the nuances that Irigaray is working towards the configuration of the dissolution of the Western "ego" through her ongoing theories. However, coming from an Indian Hindu philosophical background, I offer a rereading of Irigaray's theory from the Indian cultural/psychoanalytical/philosophical concept of *ānanda*. My hope is that this cross-cultural dialogue would enrich the Western theory of jouissance which is now inscribed in a partial way. In order to valorize Irigaray's theory, I introduce the modern Indian philosopher Sri Aurobindo's theory of "supramental consciousness" which complements Irigaray's theory of jouissance by its two basic principles: dissolution of the ego and undoing of the body-mind divide which are conditions for the materialization of jouissance and *ānanda*.

Unlike Freud and Lacan, Sri Aurobindo observes, "Man, because he has acquired reason and still more because he has indulged his power of imagination and intuition, is able to conceive an existence higher than his own, and even to envisage his personal elevation beyond his present state into that existence" (54). According to Sri Aurobindo, the state of "supermanhood" or the highest peak of human perfection is not only conceivable, but also achievable on earth. What then is the impediment to that supreme state? He identifies the stumbling block as the ego, and thus characterizes its limitation, "the nature of the ego is a self-limitation of consciousness by a willed ignorance of the rest of its play and its exclusive absorption in one form" (58). He interprets ego as the factor which determines the reactions unleashed by error, sorrow, pain, evil and death. Ego assigns negative values to movements that otherwise could be represented in their right relation to the "one Existence, Bliss, Truth and Good."

As Sri Aurobindo posits ego as "the limited ego" and as an intermediate phase for the development of human consciousness, his theory dismantles the Freudian concept. The ego is one step to the state of ultimate bliss. How does the dissolution of the ego—necessary to achieving the final state—take place? It occurs when one concentrates on Brahman or the concept of the Pure Absolute as inscribed in ancient Vedanta philosophy. In a chapter entitled "The Ego and the Dualities," in his *Life Divine*, Sri Aurobindo concludes:

> We have the dissolution of this egoistic construction by the self-opening of the individual to the universe and to God as the means of that supreme fulfillment to which egoistic life is only a prelude even as animal life was only a prelude to the human. We have the realization of the All in the individual by the transformation of the limited ego into a conscious center of the

divine unity and freedom as the term at which the fulfillment
arrives. (59)

Such fulfillment is also defined as *ānanda* or bliss later in *The Life
Divine* and in many of his other philosophical texts. Thus when I
discuss "*ānanda*" in my book and when I inscribe jouissance as
ānanda, I introduce a connection between Irigaray's theory of the
female jouissance and Sri Aurobindo's theory of the divine.

The book is designed in two parts: "Jouissance in Theory," and
"Jouissance in Literature." Part One contains five chapters, with
the first chapter providing a theoretical foundation in its discussion
of Irigaray's theory of "female jouissance" from the French
feminist perspective, and of the concept of *ānanda* via ancient and
modern Indian philosophy. Part two, "Jouissance in Literature"
moves from theory to praxis. Here I apply the several theories of
jouissance in literary textual analysis.

Thus, the book embraces theory and philosophy as well as
literature, and explores how one illuminates the other. Section One
is engaged in a theoretical discussion of jouissance through
Irigaray (as constructed on Freud and Lacan), from the West and in
a cross-cultural and global context through India in the East.
Section two explicates via colonial and postcolonial literature, East
and West, the central message of the book—which is jouissance
both as fulfillment and *ānanda*.

NOTES

1. Unless otherwise noted, all translations are my own.

2. For more information on the theory of "sexual difference" see Margaret Whitford, ed., *The Irigaray Reader* (Cambridge, Massachusetts: Basil Blackwell Inc., 1991) pp.165-77.

Chapter 2

Rādhā's Jouissance[*]

> The/a woman cannot be collected into one volume, for in that way she risks surrendering her own jouissance, which demands that she remain open to nothing utterable but which assures that her edges not close, her lips not be sewn shut. (*Speculum of the Other Woman* 240)

Rādhikā or Rādhā is both a goddess and an ordinary woman[1] and the two distinctive features of being both a goddess and a woman make her the favorite heroine of most women in India. That she is both the human partner and the divine consort to Lord Kṛṣṇa permits me, a postcolonial feminist, to perceive her through "jouissance," as the theory of jouissance is posited by Luce Irigaray. But my essay is more complex. It is an attempt to translate jouissance in terms of the Indian notions of *ānanda* and *prema,* which I offer as a postcolonial gesture to psychoanalysis, as I look at Rādhā through *ānanda* and *prema.*

Jouissance has been inscribed so far according to the norm of Western phallocratic discourse. Luce Irigaray's theory of the female jouissance is revolutionary in this regard. It foregrounds the divinity of the female body and gives women a new definition. Irigaray's theory of female jouissance, which has a celestial dimension to it, can be related to the Indian notion of the *ānanda,* "supramental consciousness" and *prema,* love both as immanent and transcendent. The psychoanalyst Lacan, as well as psycho-analysis in general, overlooks the naked truth that they are still promoting the role of the Father;[2] what Luce Irigaray tries to do is to reinscribe the divine.[3] Whereas Lacan associates God with supplementary jouissance in women or the absence of God as women's vagina hidden, Irigaray perceives that the concept of God, or God, is the only one who can save women.[4] To me

*An earlier version of this chapter was presented during the 1996-1997 seminar (The Future of Gender) at the Pembroke Center for Study and Research on Women, Brown University, Providence, RI, USA. Unless otherwise noted, all translations are my own

Irigaray uses the concept of God and jouissance to give women whatever they need and whatever is not given to them by the so-called patriarchy, which is always already constructed for women. In "La Mysterique" (in *Speculum of the Other Woman*) Irigaray defines divine love, which could save women in a way reminiscent of the Hindu religious love for the divine. The modern Indian poet Rabindranath Tagore's work *Gitanjali* contains poems and songs, which refer to this kind of loving bondage with the divine. The theme of all the songs is the total identification with God in surrender, love and giving, and vice versa. In *Speculum of the Other Woman* Irigaray foregrounds a similar type of union with God as follows, "Each becomes the other in consumption, the nothing of the other in consummation. [. . .] Thus I am to you as you are to me, mine is yours and yours mine, I know you as you know me, you take pleasure with me as with you I take pleasure in the rejoicing of this reciprocal living—and identifying-together" (196).

Luce Irigaray's ethics of sexual difference invokes this kind of love, in which one partner does not consume the other, and there is always a residue.[5] She uses the relationship between God and women as prototype for the relationship between men and women. But she refers to God in purely religious terms, and critiques the Western logocentric culture, according to which there is only God, and no Goddess. She suggests: "Man is able to exist because God helps him to define his gender (genre), helps him orient his finiteness by reference to infinity. The revival of religious feeling can in fact be interpreted as the rampart man raises in defense of his very maleness" ("Divine Women" 61). So, women need the help of infinity to measure their finiteness and Irigaray provides this through her theory of female jouissance.

There are two parts to this chapter: in the first part, I justify Irigaray's theory of the divine and jouissance and interpret it from the Indian cross-cultural perspective as *ānanda*. In the second part, I discuss Rādhā, the Indian Goddess, and the love-relation between Rādhā and Kṛṣṇa in light of Irigaray's theory of jouissance by showing the resemblance between Irigaray's theory of jouissance and the interpretation of that term in Bengali as *ānanda* (meaning bliss) and *prema* (meaning love as both corporeal and celestial).

Jouissance and Ānanda

Irigaray's theory of female jouissance could be inscribed from the cross-cultural Indian perspective as *ānanda*. It means pleasure, joy, bliss, or ecstasy. I start with the Sanskrit śloka: *"Madhu vātā ṛtāyate, madhu kṣaranti sindhavaḥ*: [. . .] *madhumat pārthivam rajaḥ* [. . .]. *"(Brihadaranyaka Upaniṣad* 318). The entire śloka symbolically means that the air is full of joy—the ocean is full of joy—the entire earth is full of joy. There are many similar expressions in *Upaniṣads* and one of the most significant ślokas is the following: *"anāndhādhyeva khalvimani bhūtāni jayante,"* (*Taiteriya Upaniṣad* 313) that *ānanda*, joy or bliss is the source of all being. In this regard, I would also like to refer to the poems of Rabindranath Tagore in Bengali: *"ānanda dhārā bahiche bhūbane,"* (*Māyār Khelā* 185) (the world is flooded with waves of joy) or *"ānanderi sāgar hate aseche āj bān"* (*Māyār Khelā* 283) (that joy overflows and the flood has come from the ocean of joy). Thus, the theme of all these songs is that a stream of joy flows over the world and there is an overflow of the flood of joy. This *ānanda* could be equated with a spiritual joy or divine bliss, which is in harmony with the Ultimate Reality. Sudhir Kakar points out that the relation between self and other, considered crucially important in the Western world, is considered as *maya* or illusion in the East (India). The ultimate goal of life is to achieve the Ultimate Reality, which could be inscribed as *ānanda*, "joy" or "bliss." Sri Aurobindo, one of the modern philosophers of India has redefined this *ānanda* as "supramental bliss" or "supramental conscious-ness." He writes:

> An aspiration, a demand for the supreme and total delight of existence is there secretly in the whole make of our being. In the body-consciousness this demand takes shape as a need of bodily happiness, in our life-parts as a yearning for life-happiness a keen vibrant response to joy and rapture of many kinds and to all surprise of satisfaction; in the mind it shapes into already reception of all forms of mental delight; on the higher level it becomes apparent in the spiritual mind's call for peace and divine ecstasy. This trend is found in the truth of the being; for Ananda is the very essence of the Brahman, it is the supreme nature of the omnipresent Reality. The Supermind itself in the descending degrees of the manifestation emerges from the

Ananda and in the evolutionary attempt merges into the ananda.
(*The Life Divine* 989-90)

Thus *ānanda*, or the demand for the supreme delight, is rooted in our being. Sri Aurobindo has divided our being into different parts: the body-consciousness, life-parts, mind and the higher level of the mind or the supermind. The *ānanda*, or the delight, could be felt through body, mind and higher mind and is the source of our being—once we have to set aside our ego or ignorance.

It is not possible to replicate exactly the imaginary and the symbolic orders of Hindu culture: the imaginary, which corresponds to the unconscious of the Western discourse, could be best represented in the Hindu culture as the unconscious, the "origin" and the "constitution" of which are not beyond sublimation. What Sri Aurobindo emphasizes is that *ānanda* could be present from the corporeal organs to the supermind. I find it very intriguing in terms of its connection to Irigaray's definition of female jouissance, which can be felt through the multiple sexuality of the female body and which could also range from the corporeal to the celestial. Irigaray does not banish man from her philosophy and ethics ("the genealogies of the two sexes need to be divinized"). The symbolic order is the order of consciousness (my term) because it is associated with language and the phallus. Now both Sri Aurobindo and Irigaray allude to the consciousness. Sri Aurobindo elucidates the ascent of the consciousness in terms of *ānanda* and Irigaray posits a new symbolic order or the order of consciousness, where women would be inscribed in symbolic order or the conscious world and not frozen into the imaginary.[6] The *ānanda* which is the source of our being, is the source of our pleasure or "jouissance."

Jouissance and Love

The best way to understand the connection between jouissance, *ānanda* and love would be to say that the *ānanda*, which is considered to be the source of life, could be approached through prema—love which is both immanent and transcendent.[7] In Hindu culture, the proper translation of Irigarayan definition of jouissance would be *prema*, in which, contrary to *kāma,* pleasure is always present in terms of *ānanda* but it is beyond procreation. However, it must be remembered here that the Hindu view of love is also expressed abundantly in terms of *kāma*.[8] As a matter of fact, the Hindu concept of marriage or sexual union is rooted in procreation. Panikkar writes:

> The Hindu view of sex differs fundamentally from that of most other civilizations. It is not only considered normal and necessary but almost sacramental. It is conceived as the human counterpart of creation and the religious symbolism of the Hindus emphasize this at all levels. It is the union of Purusha with Prakriti symbolised as the union of Shiva and Shakti, that is said to create the world. The symbol of Shiva is the lingam or phallus, the symbol of Shakti is the yoni. It is for this reason that every aspect of godhead in Hinduism is represented with a female counterpart. (Introduction; *Vātsayana's Kāmasutra* 21)

If pleasure is said to be related only to procreation, love cannot take place in terms of *ānanda*. In this regard, the relationship between Rādhā and Kṛṣṇa is unique and exceptional, in the sense that although they are consorts, Rādhā is not Kṛṣṇa's wife. They are thereby liberated from seeking pleasure through procreation. What I translate as the Hindu view of jouissance could be well represented through the relationship between Rādhā and Kṛṣṇa. I choose to portray Rādhā's jouissance in the light of Jayadeva's *Gitagovinda* (twelfth century). Therein Rādhā is portrayed as an independent heroine but their relationship is interdependent—one does not consume the other—rather they complement each other.[9] Although it has been argued by W. G. Archer that Jayadeva is prejudiced towards Kṛṣṇa, or that Kṛṣṇa dominates *Gitagovinda*, I would say that the union between Rādhā and Kṛṣṇa has been portrayed in a manner in which one does not dominate the other. On the contrary, it is based on mutual passion.

Amorous Exchange

The mutuality of their passion is best expressed through their lover's quarrels, or, in Irigarayan terms, through "amorous exchange." The Bengali word for amour is pīrītī, which alludes to the playfulness in love, which consists of different gestures, and different phases of love, and of the two partners quarrelling with each other and making up. Such a lover's quarrel starts in the

second part of *Gitagovinda,* entitled Careless Kṛṣṇa, in which
Rādhā imagines making love with Madhu's killer (Kṛṣṇa has a
hundred names and one of them is Madhu) because she is angry
and impatient while waiting for him. Keśī is the other name of
Kṛṣṇa, and addressing him Rādhā angrily expresses her desire for
Kṛṣṇa's foe. Here we see Rādhā as very strong, desperate and
audacious. According to the customary Hindu portrayals in the
tradition, women are expected to be quiet and submissive. But this
is debatable and we must not forget the ambivalent attitude
expressed toward women in Hindu society. On the one hand, we
have Draupadī of the *Mahābhārata* (who has five husbands), and
Jabālā of the *Upaniṣads*[10] On the other hand, we have Sītā of the
Rāmāyana, who was victimized by the patriarchal norms of
chastity. Rādhā is more like Draupadī than Sītā. Like Draupadī,
Rādhā is bold, aggressive and passionate and is capable of carrying
on a lover's quarrel. She does not give in, or withdraw like Sītā.
Rādhā, like Draupadī, knows how to fight back. The refrain of the
sixth song of the second part runs as follows: "Friend, bring Keśī's
sublime tormentor to revel with me! / I've gone mad waiting for
his fickle love to change" (Miller 80). In the above refrain,
Rādhā's desperation and anger are expressed; she is not inhibited
for a single moment by the fact that she is not married to Kṛṣṇa.
On the contrary, the relationship beyond marriage seems to give
her extra strength, power and claim over Kṛṣṇa. She could also
threaten him by making love with one of his foes. She imagines the
whole situation and visualizes how she would make love to
Kṛṣṇa's foe. She imagines that she would fall on the bed of tender
ferns and he (Madhu's foe) would lie on her breasts forever; she
would embrace him and kiss him and he would cling to her
drinking her lips. Rādhā teases Kṛṣṇa in order to draw his attention
to her. She also feels free to scold Kṛṣṇa and to duel with him, by
attributing his absence or delay to the presence of another woman
in his life. Love's quarrel, Rādhā's longing for Kṛṣṇa is intensified
in the eighth part of *Gitagovinda* called "Cunning Kṛṣṇa" where
Rādhā visualizes her rival and she tells her friend:

> She is richly arrayed in ornaments for the battle of love;
> Tangles of flowers lie wilted in her loosened hair.
> Some young voluptuous beauty

Revels with the enemy of Madhu.

Her body writhes with tingling flesh and trembling.
The ghost of love expands inside with her sighing.
Some young voluptuous beauty
Revels with the enemy of Madhu. (Miller 100)

But we need to read the subtext. Rādhā is so intensely angry and possessive of Kṛṣṇa that she is behaving in a fashion any jealous beloved would do, but it is this jealousy which gives her the attribute of being a human lover and not just a goddess. The lover's quarrel is best revealed in the character of Kṛṣṇa through his confession that his wanton ways made Rādhā leave him in anger. He describes that she saw him surrounded by women and left and he was too afraid and ashamed to stop her. In a refrain he soliloquizes, "Damn me! My wanton ways / Made her leave in anger" (Miller 82). Reminiscing about her beauty and his experience of love with her, he asks for her forgiveness, "Forgive me now! / I won't do this to you again! / Give me a vision, beautiful Rādhā!" (Miller 83). He implores the God of Love, *Kamadeva*, not to aim his bow at him. Kṛṣṇa uses the word "games" alluding to this lover's quarrel and confesses that Rādhā is victorious in this game of love: "Our games prove your triumph, Love" (Miller 84).[11]

Lovers' Longing for Each Other and Mutuality in "Sexual Difference"

Irigaray says in "Sexual Difference": "To arrive at the constitution of an ethics of sexual difference, we must at least return to what is for Descartes the first passion, wonder" (*Irigaray Reader* 171). Wonder or admiration is connected to female jouissance in the sense that because of her own feminine jouissance a woman is able to participate in the game of love, which is based on wonder, a game in which her male partner would look upon her with a sense of admiration and vice versa. In "The Passions of the Soul," Descartes elucidates this as, "the first of all the passions. It has no opposite, for, if the object before us has no characteristics that surprise us, we are not moved by it at all and we consider it without passion" (*Irigaray Reader* 170). Irigaray's comments that this passion has been reserved so far for the appreciation of art or even God, but has never been realized in any man-woman relationship. But a relationship based on wonder could make that love possible, in which each does not consume one another, and which always leaves a residue. This kind of love is said to be present in Kṛṣṇa's amorous relationship with Rādhā. None of the partners consume the other. Rādhā, keeps open the infinite possibilities of her jouissance constantly open by maintaining an amorous relationship with her partner, who is not her husband but her lover. Thus, the story of Rādhā-Kṛṣṇa automatically transcends phallocentrism.

Allow me now to explain the mutuality of this relationship through their longing for each other when they are separated. Rādhā's *viraha* (meaning sadness in separation from her lover) is expressed to Rādhā's *sakhīs* (or friends). They are reporting Rādhā's various moods of pain and anguish to Lord Kṛṣṇa. Rādhā slanders "sandal balm" and "moonbeams" because "sandal balm" is associated with Kṛṣṇa and "moonbeams" are associated with her meeting him on a moonlit night. She clings to him in fantasy, as she feels depressed by his desertion. In a clandestine way, she draws him with deer musk to resemble the God of Love; in her admiration, she cries out that when his face turns away, even moonlight scorches her body. She evokes his presence in deep meditation, and strives to reach his distant form. Her mental pain is expressed through her bodily anguish: "She laments, laughs, collapses, cries, trembles, utters her pain" (Miller 87). Rādhā's passion for Kṛṣṇa is so intensely emotional that it is expressed in her physical activities. She presses her palms against her cheek, looking pale as a crescent moon. The following lines from *Gitagovinda* portrays her restlessness in her separation from him: "She bristles with pain, sucks in breath, / Cries, shudders, gasps, / Broods deep, reels, stammers / Falls, raises herself, then faints" (Miller 89).[12] Poet Jayadeva conveys through the voice of Rādhā's friends that her body lies sick from the burning passion of love, and her heart feels suffocated dreaming about "sandal balm, moonlight, lotus pools." In her fatigue, she meditates on the cool body of her solitary lover, and for a moment she breathes with life. It must be remembered here that the love between Rādhā and Kṛṣṇa is not to be taken literally, as it alludes to the sublime love or their divine status. Being both human and divine—having both the qualities of the corporeal and the transcendental—they represent the relationship in which woman and the goddess Rādhā could have access to jouissance or *ānanda*. Thus, a lover's quarrel could be looked upon as a mock quarrel. In a way, these quarrels represent Rādhā's power over Kṛṣṇa which consist of both physical and spiritual aspects.

Rādhā's Eroticism

Rādhā's strong eroticism finds adequate expression while she waits for Kṛṣṇa. The corporeality of their love is revealed through her various expressions. I would say that the corporeal part of Rādhā's jouissance comes out in this separation. Irigaray observes that women could experience their own jouissance through the multiple sexuality of the female body. A little girl is not necessarily a little man; on the contrary, she has her own sources of sexual pleasure. Her whole body is prone to that pleasure which could not be realized through the phallus.[13] Here we see Rādhā experiencing her body in terms of pleasure or corporeal jouissance. She plays the role of an active and not a passive partner, and thus maintains her own difference and identity. Rādhā's passionate longing and desire are expressed through erotic images. Her body bristles with longing, her voice cracks in fear, and obsessed with corporeal passion, she sinks into an erotic mood. She puts different ornamentation on her body, spreads the bed and waits meditatively for Kṛṣṇa, evoking a hundred details of him. Even when Rādhā contemplates her own death, she thinks in terms of her corporeal passion, "Death is better than living in my barren body" (Miller 98). Love is compared with fire and she desires her own death instead of living in a barren body deprived of corporeal pleasure. I will discuss Rādhā's jouissance in greater detail in the next section. Here I quote one of Rādhā's soliloquies:

> I will not go home for refuge again!
> Jamuna river, sister of Death,
> Why should you be kind?
> Drown my limbs with waves!
> Let my body's burning be quenched. (Miller 105)

Rādhā's passionate yearning for death is best expressed in a modern Indian style by the poet Rabindranath Tagore in his *Bhanusingher Padavali*.[14] But the difference between Tagore and Jayadeva is that whereas, in Tagore, Rādhā is always in a state of mourning, in Jayadeva's verse her mourning is but a temporary phase prior to her union with Kṛṣṇa.

It would be interesting here to bring in Caṇḍīdās's portrayal of Rādhā by way of contrast. In Caṇḍīdās's creation Rādhā's longing for Kṛṣṇa could be characterized as of a somewhat pious nature. Caṇḍīdās's Rādhā claims, "The lord of my life alone is my goal, / I have no interest in another man" (*Love Songs of Caṇḍīdās* 90). Obviously, Rādhā's lord here is Kṛṣṇa. She is committed to him. It is difficult not to quote a passage from Caṇḍīdās in which Rādhā expresses her love for Kṛṣṇa like that of a devotee pining for the union with God:

> I want to forget
> But I cannot forget.
> I do not see him
> But I am devoted to him.
> Even when I sleep
> I repeat his name.
> When I walk in the streets
> I stare at the people
> And I feel like crying
> If they do not mention his name. (*Love Songs of Caṇḍīdās* 91)

Caṇḍīdās's Rādhā is submissive, unlike Jayadeva's Rādhā. Whereas Jayadeva's Rādhā is more aggressive and more articulate, demanding that the relationship flourish at the level of mutual dependence, Caṇḍīdās's Rādhā is ready to give up and resign, and to look up to Kṛṣṇa filled with religious piety. But we must not be misled into thinking that Caṇḍīdās's Rādhā is driven solely by religious piety. Because their corporeal relationship has also been portrayed quite deftly through such expressions as, "My lover was up and hastily left / Fixing his disheveled hair," or through Rādhā's confession about lovemaking: "My eyes were heavy / As I discovered his clothes on me" (*Love Songs of Caṇḍīdās* 112). This combination of corporeality and spirituality, which is a universal quality of the Rādhā-Kṛṣṇa relationship, could be best understood in Caṇḍīdās's poetry through the fifteenth century Sahaja movement. It preached "erotic love as the easiest and quickest means to that self-realization which is the ultimate aim of the Hindu religious belief" (*Love Songs of Caṇḍīdās* 46). But I must clarify that in spite of its combination of corporeality and spirituality, the Sahaja movement is different from the way I interpret Irigaray's theory of jouissance in terms of *ānanda* and *prema*. The Sahaja cult appears to be didactic in its nature—and because of its didactic quality Caṇḍīdās's Rādhā is weak in conception, compared to Jayadeva's Rādhā, who insists on establishing an equal status with Lord Kṛṣṇa. She is not hesitant or resigned like Caṇḍīdās's Rādhā, who says, "I bought poison for nectar / And ate my own joy. / My mouth burns with the taste / But I learnt Kṛṣṇa's ways. / My wish is fulfilled / And I need no longer love" (*Love Songs of Caṇḍīdās* 115). Here we see Rādhā, as a resigned heroine, who has had enough of the taste of love and wants to withdraw from love's warfare. Caṇḍīdās's heroine derives pleasure through giving up her lover: this could be interpreted through the Lacanian theory of love, but does not meet the requirements of Irigaray's theory of jouissance. It insists that love could be attained on equal terms between man and woman, that woman does not need to be looked upon as the other or inferior to man, but complementary to him or vice versa. If women succeed in establishing their own symbolic order through jouissance, then they are freed from phallocentrism. Jayadeva's Rādhā conforms to the attributes of jouissance and transcends phallocentrism when she claims equal status with Kṛṣṇa.

Kṛṣṇa's Longing for Rādhā

The mutuality of love is best expressed in Jayadeva's poetry when we see that it is not only Rādhā who is in mourning, but that Kṛṣṇa also suffers greatly through his separation from Rādhā.[15] Rādhā's friends play the role of messengers and describe to Rādhā that in his separation or *viraha*, Kṛṣṇa dwells in a dense forest, abandoning his luxurious house. In his mourning, he tosses and turns on his bed of earth and frantically calls her by name. He plays her name on his flute to call for her and desires for the touch

of Rādhā through the air-blown pollen. Kṛṣṇa eagerly waits for
Rādhā and any mild sound, like the stirring of a leaf or the
dropping of a bird feather, is enough to make Kṛṣṇa imagine that
Rādhā is on her way.[16] Even Rādhā's friends tell her that Rādhā
rules at the moment of climax in love. Kṛṣṇa sighs incessantly, and
mourns, although this is very similar to the way girls mourn. He
searches for her in empty directions and like Rādhā, he also makes
the bed of love again and again, being completely lost in pain.
Rādhā as the dominating partner in love, is depicted by her friends
in the section called "Languishing Kṛṣṇa":

> When he is tender you are harsh,
> When he is pliant you are rigid
> When he is passionate you are hateful,
> When he looks expectant you turn away,
> You leave when he is loving. (Miller 110)

Thus, there is a residue in their love. There is a balance expressed
in her attitude to Kṛṣṇa; when Kṛṣṇa is polite, she is rude, when
Kṛṣṇa is loving and passionate, she is hateful, when he is flexible,
she is stiff. Rādhā knows how to keep her jouissance intact by
allowing herself freedom in her alliance with Kṛṣṇa. Their love is
based on both alliance and freedom and I would claim that
Jayadeva's Rādhā could be conceived as positing a new order in
the ethic of "sexual difference" where a woman could exist in her
own right.

Union as Corporeal and Celestial

In the last three sections of the *Gitagovinda*, in the union between
Rādhā and Kṛṣṇa, the corporeal and the spiritual nature of this
union is fully revealed. This love is revealed from different angles:
first of all, we see that Rādhā is present in Kṛṣṇa's imagination in
both sexual and erotic images as well as in transcendental terms. In
the section "Four Quickening Arms" of the *Gitagovinda*, Kṛṣṇa
adores Rādhā as a Goddess. He praises her "hibiscus-blossom feet"
and wants to dye them with *lac* (a Hindu custom which involves
dyeing women's feet with red *alta*, meaning *lac* both for beauty
and, at times religious purposes); he asks her to place her feet on
his head and thereby quench the passion of love (Miller 113). In

Gitagovinda Kṛṣṇa adores Rādhā's feet quite a number of times, "Place your foot on my head— / A sublime flower destroying poison of love!" (Miller 113). In the section entitled "Ecstatic Kṛṣṇa," we see him worshipping Rādhā by asking her to leave her lotus footprints on his bed, and cherish the place about to be ravaged by her tender feet. He is full of admiration and wonder for Rādhā as he persuades her to accept him by asking her to set her golden anklet on his bed, which he compares to sunlight.[17] Kṛṣṇa implores her: "Rādhā cherished love, / Abandon your baseless pride! / Love's fire burns my heart. / Bring wine in your lotus mouth" (Miller 113). What is amazing is to see how Kṛṣṇa's adoration of Rādhā, as a divine figure, is juxtaposed with his erotic longing for her. Addressing her as an angry Goddess, he implores her to bite him with her cruel teeth, to chain him with her arms, to crush him with her hard breasts. Kṛṣṇa sees Rādhā, as a wonder, as both human and divine:

Your eyes are lazy with wine, like Madalasa
Your face glows like the moonlight nymph Indumati.
Your gait pleases every creature, like Manorama.
Your thighs are plantains in motion, like Rambha.
Your passion is the mystic rite of Kalavati.
Your brows form the sensual line of Chitralekha.
Frail Rādhā, as you walk on earth,
You bear the young beauty of heavenly nymphs. (Miller 114)

That Rādhā is adored by Kṛṣṇa as a deity and a beloved is joyfully expressed by Rādhā's friends. They try to persuade Rādhā to join him. They tell her that his wait has been so long that it has wearied him and inflamed his love. In his imagination, Kṛṣṇa not only drinks her "sweet berry lips' nectar," he also worships her lotus feet as well. And finally comes the moment of their union in which they enter into a fluid universe, "where the perception of being two persons becomes indistinct, and above all, acceding to another energy, neither that of the one nor that of the other, but an energy produced together and as a result of the irreducible difference of sex." *Irigaray Reader* 180).[18] This kind of union could take place only if the female partner is acknowledged through her female jouissance—having both the corporeal and celestial elements in it.

The nature of female jouissance is such that it has to range from the corporeal to the celestial—or establish the divine identity of the body. Once the divine identity of the body in general and especially the female body is accepted as divine, perfect union could take place. In this regard, I would like to recall jouissance in terms of *ānanda*, as well as in terms of Sri Aurobindo's theory of supramental consciousness—which ranges from body consciousness to supermind. In the union between Rādhā and Kṛṣṇa, this kind of bliss or *ānanda* is achieved.

> All his deep-locked emotions broke when he saw Rādhā's face
> Like sea waves cresting when the full moon appears.
> She saw her passion reach the soul of Hari's mood
> The weight of joy strained his face; Love's ghost haunted him.
>
> Her passion rose when glances played on his seductive face,
> Like an autumn pond when wag tails mate in lotus blossom
> hollows. (Miller 120)

Both Rādhā and Kṛṣṇa's passion is described in terms of water: like "sea-waves" or "an autumn pond," which has a connection to the fluid universe they are entering. The word "fluid" has a range of connotations. The fluid universe could stand for the world of *ānanda*, or "supramental bliss," much as for a state of union between lovers, in which "pleasure is a mere expenditure of fire, of water, of seed, of body and spirit [. . .]. It is ineffaceable, unrepeatable, even by child." The access to the fluid universe, or the world of *ānanda*, or real *prema* occurs through the corporeal union in which Rādhā triumphs over her lover. Drawing upon the words of Sri Aurobindo, I would say that Rādhā's *ānanda* takes place not only at the level of body-consciousness, but at the higher level of intellectual or spiritual consciousness. In Irigarayan terms what takes place is the relocation of the female imaginary in the symbolic or the phallic world through the corporeal and the celestial union between Rādhā and Kṛṣṇa. In an Upanishadic sense Rādhā and Kṛṣṇa attain *ānanda* through their *prema*.

In this world of *ānanda*, Rādhā is portrayed by Jayadeva as the active partner in lovemaking. But being an active partner in lovemaking valorizes her position in terms of divinity because, according to the theory of female jouissance, real love could take place only when the female partner plays an active role, instead of being a merely passive and submissive partner. In the concluding section of *Gitagovinda* not only Rādhā's hibiscus-blossom feet are stroked and worshipped by Kṛṣṇa's lotus hand, Rādhā commands Kṛṣṇa to ornament her after lovemaking:

> "Yadava hero, your hand is cooler than sandal balm on my breast.
> Paint a leaf design with deer musk here on Love's ritual vessel!"
> She told the joyful Yadu hero, playing to delight her heart.
>
> Lover, draw kohl glossier than a swarm of black bees on my eyes!
> Your lips kissed away the lampblack bow that shoots arrows of love.
> [. . . . .]
> My beautiful loins are a deep cavern to take the thrust of love—
> Cover them with jeweled girdles, cloths, and ornaments, Kṛṣṇa!
> (Miller 133)[19]

Rādhā is triumphant here; she has established her sole authority, she is not a coy heroine pining for her lover. She has her own ambience and she knows how to control her lover—that does not mean that she trespasses Kṛṣṇa. On the contrary, the relationship is based on harmony and mutual dependence. In contrast to Caṇḍīdās's Rādhā, who mournfully says that the "ocean of nectar" that filled her with joy, was only poison when she drank it and in this sense alludes to her passion for Kṛṣṇa, which is detrimental to her, Jayadeva's Rādhā is triumphant, aggressive and active. Unlike Caṇḍīdās's Rādhā, Jayadeva's Rādhā is never perturbed by the fear of "kalanka" or scandal. Whereas Caṇḍīdās's Rādhā is haunted by the fear that her caste and her home are totally destroyed by her scandalous love affair with Kṛṣṇa, Jayadeva's *Gitagovinda* ends with Rādhā commanding Kṛṣṇa to ornament her body after lovemaking. She asks him to "paint a leaf" on her breast, to "put colour" on her cheeks, to "lay a girdle" on her hips, to twine her "heavy braid with flowers," to "fix rows of bangles" on her hands, and "jeweled anklets" on her feet. Kṛṣṇa the "yellow-robed" lover accomplished what Rādhā asked him to do. If Vidyapati is partially successful in portraying the union between Rādhā, and Kṛṣṇa, Jayadeva's depiction of love between Rādhā and Kṛṣṇa in terms of jouissance and *ānanda* is unique.

Does Jayadeva's Rādhā attain the Hindu notion of jouissance in terms of *ānanda* and *prema*? The answer is yes. Rādhā attains jouissance, or *ānanda* through *prema*, that is her love relationship with Kṛṣṇa, in which her "body-consciousness," "life-parts," "the mind," and "the higher level of mind"—all become permeated with *ānanda* or ecstasy. It is possible for this to happen, because Rādhā keeps open the infinite possibilities of jouissance by not submitting to the phallocentric norm of Hindu Indian culture, according to which her relationship with Kṛṣṇa is an aberration, as it goes beyond the infrastructure of marriage and procreation. One more significant point is that their love is not portrayed as platonic or psychic. It is both corporeal and spiritual, and Rādhā's reputation remains intact. There is no stigma attached to this relationship, or to Rādhā, which gives her even more access to jouissance.[20] Jayadeva's *Gitagovinda* demonstrates that their relationship is based on both corporeal and spiritual love. Irigaray's rereading of the female imaginary and of the Western unconscious in terms of the female jouissance, dovetails with the Hindu attempt to define mind in terms of consciousness rather than the unconscious. Unconscious is acknowledged only through sublimation in Hindu thought. In this essay, I am not out to impose a Western theory on Hindu culture, rather I have tried to demonstrate I hope through an exploration of nuance that Irigaray's theory of jouissance has the potential of being applied to the Hindu theory of consciousness and is helpful in understanding the Hindu Goddess Rādhā and her relationship with her consort Sri Kṛṣṇa.

NOTES

1. See Donna M. Wulff's "Rādhā: Consort and Conqueror of Krishna" in *Devi and the Goddesses of India* for a detailed description of Rādhā, and her status in medieval poetry.

2. See Luce Irigaray's "The Blind Spot of An Old Dream or Symmetry" in *Speculum of the Other Woman*, where Freud and psychoanalysis in general have been criticized for phallogocentrism.

3. Lacan almost makes fun of the 'good old God,' by identifying both God and the Woman as Other. He attributes the position of a second-class citizen to both God and the Woman. He describes God as a third party between a man and a woman. See, for example, Jacques Lacan's "God and the Jouissance of the Woman" in *Feminine Sexuality*. It thus reads, "Today my objective is rather to show you precisely, in what he exists, this good old God. The mode in which he exists may well not please everyone, especially not the theologians who, as I have been saying for a long time, are far more capable than I am of doing without his existence. Unfortunately, I am not quite in the same position because I am dealing with the Other. The Other, while it may be alone, must have some relation to what appears of the other sex" (140-41). He is quite certain to distinguish him from the theologians, but he accomplishes more than that. He makes it quite clear that he is dealing with the Other—or in other words God is positioned as an other to him, or God is a mode of defining woman as an other. What is most disturbing is the fact of woman being inscribed as non-existent. Even when Lacan mentions God as Aristotle's supreme being from which everything originates—he (God) is situated in the 'opaque place of the jouissance of the other' again connecting that other with woman, "that other, which if she existed, the woman might be."

4. See Luce Irigaray's "Divine Women," in *Sexes and Genealogies*. Here she reiterates her conviction that women need a "horizon of accomplishment" to liberate themselves.

5. For more information on the theory of "sexual difference" see Margaret Whitford's *The Irigaray Reader*, (165-77).

6. What is amazing is the similarity between the Hindu concept of consciousness and the uplifting of it through the conquering of the unconscious, and Irigaray's concept of relocating of the "female imaginary" of the Western unconscious through the process of sublimation, which she defines as jouissance. In this regard, see Ashis Nandy's "The Savage Freud: The First Non-Western Psychoanalyst and the Politics of Secret Selves in Colonial India," in *The Savage Freud and*

Other Essays on Possible and Retrievable Selves. He refers to Girindrashekhar Bose as the first Indian psychoanalyst who practiced psychoanalysis as "science as a philosophy of consciousness." Let me quote a relevant observation from this piece: "Acceptance of the unconscious does not secularize one's world, for the unconscious is not particularly incompatible with spirituality, but it cures one of pseudo-spirituality" (129). In Indian Hindu culture, the emphasis is on the conquering of the unconscious, or using unconscious as the source of intuition. See, in this regard Girindrashekhar Bose's essay "Sattva, Rajah, Tamah," (1-5). Bose had correspondence with Freud, and as Ashis Nandy tells us Bose like Freud believes that "the unconscious" stands for a lower level of "personality functioning," but, contrary to Freud and like a Hindu believed in the conquering of the unconscious and self-knowledge. Bose said in his "Sattva, Rajh, Tamah," that the realization or the awareness of the self is identical with the "awareness of the Ultimate Reality of being and God." Sri Aurobindo also discusses the same concept of self-knowledge through his philosophy of supramental consciousness—where he advances the theory of mind further by suggesting different gradations of mind in terms of the level of consciousness. Finally, he talks about supermind and the attainment of the highest level of consciousness and *ānanda* through the conquering of the ego and the superego.

7. See Frederique Apffel Marglin's "Types of Sexual Union and their Implicit Meanings" in *The Divine Consort: Rādhā and the Goddesses of India.* The article is unique in giving the definition of *kāma* and *prema*, and in explaining the distinction between the two, "Furthermore, the opposition between the realm of lordship and the realm of sweetness is also expressed in this opposition between sexual love (*kāma*), which entails relinquishing the seed, and that other, continuous love (*prema*)" (306).

8. It would be worthwhile to mention here the Introduction to *A New, Complete English Translation of the Sanskrit Text Kamasutra* by Wendy Doniger and Sudhir Kakar as it offers a very modern view on the Hindu concept of *kāma*: "The *Kamasutra* recognizes that a woman who actively enjoys sex will make it much more enjoyable for him. One might speculate that this more active role of the woman in sex was enhanced, if not inspired, by the more active nature of the Goddess in the religious sphere, since the glorification of the Goddess (*Devi Mahatmaya*), the earliest Sanskrit text in praise of the Goddess, was composed during this same period" (xIiii).

9. The amorous relationship between Rādhā and Kṛṣṇa needs some clarification for the Western readers who might misread the relationship. It must be noted here that the relationship must be understood in the light of the divine origin of both Rādhā and Kṛṣṇa and it needs to be understood as something beyond a mundane love affair where one partner has a tendency to consume the other. Their love could also be understood as the devotion of a devotee to a God or a Goddess. It must not be misunderstood as an ordinary love affair, as one of my Western friends commented that the amorous relationship between Rādhā and Kṛṣṇa seems to be a soap opera relationship; as Kṛṣṇa has affairs with Rādhā's friends to make Rādhā jealous of him. Kṛṣṇa's relationship with Rādhā's friends indicate the divine love which is cosmic. And it is also in this sense that "jouissance" could be realized in terms of ananda— Rādhā and Kṛṣṇa attaining a divine ānanda or "jouissance" in their relationship. In this regard, see Sudhir Kakar's "Tracings: The Inner World in Culture and History" in *The Inner World: A Psycho-analytic Study of Childhood and Society in India*. In this article he states, "The love of Rādhā and Kṛṣṇa, which has been one of the central features of the cult from the eleventh century A.D. to the present, is celebrated in legends and poems as an idyllic affair beyond the norms of traditional courtship. It is full of playfulness and joy, of mock quarrels and passionate reconciliation in which Rādhā often takes the initiative" (140).

10. Please see "Chāndogya Upaniṣad" in *Source Book in Indian Philosophy*. It alludes to the stage of a society in the Vedic period where patriarchy did not seem to play a dominant role as exemplified by the story of Satya *kāma* and Jābāla described in this *Upaniṣad*:

i. Once upon a time *Satya kāma* Jābāla addressed his mother Jābāla: "Madam! I desire to live the life of a student of sacred knowledge. Of what family, pray, am I?"

ii. Then she said to him: "I do not know this, my dear—of what family you are. In my youth, when I went about a great deal serving as a maid, I got you. So I do not know of what family you are. However, I am Jābāla by name. So you may speak of yourself as Satya *kāma* Jābāla."

Satya *kāma*'s mother tells him that he can be introduced to society by his mother's name since she does not know what family he belongs to, since she conceived him as a maid when she was serving various people. But she was hesitant to articulate the truth that her son did not have an acknowledged father. Even more interesting is the way Satya *kāma* is accepted by his Guru, (teacher). When he tells him the story of his genealogy that his mother does not know who his father is and he should go by his mother's name, Haridrumata Gautama was pleased, "A non-brahmin would not be able to explain thus. Bring the fuel, my dear. I will receive you as a pupil. You have not deviated from the truth." (66)

11. For further discussion on this scene see Barbara Stoller Miller's essay, " The Divine Duality of Rādhā, and Kṛṣṇa."

12. Her torment at Kṛṣṇa's desertion is highly reminiscent of Shakespeare's heroine Cleopatra who was tormented and raged at her lover Antony's desertion.

13. For further reference see Luce Irigaray's "The Blind Spot of the Old Dream of Symmetry" and "Volume-Fluidity" in *Speculum of the Other Woman*. Critiquing   Lacan's phallocentrism Irigaray offers her theory of female jouissance in which women can experience pleasure through their multiple sexual organs. Irigaray says: "Now, the/a woman who doesn't have one sex organ, or a unified sexuality (and this has usually been interpreted to mean that she has no sex) cannot subsume it/herself under one generic or specific term. Body, breasts, pubis, clitoris, labia, vulva, vagina, neck of the uterus, womb [. . .] and this nothing that already gives pleasure by setting them apart from each other: all these foil any attempt to reduce sexual multiplicity to some proper noun, to some proper meaning, to some concept" (233).

14. See Rabindranath Tagore's "Bhanu Singher Padavali." It expresses Rādhā's intense longing for Kṛṣṇa in terms of death.

> Maranare, tnhu mama shayma saman.
> Meghabarana tujha, meghajatajuta,
> Rakta *kāma* lakara, raktoadharaputa,
> Tapabimochan karunokorotaba
> Mrityu Amrita kare dan.
>> Akulo Rādhā, -rijha ati jara, jara
>> Jharai nayanadau anukhana jharajhara—
>> Tnhu mama madhva, tnhu mama dosara.
>> Tnhu mama tapa ghuchao.
>> Marana, tu aou re aou. (48)
> Death you are my beloved Shayma.
> Your complexion is of dark blue cloud,

Your hair is tangled like cloud,
        Your palms are like red lotus,
Your lips are bloody red,
You pacify the heat of pain, you are kind
And Death could bestow peace, and bliss.
Rādhā is intensely pining for you,
Shedding tears constantly,
You are my beloved, you are my friend,
Quench my body's thirst,
Death, O my beloved come. (my trans.).

Rabindranath Tagore's Rādhā could be better interpreted through Freudian theory of mourning and melancholia, because her longing for Krishna is usually expressed through pain and suffering.

15. Like Jayadeva, but unlike Caṇḍīdās and Rabindranath Tagore, Vidyapati also describes Kṛṣṇa's longing for Rādhā, in their separation. Krishna's pain is so intense that he swoons "again and again." The "forests," and the "gardens," "the groves," and the "huts" are permeated with Rādhā's presence. The poem called "Waiting" by Vidyapati is remarkable in this regard.

16. See Donna Marie Wulff's "Rādhā: Consort and Conqueror of Krishna" in *Devi and Goddesses of India*, (109-34).

17. See *Love Songs of Caṇḍīdās: The Rebel Poet-Priest of Bengal*, (92). In contrast to Jayadeva's *Gitagovinda*, where Krishna mentions worshipping Rādhā's feet a number of times, it is Rādhā who worships Krishna's feet:

Not a soul is there.
In all the three Worlds
That I can call to be mine.
So calming I know your lotus feet,
I beg my shelter there [. . .]. (18-22)

18. For further clarification of Irigaray's theory of the "fluids" see "This Essentialism Which is Not One: Coming to Grips With Irigaray," in Differences: *A Journal of Feminist Cultural Studies*, where Naomi Schor suggests that Irigaray is rereading the mechanics of solid or metaphysics in terms of a physics of the liquid or fluids.

19. Here, I could not help recalling Vidyapati's depiction of Rādhā. See Sumanta Banerjee's *An Appropriation of a Folk Heroine: Rādhā in Mediaeval Bengali Vaishnavite Culture.* Vidyapati's depiction of the union of Rādhā and Kṛṣṇa is more erotic than the depiction of Jayadeva. He does not portray sexual union directly, but through nuances or in terms of passion, but Vidyapati's depiction is more explicit in this regard:

> Exquisite today,
> This sport of love,
> As Rādhā rides on Krishna.
> Beads of sweat glisten on her face
> Like pearls on the moon
> A present to her
> From the god of love.
>
> With all her force
> She kisses her lover's lips,
> Like the moon swooping
> To drink a lotus bloom.
> Her necklace dangles
> Below her hanging breasts,
> Like streams of milk
> Trickling from golden jars.
> The jingling bells around her waist
> Sang glory to the god of love. (*Ecstasy 8-24*)

20. Jayadeva's portrayal of Rādhā is unique in this regard. He never alludes to the Rādhā-Krishna relationship as an illicit one or as such never alludes to any conflict in Rādhā's mind for her would-be marital status or the case of her being married to another man someday. Thus, Jayadeva's depiction of Rādhā is more appropriate for the experience of jouissance. But, Vidyapati and Caṇḍīdās seem to be little troubled by Rādhā's *kalanka* (meaning stigma) and contrary to Jayadeva portray that. Here I would like to refer to Sumanta Banerjee's discussion on these two poets. About Vidyapati's creation of Rādhā he comments, "Vidyapati solves the conflict in a charming verse. Like Rādhā explaining away the evidence of her liaison (the marks of lovemaking) to hoodwink her sister-in-law, her creator Vidyapati also takes recourse to rationalizing the eroticism of his verses by a spiritual allegory (to hoodwink the moral guardians of his society)? In a verse that glides through an earthly paradise, he endows the voluptuousness of Rādhā's body with

suggestions and overtones of remote and greater powers that are divine. He makes her describe her body as a temple" (Banerjee 25). Caṇḍīdās seems to be little perturbed by Rādhā 's kalanka or scandal and I refer to Banerjee's comment on Caṇḍīdās: "Kalanka, or scandal, is Rādhā's constant companion in the verses of Caṇḍīdās. She is under perpetual surveillance by a fault-finding society which brands her as a whore (*Gharey parey bahirey kulat boli khyati*)" (27). I would like to suggest that although Vidyapati and Caṇḍīdās's Rādhā are capable of having jouissance, these depictions are not as strong as Jayadeva's portrayal of Rādhā which excels in attaining "female jouissance."

Chapter 3

Body in Transcendence: Jouissance and Kali[1]

As the summits of human mind are beyond animal perception, so the movements of Supermind are beyond the ordinary mental human conception: it is only when we have already had experience of a higher intermediate consciousness that any terms attempting to describe supramental being could convey a true meaning to our intelligence; (*The Life Divine* 920)

For a real transformation there must be a direct and unveiled intervention from above; there would be necessary too a total submission and surrender of the lower consciousness, a cessation of its insistence, a will in it for its separate law of action to be completely annulled by transformation and lose all rights of our being. (*The Life Divine* 922)

In the West, especially in America an undue emphasis is being given to the term psychoanalysis and to my dismay I find that at this moment when we have entered the twenty-first century the American feminists still foreground psychoanalytic theory extended by both Freud and Lacan and attach little importance to Luce Irigaray's version of psychoanalysis—which is often rejected as incorrect.[2] Western psychoanalysis still places very little importance on the term "consciousness" especially with reference to women. In the Western logocentric culture, women are not only alienated from the phallic order by being the other, but women are also associated with matter, inconscience and unconscious.[3] The extent to which psychoanalysis places undue emphasis on the unconscious has been commented on by the French philosopher Satprem[4] (1923) in his book *The Adventure of Consciousness*, where he quotes from the Indian philosopher Sri Aurobindo:

The psychoanalysis [specially] of Freud [. . .] takes up a certain part, the darkest, the most perilous, the unhealthiest part of the nature, the lower vital subconscious layer, isolates some of its most morbid phenomena and attributes to it and them an action out of all proportion to its true role in the nature [. . .] . To raise it up prematurely or improperly for experience is to risk suffusing the conscious parts also with its dark and dirty stuff and thus poisoning the whole vital and even the mental nature. (242-43)

Here, Freud has been charged minimally. Freud not only deals with "the lower vital subconscious layer"[5] and focuses on the morbid aspects of it, he is offensive to women, because he inscribes women's world in terms of the male organ, "the penis." The "little girl" according to Freud is always a "little man" and she does not have access to the Phallic world through her own female sexual organs. However, Lacan goes one step further by inscribing women's world through linguistic interpretation of the "penis" as the "phallus" and by not referring to the male organ, but by rendering it linguistically as the signified. Lacan thus divides the world into the imaginary and the symbolic orders, by associating women with the imaginary, and therefore, the unconscious, the inconscience. The fundamental problem remains—women are associated with the unconscious. But, unfortunately, Luce Irigaray is not being heard for her groundbreaking work to inscribe women in terms of "consciousness." What Irigaray establishes through her theory of corporeal and spiritual jouissance,[6] I translate in Indian terms as "consciousness," "feminine power," "Kali" or "Kali's power" as inscribed in Tantric philosophy. I not only associate Kali with jouissance or consciousness, I also make the claim that Kali's "yoni" (the female sexual organ which is marked as a lack in Western culture) controls the phallus[7] through my reading of the Tantras (which dates from the ninth to the nineteenth century).

Jouissance in the Western and Indian Context
What Irigaray defines as jouissance is mostly revealed in *Irigaray Reader*, (edited by Margaret Whitford) in *Speculum*, and in *Ethics of Sexual Difference*. Jouissance in a word is what women feel both with the body and the mind. Irigaray's definition of jouissance opposes the Western psychoanalytical definition of

jouissance which according to Lacan is impervious to women or occasionally accessible to her. Lacan also denigrates the definition of jouissance by alluding to a kind of "mystical jouissance" that is triggered only by the Statue of Bernini which is a rather derogatory definition of jouissance because it does not encompass the whole implication of jouissance with its elements of both "corporeality" and "spirituality." Alice Jardine's *Gynesis* is extremely useful in delineating the inadequacy of the Lacanian theory of jouissance. The main attribute of Irigaray's definition of jouissance is that it contributes to the feminist philosophy of the female body. Irigaray introduces the concept of "divinity" in the female body—a concept which has been neglected in Western phallocentric culture for centuries. Although any discussion of the female body introduces the debate about "essentialism" (which by now is an exhaustive field)—we should be past the debate of it. The most important contribution of this theory of jouissance is that it goes beyond psychoanalysis and embraces other culture like Indian culture, although Irigaray is not explicit about it.

Irigaray's theory of jouissance could be translated in Indian terms both as *ānanda* meaning bliss and "consciousness" meaning the knowledge of the Ultimate Reality or Brahman—a detailed discussion of which follows. The notions of *ānanda* and "consciousness" which are embedded within Irigaray's notion of jouissance when juxtaposed against the Western psychoanalysis, clarifies Irigaray's quarrel with psychoanalysis. Irigaray offers the theory of jouissance, and the theory of divinity (they overlap) as emancipatory strategies. The theory of jouissance offers women the ability to feel with both their bodies and their minds. This gross disrespect for the imaginary and the body, which associates it with the feminine by Lacan, has been positively rendered by Irigaray in terms of the female jouissance.[8] Irigaray's definition of female jouissance could be characterized as an attempt to redefine the imaginary or the female imaginary of Western discourse in terms of the Symbolic—or an attempt to define the female unconscious in terms of the conscious. This gesture to reinterpret Western psychoanalysis is Irigaray's unique contribution to the Western phallogocentric culture and binds her to the Indian philosophy of *ānanda* and "consciousness." According to Irigaray, jouissance has two dimensions—corporeal and spiritual. Her theory of corporeal jouissance advocates that the multiple sexuality of the female body is the site of her jouissance. Thus, the corporeal aspect of jouissance helps women to valorize the body which has been abnegated by the Western theological tradition. The spiritual aspect of jouissance could be inscribed as "An indefinite overflowing in which many a becoming could be inscribed [. . .] . Without any conceivable end. With neither telos or arche" (*Irigaray Reader* 55). It is possible only if women have their jouissance, their own jouissance which they could feel through different parts of their body—and then connect it to their inner heart, and make a journey upward (or ascend as necessary) for their survival.

Jouissance As Consciousness

I inscribe jouissance[9] as consciousness in Indian terms. In the West or according to the Lacanian definition in the North American context, jouissance of women is still enigmatic. But in India it could be inscribed as consciousness, since contrary to Western psychoanalysis, consciousness in the Indian Hindu culture could be defined as either independent of gender or more precisely as the power of the Shakti or the Kali (Indian Goddess, cf. the *Mahanirvanatantram*, the *Yoginitantram*). Consciousness has a long tradition and history in India. Consciousness is identical with a feeling of bliss or happiness in harmony with the Ultimate Reality. This Ultimate Reality is no other than Brahman and according to the Tantric philosophy this Brahman is identical with Kali which I want to enunciate here as jouissance or Kali. Why is this Shakti identical with jouissance or vice versa? My point is that whereas jouissance in the West is impervious to women, or they can only feel it occasionally, in the Hindu culture jouissance could be inscribed as consciousness which means being in harmony with the Ultimate Reality or Brahman. But why do I valorize Irigaray's theory of jouissance over the Lacanian interpretation of it? I valorize Irigaray's theory of jouissance over Lacan for the reason that it delegitimizes Lacan's interpretation of women as unconscious/imaginary and situates women instead in the conscious/symbolic plane by establishing women's connection with the divine. Specifically, as I mentioned earlier establishing women's connection with the symbolic plane is the main contribution of Irigaray's theory of jouissance. According to the Western phallogocentric definition, this symbolic plane which is associated with consciousness has been denied to women and that is where Irigaray vocalizes her claim for empowerment of women by giving her access to the conscious symbolic plane. Both the corporeal and spiritual jouissance are imperative for women's empowerment as Irigaray tells us and it is where as a third-world feminist and as a postcolonialist I feel that it intersects with Indian philosophy and psychoanalysis.

The question is what is the connection of jouissance or Irigaray's theory of jouissance with the Indian philosophical notion of "consciousness" and "Kali?" I have established earlier in my discussion the connection of Irigaray's theory with "consciousness" in the Western psychoanalytic context but what remains to explore is its relevance and implication in the Indian philosophical context—since that is what I intend to discuss in the article. The connection of Irigaray's theory of jouissance with the Indian notion of consciousness, I enunciate via the concept of Brahman initially and then via the concept of Kali. What is the connection of jouissance with the concept of Brahman? The connection of Brahman with jouissance takes place via the Indian philosophical theory of "consciousness" according to which attaining consciousness is the ultimate goal of human life. The fundamental distinction between Western psychoanalysis and Indian psychoanalysis/philosophy resides in the fact that in the latter the emphasis is on the "consciousness" as opposed to the unconscious. What is more according to Hindu culture is that the unconscious has always been sublimated and the focus is on sublimation via yogic process rather than mechanical control as proposed by Freudian theory of the tying of the primary process. Irigaray's theory overcomes the drawbacks of both Freudian and Lacanian theories by its transcendental dimension which elevates women's position from the state of the unconscious to consciousness and intersects with the Indian theory of psychoanalysis/philosophy. Thus, both Irigaray's theory of "female jouissance" and Indian philosophy/psychoanalysis foreground the term "consciousness" rather than the unconscious and thus I establish the initial connection of the implication of the word jouissance with "consciousness" or jouissance with Brahman. Thus, jouissance is

identical with "consciousness" and "Brahman" as far as Irigaray's
definition of it is concerned. Now the connection of
"consciousness" with Brahman remains to be seen. According to
Indian philosophy, attaining the supreme form of "consciousness"
is the ultimate goal of human life and this supreme form of
consciousness is identical with the concept of Brahman or the Pure
Absolute. Thus, the concept of Brahman as the Pure Absolute has
been enunciated in the Indian Vedanta philosophy. Finally, what
remains to study is the connection of the concept of Brahman with
Kali—which I explain through Indian Tantric philosophy.
According to the *Mahanirvanatantram*, Brahman has been
explicated as identical with goddess Kali—which means that the
concept of Brahman or consciousness is independent of gender.
This idea that the concept of Brahman or consciousness is
independent of gender is quite radical to the advancement of
feminist philosophy—especially in the context of the Western
world where women are denied access to consciousness according
to Lacanian psychoanalysis. Thus, I hope the concept of jouissance
as consciousness or as inscribed by Irigaray rendered through the
Indian philosophical/psychoanalytical theory of "consciousness,"
thereby as Brahman and as Kali would further feminist philosophy
and add a cross-cultural dimension to Irigarayan theory.

I think what is imperative here is a brief discussion of the
theory of consciousness from an Indian perspective and the
relevance of it according to Indian psychoanalysis. Ashis Nandy in
his article, "The First Non-Western Psychoanalyst and the Politics
of Secret Selves in Colonial India," foregrounds the view that the
first Indian psychoanalyst Girindra Shekhar Bose tried to
incorporate Indian Hindu philosophy into psychoanalysis. Nandy
writes:

> Obviously, Bose is here [Ashis Nandy refers to the situation
> where Bose emphasizes on attaining self-knowledge] trying to
> locate contemporary psychology in the Indian experience and to
> legitimize the discipline as a natural outgrowth of traditional
> knowledge. As it happens, the space thus created for psychology
> also accommodates a heavily textual version of adaivta as the
> core of Indian consciousness. The psychologist is the ultimate
> scientist because he or she tries to look within. (127)

The excerpt emphasizes that *adaivta* had impact on psychology in terms of attainment of consciousness, according to which the Ultimate Reality is Brahman and the aim of human life is to attain that self-knowledge or consciousness which is identical with Brahman.[10] Thus consciousness or attainment of consciousness which is identical with Brahman or the Ultimate Reality reigns supreme in the Indian Hindu culture rather than the unconscious. It is for this reason, that Girindra Shekhar Bose alludes to attainment of self-knowledge and another Indian psychoanalyst Sudhir Kakar remarks: "Reality, according to Hindu belief, can be apprehended or known only through those archaic, unconscious, preverbal processes of sensing and feeling (like intuition, or what is known as extra-sensory perception) which are thought to be in touch with the fundamental rhythms and harmonies of the universe" (20). What I want to highlight about this observation is that like Girindra Shekhar Bose, Sudhir Kakar also puts emphasis on a Hindu coming to terms with the "fundamental rhythms and harmonies of the universe." That Hindu culture places emphasis on the sublimation of the unconscious, or even attaches an intuitive value to the unconscious is also clear in Kakar's statement. But, the limitation of the statement is that he suggests "reality" according to Hindu belief can be apprehended only through an unconscious intuitive process. It is true that Hindus always believe or emphasize the principle that one needs to come into terms with the Ultimate Reality which is Brahman or consciousness, but it does not foreclose the notion of leading a mundane life. What Hindu culture talks about is the synthesis between the two.[11] A Hindu believes in the supreme goal of attaining the Ultimate Reality, but that does not mean that he apprehends reality only in one particular way. It is far more complicated than the way Sudhir Kakar perceives it. But, I agree with Kakar's view that the unconscious is not given much importance in Hindu culture—rather what is emphasized is the sublimation of the unconscious and as such philosophy impacts psychoanalysis (cf. Girindra Shekhar Bose). It is quite pertinent here to see Sri Aurobindo's view on psychoanalysis and his theory of "supramental consciousness."[12] In critiquing psychoanalysis Sri Aurobindo observes:

I find it difficult, [. . .] to take these psychoanalysts at all
seriously—yet perhaps one ought to, for half-knowledge is a
powerful thing and can be a great obstacle to the coming in front
of the true Truth [. . .]. They look from down up and explain the
higher lights by the lower obscurities; but the foundation of these
things is above and not below. The superconscient and not the
subconscient, is the true foundation of things. The significance
of the lotus is not to be found by analysing the secrets of the mud
from which it grows here; its secret is to be found in the
heavenly archetype of the lotus that blooms Forever in the Light
above. (*The Adventure of Consciousness* 244)

Sri Aurobindo accuses psychoanalysis of offering half-knowledge;
according to him the loophole of psychoanalysis is that it starts
from the unconscious and explains "the higher lights by the lower
obscurities," whereas the process should be reverse. One should
start from above in the superconscient (meaning intuitive mind or
the highest plane of consciousness) and descend below to clear up
the confusion of the subconscient (meaning the subconscious)
mind. What he refers to here is his philosophical theory of supramental consciousness, according to which at first a person should
try to connect to the Ultimate Reality of the universe which is
defined as Brahaman in the Hindu culture, then bring it down to
his/her material or corporeal self and only then could the
transformation in oneself take place. But, if the process starts at the
subconscient or subconscious level—the evolution of consciousness or the descent of the "supramental consciousness"[13] does not
take place. What is significant here is to see how Sri Aurobindo's
philosophy of the supramental consciousness qualifies Sudhir
Kakar's perception or the traditional Hindu notion of the Ultimate
Reality? According to Sri Aurobindo's philosophy the Ultimate
Reality is not merely confined to the superconscient or intuitive
level of mind, but could be brought down to the material plane and
the ultimate evolution of consciousness depends on how deftly one
can synthesize this material with the spiritual. Unlike Kakar, Sri
Aurobindo suggests that the Hindus do not necessarily need to rely
on the unconscious intuitive process to be in harmony with the
Ultimate Reality—but that intuitive process could start at the
conscious mental plane and does not have to occur as sudden
flickering of light.

Mind has to make room for another consciousness [obviously Sri Aurobindo alludes here to the Supra-mental consciousness] which will fulfill Mind by transcending it or reverse and so rectify its operations after leaping beyond it: the summit of mental knowledge is only a vaulting board from which that leap can be taken. The utmost mission of Mind is to train our obscure consciousness which has emerged out of the dark prison of Matter, to enlighten its blind instincts, random intuitions, vague perceptions till it shall become capable of this greater light and this higher ascension. Mind is a passage, not a culmination. (128)

What has been emphasized in this observation is that not the unconscious but the conscious Mind is the starting place for the realization of the Ultimate Reality, the higher consciousness or even the Supra-mental consciousness. However, my point is that all these three thinkers agree on one thing—that is the attainment of consciousness in terms of the Ultimate Reality—it could happen just intuitively and stay in an unconscious intuitive realm, or it could happen intuitively and be brought down to the material plane or the level of the mind. Unlike Western psychoanalysis which considers women as men's unconscious, or even questions if women have their own unconscious, Indian psychoanalysis starts with the assumption of sublimation of the unconscious. I am not trying here to disparage Western psychoanalysis or Western culture, but rather I am pointing out the distinction between two cultures regarding consciousness and the unconscious and the way in which women are positioned in both cultures. My finding is that according to Hindu Indian culture, in which attainment of consciousness in terms of Brahaman constitutes a great part of reality, Irigaray's definition of jouissance could be translated not only as consciousness but as Brahman and as Kali, since consciousness which is identical with Brahman is identical with Kali.

Jouissance as Feminine Energy or Kali

Mahanirvanatantram enunciates Kali as Brahman or vice versa and talks about the sameness in this conception. In the fourteenth chapter of *Mahanirvanatantram*, this theory or philosophy has

been explained very well in a discourse between Bhagavati
Bhavani (a different name of Goddess Kali) and Shankara or
Shiva. Bhagavati Bhavani asks Shankara how is it so that
brahmasajujya, that is attainment of the Ultimate Reality, is
possible both through worshipping her which is defined as
"adyashakti" and worshipping "Brahman"! The answer to that
clarifies my thesis as well as that Brahman is identical with Kali.[14]
Shankara answers Bhavani that the same Ultimate Reality is
worshipped by adoring either Brahman or Adyashakti, because, in
this context Brahman means Brahman who resides in *Prakṛti* and
Adyashakti means just the reverse—*Prakṛti* in conjunction with
Brahman. Adyashakti or *Prakṛti* has been given different names as
Mahamaya, Kali, Mahakali, and Adyashakti. *Mahanirvanatantram*
reiterates the concept that Brahman and Maya (another name given
to *Prakṛti*) are not different but the same. Both Brahman and *Prakṛti*
or Maya will turn into static objects if they are separated—they are
intimately connected and cannot exist without each other.

When one worships Brahman one really worships Shakti
with Brahman and when one worships Shakti, one worships
Brahman with Shakti, because Shakti with Brahman and Brahman
with Shakti are identical. The conclusion is that the worship of
Brahman is identical with the worship of Shakti, so the same result
could be obtained by worshipping either of those deities. This
Brahman who is identical with Shakti or Kali and this power which
is similar to attainment of the Ultimate Reality or consciousness
(*chaitanya*) is genderless, and could be conceived both as male and
female. The third chapter of *Mahanirvanatantram* explicates that
Prakṛti has authority and executive energy, whereas Brahman has
chaitanya meaning consciousness but when they are united
together energy and consciousness work together. For this reason,
Prakṛti vis-a-vis Brahman are conceived in a genderless way by
various Hindu sects. Some sects conceive it as worship of a male
god, some of a female god. Thus, some Hindus worship it as Lord
Shiva or the male God, some Hindus worship it as Shakti or the
female god, some Hindus worship it as both, and some even
worship it as the Brahman or the Ultimate Reality. Moreover this
united genderless power is also conceived as Visnu, Gopal,
Krishna by the Vaisnavites, and as Kali, Tara, Tripura (various
other names of the Goddess Kali) by the Shaktas (worshippers of

Shakti or Kali), worshippers of the Sun worship this as Sun, Ganapatyas (worshipper of Lord Ganapati or Ganesh) worship this as Ganesh. Some people even worship *nirakar* meaning just the imaginary form of it with no image. The main point is that whatever one worships, (*sakar* meaning with form, or *nirakar* meaning without form, it is actually worshipping this Sacchidānanda Brahman with *Prakṛti* or *Mula-prakṛti*.

Prakṛti, Shakti and Kali

Prakṛti or nature has been attributed a very high status in the Hindu philosophy, since *Prakṛti* according to the Hindu concept is superior to what is called Nature in the Western culture. In the Indian Hindu culture, *Prakṛti* or Nature has a great role to perform. In discussing *Prakṛti* one should not forget the fundamental distinction between the East (India) and the West. Whereas, in the West *Prakṛti* or Nature is approached in an empirical way, in Indian culture the whole concept of Brahman and *Prakṛti* is approached in a philosophic way and it corroborates my former statement that there is a great deal of philosophy, even religion in psychoanalysis contrary to the West. *Prakṛti* keeps the universe moving because Brahman without *prakṛti* is static. With relation to, I would also refer to another term *Mula-prakṛti*, meaning basic nature, which according to *Mahanirvanatantram* refers to a state where balance has been achieved between different *gunas* (different states or phases of body and mind). According to the Hindu Indian culture, there are three different types of *gunas*: *sattwic, rajashik, tamashik* which correspond to different mental and physical states. The *sattwic* state corresponds to an ideal state of mind and body, *rajasik* corresponds to a state where one is controlled by worldly and vital desires, and the *tamasic* corresponds to a state when one is under the grip of a dark mental power or inconscience. According to the definition of the *Mahanirvanatantram*, *Mula-prakṛti* stands for the phase in which equilibrium has been achieved in these three *gunas* or qualities.[15] *Mula-prakṛti* as a balance of different mental and physical states has quite a positive status compared to the term nature in the Western phallogocentric culture. However, my intention is to emphasize that Shakti originates from *Prakṛti*, which is also defined as *Mula-prakṛti*. That Shakti or Adya-Shakti originates from the *Prakṛti* has been made clear in various places of the *Mahanirvanatantram*. Thus, Adya-Shakti which originates from the *Mula-prakṛti* dwelling in Brahman creates the entire world which is the manifestation of the Brahman identical with consciousness and again this manifestation is controlled by Shakti who devises this world as manifestation of Brahman or consciousness.

The creation of the Shakti or the Adya-Shakti is construed as the first creation, after that the universe as the manifestation of Brahman devised by Shakti is called the Second creation, and after that what follows is the creation of *ahankara* (meaning ego) which consists of the three *gunas* (*sattawa, rajah, tamah*). From *tamasik guna* arises the five senses (sound, touch, shape, fluidity and smell), from *sattwic guna* arises the five sensory organs, after that from the five senses arise the five elements: earth, water, fire, air and sky.[16] Shakti or Adya-Shakti or the feminine power thus controls the creation of the universe. In the fourth chapter of *Mahanirvanatantram* it has been described in great detail how powerful this Adya-Shakti or Kali is. It has been suggested that She is the power from which the entire universe has emanated; she is the mother[17] of the entire universe. She has also been addressed as "Adya" meaning original power from which all five senses, and all five elements originated. She has also been addressed as the creator of Brahman, Vishnu and Maheswar—the Hindu holy trinity[18] and the three male gods also originated from her. This theory is similar to what has been said in the Devi Mahatmaya[19] (part of the *Markandeya Purana*) about the Devi and her four manifestations, with the difference that this Devi has not been described or explained as being identical with Brahman and *Prakṛti*, as has been done in the *Mahanirvanatantram*. This Shakti has been described as both subtle and manifest and adored in various ways. She has also been described as the *tama* or the dark power beyond words prior to creation and came to create with Brahman with her transformed energy as Shakti.

Unlike the Western phallogocentrism in which women are always already constructed as men's unconscious, as darkness, this *tama* or darkness through which she is sometimes described prior to creation, did not stay forever as the dark power, but transformed itself into creative energy in conjunction with Brahman. The truth of the matter is that Brahman or Parambrahman is just the cause. He is all-pervading and he is static. Although his presence is all-pervading, he is not attached to anything. He is inactive, he does not execute anything, and he does not have any authority. Instead, she is the supreme creator who has created the entire universe, sustains it and destroys it accepting the desire of Brahman. Unlike the concept of female in Western psychoanalysis she is not men's or Brahman's unconscious; rather, she is the conscious executive energy operating the universe. That she is the executive power or energy has been reiterated in the *Mahanirvanatantram*. The entire universe becomes static without her. Contrary, to the Western concept of phallogocentrism, in Indian Hindu culture the Shakti or the Kali or the feminine energy thus controls creation; Brahman, Vishnu, Maheswar remain as static objects if they are not roused by the Shakti.

Kali's Body as the Site of Both Corporeal and Spiritual Jouissance

I also argue that Kali's body is the site of both corporeal and spiritual jouissance. The iconography of Kali is quite complicated and normally it is associated with fear, fierce energy, destruction, speed, war, death, and sexuality.[20] In *Yoginitantram* the goddess Kali has been described in the following way: Her teeth are shining like lightning, her body is decked with a garland of human heads (obviously the nuance is that she has killed many but these are devils), her hair is open, and her complexion shines like a dark cloud. There is more detailed description of her in the same book. She has a lolling tongue, her eyes are blood-shot, millions of moons are melting from her face, her head is decked with a glistening crown; her entire body is ornamented with jewels, but at the same time her ears are decked with corpses, her waist is garlanded with the hands of the corpses, blood is trickling down her mouth, she has a resounding laughter, her image is tinged with the color of blood, and she is standing on the corpse of Lord Shiva. I think Kali's sexuality is all-pervasive—it is in her entire body image. The sexuality could be seen expressed in her lolling tongue, in her shining teeth, in her complexion which is dark tinged with the halo of red, in her hair which is open, in her wide ecstasy alluding to her loud laughter, and in the standing posture that she assumes while standing on the corpse of Shiva, her husband. As opposed to Western psychoanalysis in which women are looked down upon as having no sexual organ of their own, and the feminist philosopher Luce Irigaray[21] has to establish her theory that female sexuality is not confined to one sex organ, the vagina, but it is all over her body, in Hindu Indian culture Kali's body, the body of the female divinity has been looked upon as the source of multiple sexuality or corporeal jouissance.

What is even more intriguing is that the body of the goddess Kali which has been the site of corporeal jouissance in Hindu culture is spiritual and divine as well.[22] Thus, unlike in the West where women are mourning the lack of a goddess in their phallogocentric culture, and also mourn the fact that the female body has not been looked upon as divine,[23] in the Indian culture the divine body of the goddess has been conceived of as human as well—thus Kali's body is both corporeal and spiritual. About this juxtaposition of the corporeal and the divine I would like to give another example from *Yoginitantram*, which could also be defined as the juxtaposition of the terrible and the divine. She looks like the image of destruction, and she is intoxicated with the drinking of wine being surrounded by *yoginis* and *bhairabas*, meaning her companions who roam in the *sasan* (crematory), she also dwells in crematories, but having these ghastly companions, or being fierce, or intoxicated does not take away her status of the divine, since she is worshipped by all the gods including Brahman. Kali's body has thus been the site of both corporeal and celestial jouissance.

Kali's body has not only been the site of corporeal and spiritual jouissance, Kali's yoni is worshipped as sacred. There is no difference between corporeality and spirituality—what is corporeal is considered spiritual and vice versa. It has been said in the eleventh chapter of *Yoginitantram* that one has to worship *Kama* as signifying the worship of yoni. Whoever worships the yoni which is dwelling in a cavern gets cleansed of sin. This yoni which is called *kamakhya* is also surrounded by a lake which is filled with the grace of Brahman, Vishnu and Maheswar. This water is so sacred that whoever worships it is liberated from sin and reincarnations. The Goddess Kali resides here not only with her companions but with Brahman, Vishnu and Maheswar as well; the universe is created out of Brahman and Kali; Brahman, Vishnu, and Maheswar are also created by Kali and Kali dwells in these three gods as Shakti. However, worship of this yoni expiates one of sin. In the fifteenth chapter of *Yoginitantram* the story of Kali's yoni or Kamakhaya has been reported in great detail. Brahman who created the universe with *Prakṛti* or Kali once became too haughty regarding his creation, when Kali perceived this she created a demon called Kesi out of his haughtiness, and Kesi threatened to kill Brahman. At this, Brahman returned to his senses and started worshipping the Goddess Kali; when Kali was satisfied with his prayer, she turned him into ashes and with the sprinkling of water a small mountain was created from Kesi's ashes. The small mountain was covered with grasses and a lot of cows ate; the more the cows ate the grasses, the more Brahman was expiated of his sin, until finally he was expiated of all his sins. After expiation of all of his sins, Brahman started praying again for the Goddess Kali; Kali appeared and asked him why he is praying. Brahman expressed his wish that he wanted to start the worship of the liberatory, transparent, invisible, formless, hidden feet of the goddess Kali. Kali answered that the spot where she destroyed Kesi had turned to a spot of infinite power. She also assured Brahman that the place where he worshipped her to destroy the demon Kesi was the very place where her *Yoni* had just been created. She further said that this *Yoni* is full of her power; this is the origin of everybody's creation, her nature could be identified as *Yoni* and whoever worships Kamakhaya attains *ānanda*.

Kali's Yoni Controlling the Phallus
How does Kali's *Yoni* control the Phallus? In order to clarify this first I need to explain the word "phallus" in Indian Hindu culture. Unlike Western culture in which phallus stands for the supreme signified, and also the supreme symbol of the patriarchal world, in Indian culture it stands specifically for the phallus of Lord Shiva. Phallus or Shiv's phallus since that is the way the word phallus is construed in Bengali, except that the Bengali word *linga* or the Hindi and the Sanskrit word "lingam" (phallus is the English translation of the word linga) also stands for the word "gender" in general, Shiva's phallus is always controlled by Kali's *Yoni*. There are several versions of stories or myths in the different *Puranas* and the *Tantras* narrating how Lord Shiva's phallus came to exist

as *linga* (meaning phallus) and how the worship of this "phallus" originated. As in Lacanian discourse in which phallus stands symbolically for patriarchy and not just the male sexual organ, similarly in Hindu culture phallus stands symbolically for Shiva's phallus which dwells in Kali's *Yoni*, which is being created with the help of this *Yoni*, and which is also being controlled by it. First, it must be emphasized that in the fourteenth chapter of the *Mahanirvanatantram* it is discussed that worshipping the phallus or Shiva's phallus is identical with worshipping Brahman with Kali or Brahman with *Prakṛti*. In the *Mahanirvanatantram* the creation of Shiva's phallus has been portrayed as having been created with the help of Kali's *Yoni*.

Brahman is telling the story to Narad, one of the saints who is normally famous for his restless nature, but when Brahman felt that he had become mature he started telling him the story. In the beginning of creation trees, fishes, tortoises, etc. were created; after that gods, *danabas* (giants), *daitayas* (demons), *gandharvas*, (mainly persons dwelling in heaven), *rakhasas* (giants) and human beings were created. Finally, the production of human beings started with the union between males and females. Brahman created the rule that all men including gods and giants yield to women and marry; all the gods and giants got married except Lord Shiva. Indra, who is known as the king of Gods in the Hindu religion got worried about this, and along with other gods as well as giants went to Brahman to seek the solution. Brahman along with everybody else went to Vishnu for the solution; Vishnu proposed to go to Maheswar or Lord Shiva and propose marriage to him, but he thought, prior to that, it is necessary to find the suitable bride. So, Brahman decided to go to Prajapati Dakhaya, ask him to worship and invoke the Goddess Kali to be born as his daughter, because they thought that Kali would be strong enough to captivate Shiva. Then they went to Dakhaya and all the Gods along with him prayed to Bhagavati or Kali. Bhagavati Kali appeared before them and asked if she could offer them any boon. They told Her their wish that she be born as the daughter of Dakhya (a powerful King) and entice Lord Shiva. The Goddess Kali was surprised because she thought that Shiva was not powerful enough for her. Then Brahman persuaded Kali that Shiva is the guru or Lord of all the gods, and nobody could equal him in power. As Kali was persuaded, King Dakhya asked for the boon that she would be born as his daughter. After that all the Gods along with their wives went to Lord Shiva to persuade him to marry. They argued with him that He is Lord of all the gods and as they accepted wives for creation, He should also marry to preserve the creation. They further told him that the suitable bride for Him is the Goddess Kali, who has been born as the daughter of Dakhya. Shiva told them that he would marry to please them. Finally, the great marriage took place.

What is important for our discussion for the origin of the phallus is how the union takes place between Lord Shiva and the Goddess Kali. As the Gods depart after the marriage and after some time went by, Lord Shiva engaged in coitus with Sati (the name given to Kali when she is born as the daughter of King Dakhya); Sati could not bear it and asked him to stop. But Shiva was quite indifferent to what she said and did not stop. But, the moment coitus ended and Sati planned to get up, at that time the semen of both dropped on the earth and was spread over the heaven, the earth, and the underworld. The phallus of the lord Shiva originated from that united semen of Shiva and Shakti or Kali. It has been further commented that whatever Shivalingam (the phallus of Shiva) has been built in the past and whatever would be built in the future would be created out of this united energy of Shiva and Shakti. The conclusion is that the phallus of Shiva thus being created out of the union of Shiva and Shakti, is always attached to the *Yoni*. The phallus is always accompanied by *Yoni* and *Yoni* by phallus.

Thus, the fact that the yoni always accompanies the phallus is quite a resource for women in Hindu culture. The question is if the culture and the religion provide such a non-phallogocentric infrastructure, why we women are still not liberated. My preoccupation here is to discuss the justification of the story narrated above. Unlike Western culture where the phallus is the center or the supreme signified, in the Indian Hindu culture, both phallus and *Yoni* equally contribute, although this equality is not practiced in real life. It corroborates the concept developed in the *Mahanirvanatantrm* that Brahman and Kali are identical; it also points towards the truth that in the Hindu culture / religion the concept of the complementarity between men and women is heavily emphasized; we could say that it constitutes the foundation of Indian culture. From the very ancients times, in the Indian Hindu culture yoni is associated with the phallus; Kali complements Shiva, and Kali's Yoni always holds Shiva's phallus. When the Gods conceive of the union between Kali and Shiva, or when the Gods go to Shiva to persuade him to marry Kali, it is with the mission of procreation. Thus, procreation is a major issue in the Indian culture, so is motherhood which is sometimes problematic; the theme of procreation needs to be reassessed, redefined, de-emphasized and also delegitimized to a certain extent as we cannot completely rule out the process of procreation. This is not exactly what Irigaray is suggesting that men and women would create an ecstasy through "irreducible difference of sex." Although, this pleasure is independent of procreation or childbearing, it is at the same time connected to the flesh, because, in this new logic women's body is looked upon as divine, her corporeal jouissance is spiritual as well as her flesh. But, the message that we need to emphasize from Hindu mythology is that women's bodies and sexual organs have been given a great deal of importance in Hindu culture. In this culture woman's body like Kali's body is the site of both corporeal and spiritual jouissance; women do not need to freeze to death brooding about any scorn bestowed upon the female body. If Kali's Yoni controls Shiva's phallus, then yoni instead of phallus has the potential to control the Indian culture which is rather a buried resource needing signifiers.

About Yoni controlling the phallus there are more myths in the Mahanirvanatantram. In ancient times there was a forest called the "Daruban." The hermits in this forest used to worship Lord Shiva. One day when the hermits went to a different forest, Lord Shiva appeared there in the disguise of a hermit who is extremely handsome as well as powerful and started enticing the wives of hermits with different gestures. Some hermits' wives were so attracted that they started pulling his hand or embracing him; when their husbands (hermits) returned, and saw this situation, they became extremely impatient and cursed Shiva saying that his phallus must fall on the earth—in other words let him be devoid of his sexual organ. As soon as they had said this Shiva's phallus was dropped on the earth and started burning everything that it came in contact with, since it became powerful like a burning fire. That phallus like a column of fire started roaming over the heaven, the earth, and the underworld burning everything it encountered. At the time, all the hermits along with the Gods went to Brahman for a solution, Brahman was rather displeased that they were not hospitable enough to Lord Shiva and further said that until this phallus is stabilized, there will not be peace in heaven, earth or the underworld. The hermits implored Brahman to tell them the solution; Brahman said that the only way Lord Shiva would be pacified would be if they worship Devi Bhagavati (another name of the goddess Kali) and she takes the form of the *Yoni*; she has to hold that phallus in her *Yoni*, and that this is the only way to make the phallus steady. Then the hermits approached Maheswar or Lord Shiva and worshipped him with the greatest devotion whereupon he told them the same solution that save for Parvati (another name of Kali) no other woman would be able to hold his phallus; as soon as she holds it in her Yoni peace would be established in the three worlds. At this, all the Gods along with the hermits went to Parvati, prayed to her, and implored her; as she consented, they chanted one hundred mantras from *Samveda*[24] and placed the phallus in the *Yoni*. They worshipped Shiva to a great extent; Shiva was pleased and told them that now peace would be established in the three worlds. From that time onward the worship of the phallus was introduced into the heaven, the earth, and the underworld. That is the story behind phallus worship. What is important for our discussion is that the phallus could not exist without the *Yoni*; not only that, the *Yoni* or the Kali's *Yoni* only has the power to pacify Lord Shiva. That means, at least according to religion and mythology that Hindu women have great potential for having jouissance even though themselves are unaware of it. In a culture in which philosophy is behind psychoanalysis, and the power of consciousness controls one's sense of reality, Kali or the power of Goddess Kali who is identical with Brahman, thereby with the Ultimate Reality, thereby with consciousness, could be an infinite source of power and jouissance for Hindu women, and many Hindu women are not aware of it to its fullest extent. Also the trope of Kali's *Yoni* controlling Shiva's phallus could be looked upon as the reverse of the Western phallogocentric culture; we might want to rename Hindu culture as not matriarchic but as "Yonicentric" or "Yoniphallocentric."

NOTES

1. This chapter was presented at 'Science, Religion, and Philosophy Conference' in Calcutta, India in August 2000, at Bentley College in November 2001, and at Calcutta University in January 2002 as the extramural lecture in the English Department.

2. I am aware of the books written on Irigaray by American feminists in defense of her theories; but here I refer to one of the many complaints I have heard about Irigaray's work. In *Bodies That Matter*, Judith Butler writes:

> Although feminist philosophers have traditionally sought to show how the body is figured as feminine, or how women have been associated with materiality (whether inert—always already dead—or fecund—ever living and procreative) where men have been associated with the principle of rational mastery, Irigaray wants to argue that in fact the feminine is precisely what is excluded in and by such a binary opposition. (17)

3. In Indian culture nature is not necessarily associated with negative or destructive energy, but creative energy. The reason the feminine is expressed in terms of Nature in Indian culture is that in Hindu culture, men and women are believed to function in a complementary way. So, a man is configured in terms of *Puruṣa* meaning knowledge and women in terms of *Prakṛti* meaning energy or the guiding power; women are not described as associated with the unconscious.

4. Satprem is a French philosopher who lived in Sri Aurobindo Ashram Pondicherry, India and worked on Sri Aurobindo's philosophy of the Supramental consciousness. Currently he is in Mysore, India at the Mira Aditi Center. Among his other works, I would like to mention his book *The Mind of the Cells*.

5. There are different grades and subgrades at the subconscious level; for further discussion see Sri Aurobindo's *The Life Divine* and Satprem's *The Adventure of Consciousness*.

6. What Luce Irigaray meant by both corporeal and spiritual jouissance allude to her definition of the feminine jouissance. The corporeal jouissance she explained is a combination of sexual and ecstatic feeling which pervades the female body and which is expressed through the

multiple sexual organs of the female body. But, there is joy in it, and there is no sense of mourning and this joy is expressed through the celebration of the female body parts or sexuality. In this sense it is spiritual too. The spiritual jouissance advocated by Irigaray could be explicated in multiple ways: in one sense it could be expressed as Western women's attempt to connect themselves to the concept of a female divinity since that is lacking in the modern Western phallogocentric culture. It could also be inscribed as a search for infinity which is not there in the Western culture, or if it is there, it is tainted by phallocentrism. But, Irigaray's theory of corporeal and spiritual jouissance is a powerful tool not merely to undo phallocentrism in the West, but if translated to Indian culture, opens discursive space for more discussion on undoing of phallocentrism in the East (India).

7. When I make the claim that Kali's *Yoni* controls the phallus I point to the nuances scattered in the Tantric texts that the *Yoni* controls the phallus (of course symbolically), whereas in real life phallogocentrism still dominates Hindu culture.

8. Here I would like to allude to the Bangladeshi writer Taslima Nasreen's book (*Nirbachita Kalam*, meaning Selected Columns), which illustrates how gross disrespect is shown to the female body irrespective of any culture by associating it with the rottenness of milk, eggs, etc.

In Hindu culture it is not possible to find an exact parallel of the word "imaginary," since according to this culture the unconscious is not given much importance; the unconscious is primarily understood positively as "intuition" or "extra-sensory perception" in sync with the rhythm of the universe (cf. Sudhir Kakar). Thus, the unconscious is independent of any gender. The emphasis on Hindu culture is on conquering the self and merging with others in complete identification. My point is that although the unconscious is not ascribed any gender, gender distinction still remains, but in other forms, or manifestations through rigorous rituals, rights and prohibitions. The "phallus" still dominates Hindu culture in terms of "phallus-worship" by Hindu women who hope to marry good husbands and by married women who wish to give birth to sons.

9. When I make the claim that I inscribe Irigaray's theory of jouissance as "consciousness" via Indian philosophy, the question arises as to what aspect of Irigaray's theory of jouissance am I referring to. When I talk about jouissance as "consciousness" I intend to foreground Irigaray's attempt to relocate the imaginary which is associated with women and as

such unconscious in terms of the symbolic order or "consciousness" (I translate the symbolic order of Western psychoanalysis as consciousness). This is the meaning of "consciousness" at one level, at another level; I interpret jouissance as "consciousness" via Indian philosophy suggesting a rereading of the term jouissance through the lens of Indian Hindu philosophy and culture.

10. Like Indian psychoanalysts, Luce Irigaray attempted to bring philosophy into psychoanalysis, and for this reason she has been ridiculed. It would be interesting to study Margaret Whitford's comment about this:

> Irigaray is convinced then, of the powerful potential of psychoanalysis. But, it is necessary, she says, to rethink psychoanalysis from women's point of view. I will contend that one cannot understand her philosophical contribution without taking into account the insights that psychoanalysis has enabled her to formulate. (*Philosophy in the Feminine* 33).

It is obvious that Irigaray was critiqued to introduce her theory of the divine in Western psychoanalysis. Her contribution is an attempt to expand Western psychoanalysis in the light of Indian philosophical theory for women's equality. Apart from scattered nuances in her writings, Irigaray does not clarify how much she was influenced by Indian philosophy.

11. Here, I intend to refer to the Indian philosopher Sri Aurobindo whose theory of "supramental consciousness" extends the theory that materiality and spirituality go together—they are not exclusive of each other. The observation from Sri Aurobindo's book would further clarify this:

> The passionate aspiration of man upward to the Divine has not been sufficiently related to the descending movement of the Divine leaning downward to embrace eternally its manifestation. Its meaning in Matter has not been so well understood as its truth in the Spirit. The Reality which the Sannayasis seeks has been grasped in its full height, but not as by the ancient Vedantins, in its full extent and comprehensiveness. But, in our complete affirmation we must not minimize the part of the pure spiritual impulse. As we have seen how greatly Materialism has served the ends of the Divine, so we must acknowledge the still greater

service rendered by Asceticism to Life. We shall preserve the truths of Material science and its real utilities in the final harmony, even if many or even if all of its existing forms have to be broken or left aside. (24)

12. I think it is important here to define Sri Aurobindo's Supermind or the "supramental consciousness" for our discussion of the term consciousness. The terms "Supermind," "supramental consciousness" are formed by Sri Aurobindo himself to allude to the consciousness of Brahman or the Absolute in the Hindu Vedantic philosophy. But, his contribution is to add the concept of bringing the consciousness of Brahman to the material plane, to the corporeal self instead of limiting it to the realm of intuition only. In his own words, "Supermind is the vast self-extension of Brahman that contains and develops" (*The Life Divine* 128). The descent of the "supramental consciousness" means the descent of the "supermind" or the consciousness of Brahman to the material plane. The Mind plays a great role for his theory of the supra-mental consciousness. According to Sri Aurobindo, the subconscient (meaning the subconscious) and the superconscient (meaning the highest form of consciousness) are linked together through the Mind: The Mind works as the mediator between these two:

> But in the subconscient the intuition manifests itself in the action, in effectivity, and the knowledge or conscious identity is either entirely or more or less concealed in the action. In the superconscient, on the contrary, Light being the law and the principle, the intuition manifests itself in its true nature as knowledge emerging out of conscious identity, and effectivity of action is rather the accompaniment and no longer marks as the primary fact. Between these two states reason and mind act as intermediaries which enable the being to liberate knowledge out of its imprisonment [. . .].This is the highest possible state of our knowledge when mind fulfills itself in the supramental. (65-66)

13. The philosophy of supramental consciousness involves the Mind and the different levels of it: above mind, illumined mind, intuitive mind, overmind and supermind. For further information see Sri Aurobindo's *The Life Divine*, vol. 1 and 2.

14. Shankara answers Bhavani that the same Ultimate Reality is worshipped by adoring either Brahman or Adyashakti, because, in this context Brahman means Brahman who resides in *Prakṛti* and Adyashakti

means just the reverse—*Prakṛti* in conjunction with Brahman. Adyashakti or *Prakṛti* has been different names as Mahamaya, Kali, Mahakali, and Adyashakti.

15. It is interesting to note here that the Indian psychoanalyst Girindra Shekhar Bose who I discussed earlier also alluded to these *gunas* in discussing psychoanalysis. Specifically, he refers to the *sattwic* state in talking about psychology, and the *rajasik* state when talking about psychoanalysis—the underlying assumption being that the highest state of consciousness or the *sattwic* state is beyond the purview of psychoanalysis. But, *rajasik* state could be grasped by psychoanalysis and this distinction thus automatically attributes a hierarchical position to psychology and psychoanalysis. Psychology as a branch of study seems to incorporate the study of the highest mental phase, whereas psychoanalysis as a branch of science seems to be associated with a comparatively lower state of mind.

16. It is worth noting here that Irigaray often talked about these five elements in terms of Nature and how important it is for women to establish a connection with these elements.

17. I am strongly opposed to using her as mother figure as well, since it has been distorted by the concept of patriarchy in Hindu culture. By conceiving Shakti as the mother, women are brainwashed to sacrifice everything. The concept of Mother as a religious figure or the Divine mother is different from real motherhood. The picture of a real mother is subsumed by the image of the Divine mother and she is expected to do anything and everything, whereas she does not possess the power and strength of the Divine mother.

18. The power of Devi as the creator of Brahman, Vishnu, and Maheshwar has been described in the *Devibhagavata Purana.* Brahman rising from Vishnu's naval started to wonder why Vishnu was meditating since he was the creator of the world. When Brahman approached Vishnu, he explained that he is not the creator but Devi Bhagavati (who is identical with Shakti) is the creator and it is She who gave him the power to conquer the demons MadhuKaitava. If he had been free he would never have left and been born in different forms. Thus, Brahman, Vishnu and Maheswar gathered to think about the creator when they heard the oracle: "The entire universe consists of me (Shakti) and there is nothing eternal without me; then they heard another oracle: Be prepared to create." After that a carrier arrived to take them to heaven and they

arrived at a place where Bhagavati was surrounded by thousands of maids. As soon as they landed they were turned into women and they had to spend ten thousand years attending Shakti. Finally, when she was satisfied with their prayers she transformed them into males and from her own body imparted Mahasaraswati, Mahalakshmi, and Mahakali to them and asked them to create, to sustain, and to destroy with the help of these three manifestations of Shaktis. Finally, Brahman, Vishnu, and Maheswar realized that

19. Shankara answers Bhavani that the same Ultimate Reality is worshipped by adoring either Brahman or Adyashakti, because, in this context Brahman means Brahman who resides in *Prakṛti* and Adyashakti means just the reverse—*Prakṛti* in conjunction with Brahman. Adyashakti or *Prakṛti* has been given different names as Mahamaya, Kali, Mahakali, and Adyashakti.

20. For further discussion in this regard see Lina Gupta's "Kali, The Saviour." David Kinsley's "Kali" in his Tantric Visions of the Divine Feminine foregrounds this issue of Kali's sexuality, but at the same time undermines it and narrows the concept of her sexuality:

> In her sahasranama sotra (thousand name hymn) many names emphasize her vigorous sexual appetite or her sexual attractiveness. She is called She whose essential form is Sexual Desire, Whose Form is the Yoni, Who Is Situated in the Yoni, Who is Adorned With a Garland of Yonis, Who Loves The Lingam, Who Dwells in the Lingam, Who is Worshipped with Semen, and many other such names. In this respect, Kali also violates the idea of the controlled woman who is sexually satisfied by marriage. Kali is sexually voracious and dangerous because of this. (80).

David Kinsley's interpretation of Kali's sexuality does not address the issue that Kali's sexuality is grounded in spirituality and my reading is a deconstructive reading of Kinsley's reading.

21. About the concept of the multiple sexuality of the female body, it is interesting to note Irigaray's observation in the "Volume-fluidity" chapter of her book *Speculum*:

> Now, the/a woman who doesn't have one sex organ, or a unified sexuality (and this has usually been interpreted to mean that she

has no sex) cannot subsume it/herself under one generic or specific term. Body, breasts, pubis, clitoris, labia, vulva, vagina, neck of the uterus, womb [. . .] and this nothing that already gives pleasure by setting them apart from each other: all these foil any attempt at reducing multiple sexuality to some proper noun, to some proper meaning, to some concept. (233)

Another comment of Irigaray I would like to add here: "For the sex of woman is not one. And, as jouissance bursts out in each of these/her "parts," so all of them can mirror her in dazzling multifaceted difference." (239)

22. In this regard, I would like to allude to the Indian philosopher Sri Aurobindo's philosophy of "supramental consciousness" which advocates the idea of bringing supramental consciousness in the body and emphasizes the concept that the spiritual transformation must take place in the body.

23. For further reference in this regard, see the article "Divine Women" from Irigaray's *Sexes and Genealogies, "Any Theory of the Subject"* from the Speculum, and *"When Gods* Are Born," from the *Marine Lover.* Let me quote from *Marine Lover*, a very interesting paragraph which discusses this prejudice against the female body, the sexuality of which has not been recognized as divine:

Not that women are absent from the evangelists' path. But they appear there as virgins or repentant sinners. Softer, more submissive than the mother of Appollo, they listen to the lord's word, and it is enough to fill their cup with joy [. . .]. They seek Him, not He them. If He does occasionally take notice of them, it is out of his infinite benevolence, neither needed nor earned. Sex is virtually absent from their meetings, except for a few confessions or avowals of morbid symptoms. He listens, but does not marry/make merry with women, for already he is bound to his heavenly Father. At best, he takes part in some symbolic union that ignores, or defers to a time after death, the fulfillment of carnal exchange. (166)

24. One of the *Vedas* which contains religious hymns. The *Vedas* in general introduce Gods and *Rishis* (saints) of the ancient Hindu culture.

Chapter 4

Women in the East and Women in the West

Divinity is what we need to become free, autonomous, sovereign. No human subjectivity, no human society has ever been established without the help of the divine. There comes a time for destruction. But, before destruction is possible, God or the Gods must exist.

If women have no God, they are unable either to communicate or commune with one another. They need, we need, an infinite if they are to share a little. ("Divine Women" 62)

I am Durga, goddess of the proud and strong / And Laksmi, queen of the fair and fortunate; / I wear the face of Kali when I kill / I trample the corpses of the demon hordes. (*Savitri* book seven—canto four 509)

As a postcolonial feminist, I realize that we have reached a critical time when women can speak globally on certain issues. For my purpose, I intend to use the French feminist Luce Irigaray's theories of "jouissance" and "divinity" (they overlap) to read problems of women both in the East (India) and the West and to negotiate solutions. In articulating the problems of Indian women, I will take recourse to the Hindu philosophical texts. In this regard, I would like to articulate my position as a postcolonial feminist trying to bridge the hiatus between the East (India) and the West by using Luce Irigaray's theories of jouissance and divinity which have a great deal in common with the Hindu philosophy; jouissance being identical in a way with the Hindu notion of *ānanda*, and the rich tradition of the Hindu Goddesses buttressing Irigaray's concept of the female divinity.

What is the problem of the East when it comes to women? The problem of the East is that in many religious scriptures of Hinduism, woman has been given equal status with man, but, in reality, women are dominated by a patriarchal society. Although there are women goddesses and male gods who cannot exist without them, there are Books of Laws as well, which relegate women to the role of subordinates. There are two serious problems here: first of all, the Hindu religious texts are self-contradictory: second, there is a hiatus between theory and practice.

I believe the *Upaniṣads* is an authentic religious text which has much to say about the status of women. In the *Brihadaranyaka Upaniṣad*, 'the creation of the manifold world from the unitary self' is described through the splitting of the self into two pieces. It has been said: "He caused that self to fall into two pieces. Therefore, arose a husband and a wife. Therefore this [is true]: 'Oneself is like a half-fragment,' [. . .] therefore this place is filled by a wife" (*BU* 78). Here, it is being suggested that without the existence of the sexual partner, in this case, the wife, a man cannot thrive. Otherwise, 'Oneself is like a half-fragment.' One more interesting aspect is that the wife is considered to originate from the same self. It alludes to the general prevailing theory of Hinduism, that woman is the better-half of man. In the same passage of the *Upaniṣad*, it has been observed: "Verily, he had no delight. Therefore one alone has no delight. He desired a second" (*BU* 78). So, the wife is created from the same self, 'the unitary self' from which the husband is also created.

In the *Chandogya Upaniṣad*, the sexual act is described as a religious rite: "The woman is the fire, her womb the fuel, the invitation of man the smoke. The door is the flame, entering the ember, pleasure the spark. In this fire Gods form the offering, from this offering springs forth the child." This passage discusses the high status of woman's body ascribed to it by Hinduism, in contrast to the female body abnegated by Western phallocentrism. The *Chandogya Upaniṣad* also alludes to the stage of a society in the Vedic period where patriarchy did not seem to play a dominant role which is exemplified by the story of Satyakama and Jabala described in this *Upaniṣad*:

> 1. Once upon a time Satyakama Jabala addressed his mother Jabala: 'Madam! I desire to live the life of a student of sacred knowledge. Of what family, pray, am I?'

2. Then she said to him: 'I do not know this, my dear—of what family you are. In my youth, when I went about a great deal serving as a maid, I got you. So I do not know of what family you are. However, I am Jabala by name. So you may speak of yourself as Satyakama Jabala.' (*CU* 66)

Satyakama's mother tells him that he could be introduced to society by his mother's name since he was conceived when she was serving various people. But she was hesitant to articulate the truth that her son did not have a father. Even more interesting is the way Satyakama is accepted by his *Guru* (teacher), because when he tells him the story of his genealogy and that his mother does not know who his father is and he should thus use his mother's name, Haridrumata Gautama was pleased and said, "A non-Brahmin would not be able to explain thus. Bring the fuel, my dear. I will receive you as a pupil. You have not deviated from the truth" (*CU* 66).

The *Upaniṣads* contain references which testify to the high status of women in that society which does not seem to be dominated by patriarchal influences. But, there are other texts and the *Book of Laws* in Hinduism reduces women to the role of a subservient. First, however, I would like to talk about Vatsayana's *The Kamasutra*. '*Kama*' means senses and so Kamasutra, means a book of the erotic. At the outset, I must also clarify the divine or the religious origin of this book. According to the Hindu philosophy of perfect life, there are three postulates which one has to obey: *Dharma, Artha, Kama. Dharma* means a life of religious activity, *Artha* means social welfare, 'economic and political activity' and *Kama* means a life of senses or sensuous pleasure. Each of them is considered equally important and essential to pursue. The life of *Kama* or senses was considered sacred. Historians speculate that this book was written between first and fourth centuries A.D. The main point is that the book advocates the Hindu view that sex is not only 'necessary' and 'normal' but also 'sacramental.' Vatsayana's code of marriage is highly advanced and is based on the assumption that the marriage is successful only when both partners respect each other.

A man acting according to the inclinations of a girl should try to
gain her over so that she may love him and place her confidence
in him. A man does not succeed either by implicitly following
the inclination of a girl, or by wholly opposing her, and he
should therefore adopt a middle course. He who knows how to
make himself beloved by women, as well as to increase their
honour and create confidence in them, this man becomes an
object of their love. But he who neglects a girl, thinking she is
too bashful, is despised by her as a beast ignorant of the working
of the female mind. Moreover, a girl forcibly enjoyed by one
who does not understand the hearts of girls becomes nervous,
uneasy, and dejected, and suddenly begins to hate the man who
has taken advantage of her. (*Kamasutra* 130-31)

Vatsayana has described the art of winning a woman's heart and
suggests that the man-woman relation is based on mutuality. The
above-mentioned quotation postulates that a man should approach
a woman according to her desires and know how to honor her. A
man should never neglect a woman thinking her fastidious or
forcibly enjoy her. If he does, he will be held in scorn. Vatsayana
has attached a great deal of value to the mind of a woman and
advocates the importance of a woman's mind in the play of erotic
senses and how a man should be of this. He also suggests inducing
her by 'conciliatory words,' 'entreaties,' 'oaths,' and 'kneeling at
her feet': "for it is a universal rule that however bashful or angry a
woman may be she never disregards a man's kneeling at her feet"
(*Kamasutra* 129). In spite of all these positive attributes, the book
is prejudiced against women. In the chapter "On Marriage,"
Vatsayana describes that when a girl reaches the age of marriage
every afternoon she should be dressed in a becoming way by her
parents and sent to different social gatherings including marriage
ceremonies because, similar to merchandise she should be
marketed carefully. Vatsayana considers women as an object of
exchange between two families. No matter how much importance
he ascribes to women's mind and body when he talks about the
sexual relationship, he is prejudiced against women. It is a pity that
the Hindu religious texts are full of such ambivalences; it is doubly
tragic because not only are the books full of ambivalences, there is
a hiatus between theory and practice. That means even when some
of the ancient texts foreground the position of women as an active

agent, in reality, they are still subalterns. When it comes to the marital relationship between man and woman, women are most often usually given the status of the subordinates.

The most disparaging comments about women have been made in the book called *The Laws of Manu*. One of the codes of Manu suggests that a woman should be under the custody of her father during her childhood, under her husband during her youth and under her son's custody during her old age. It has been said: "a woman is never fit for independence" (*The Laws* 190). It further says, "By a girl, by a young woman, or even by an aged one, nothing must be done independently even in her own house" (*The Laws* 190). *The Laws of Manu* is highly biased by the prevailing stringent patriarchal rules. Even when the Laws talk about the duties of a wife, it leaves no space or freedom for women. It gives too much allowance to a husband at the cost of his wife. It says that a husband who is 'destitute of virtue,' 'or seeking pleasure (elsewhere),' or does not possess any good qualities must 'be constantly worshipped as a god by a faithful wife.' According to Manu, the remarriage of the widow is not allowed but the remarriage of a widower is allowed. It has been said that after the death of her husband a wife should lead a rigorous and an ascetic life surviving on 'pure flowers, roots, and fruit,' she must not mention the name of another man after her husband's death. But as far as man is concerned, it has been said, "Having thus, at the funeral, given the sacred fires to his wife who dies before him, he may marry again, and again, kindle [the fires]" (*The Laws* 192). The role of husband has been repeatedly equated with that of God and a wife is to be intimidated and controlled as noted in the following observation: "By violating her duty towards her husband, a wife is disgraced in this world, [after death] she enters the womb of a jackal, and is tormented by diseases [the punishment of] her sin" (*The Laws* 191). What is more, in the famous book *The Kama Sutra*, a man is allowed to commit bigamy or polygamy during his wife's lifetime, given the following conditions:

The folly or ill-temper of the wife
Her husband's dislike to her
The want of offspring

The continual birth of daughters
The incontinence of the husband. (147)

This above captures the status of women in precolonial India. Since then, India has gone through many upheavals and changes but the status of women has not changed even in postcolonial India, especially among certain classes. Next it would be best to understand the different categories of women during the post-colonial period. A number of women have been able to cross the boundary of patriarchy and come to the United States for higher studies. But there is another category of migrant women in the States who bought the ticket for this country by leaning on their husbands. This category of women has been deftly portrayed in Bharati Mukherjee's writing. It is not that I am castigating them but given the circumstances in India, they have no other alternative.[1] If they had rebelled they could have saved themselves but they chose not to, possibly because of patriarchal pressure. There is another category of women in India, who belong to the educated middle class and they have maintained independent positions in society, apart from their husband's affiliations. This group is comprised of doctors, engineers, high government officials, schoolteachers, and college and university professors. They are similar to those women in North America who are highly established professionals and economically independent. I cannot help alluding to a quotation from Gayatri Spivak's article, "A Literary Representation of the Subaltern" in which she alludes to a passage from the article, "The Betrayal of Superwoman" by Binita Parry and suggests that the passage which is talking about the established professionals in the USA who are suffering from a sense of history. It is implied that this article does not portray the suffering of the other non-elite classes of women. I defend Parry and critique Spivak by saying that we should always give credit to ourselves if we have been able to liberate ourselves at least to a certain extent. However, I feel now it is incumbent on me to report about the other categories of women in India. I have not talked about the lower middle-class and working-class women who suffer most through lack of education and poverty. If they are abused they do not know how to articulate themselves and they are sometimes beaten and burned to death by their in-laws and husbands when their parents fail to meet their expectations for a dowry. But, here one thing must be made clear: that any woman irrespective of her class could be the victim of this kind of situation. Dowry-death could be likened to the *Sati-daha pratha* (the custom of women being burnt along with their husbands in the eighteenth century). Spivak in her article "Can the Subaltern Speak" has spoken about this heinous rule, governing women in India, which is described by her as a form of 'self-immolation.'

Spivak has dealt widely with the issue of the subaltern and the importance of being sensitive not only to the subaltern group in general but the status of women as subaltern in the context of the entire subaltern group:

> Within the effaced itinerary of the subaltern subject, the track of sexual difference is doubly effaced. The question is not of female participation in insurgency, or the ground rules of the sexual division of labor, for both of which there is 'evidence.' It is, rather, that, both as object of Colonialist historiography and as subject of insurgency, the ideological construction of gender keeps the male dominant. If, in the context of colonial production, the subaltern has no history and cannot speak, the subaltern as female is evermore deeply in shadow. (Spivak 287)

The passage makes it clear that both as a subaltern and as a subject of Colonialist historiography, the ideological construction of gender always prioritizes the male. The truth is that women as subalterns are doubly effaced, and doubly repressed. They are once removed because they are the subjects of colonial production; they are twice removed because they are repressed by patriarchy. An interesting example of the working-class and other non-elite subaltern woman would be Spivak's representation of Jashoda in her translation of the Bengali female writer Mahashewta's story, "Stanyadayani" (meaning 'Breast-giver') where the crude reality of the subaltern woman is portrayed. In the story, everything relates to the breast-milk produced by the character Jashoda. Her job is to breast-feed the children of her master's family in addition to breast-feeding her own children and finally she becomes the victim of this situation and finally devoured by cancer.

The milk that is produced in one's own body for one's own children is a use-value. When there is a superfluity of use values, exchange values arise. That which cannot be used is exchanged. As soon as the (exchange) value of Jashoda's milk emerges, it is appropriated. Good food and constant sexual servicing are provided so that she can be kept in prime condition for optimum lactation. The milk that she produces for her children is presumably through 'necessary labor.' The milk that she produces for the children of her master's family is through 'surplus labor.' (Spivak 248)

Here is a portrait of the subaltern woman whose body is being used as a commodity, as an object of exchange. The female is being used for exchange-value when her body's use-value has been exhausted. I fully agree with Spivak that this is the picture of a subaltern woman who is a victim of a patriarchal society, yet she is ignorant of her situation. The tragedy is that women are often idolized in a manner that ultimately only serves to exploit them for patriarchal usage. Women are idolized as Divine Mothers, so that they can be taken advantage of, as exemplified in Mahashewata Devi's story. I would like to quote just one simple line from Spivak's translation of Mahashewata Devi's story, "Stanyadayani" which exemplifies this situation: "Such is the power of the Indian soil that all women turn into mothers here and all men remain immersed in the spirit of holy childhood. Each man the holy child and each woman the Divine Mother" (Spivak 225-26). Spivak interprets this as the 'hegemonic cultural self-representation of India as a goddess-mother,' and her comment is that as long as this kind of 'goddess-mother' image persists there is no hope for Indian women as they "will collapse under the burden of the immense expectations that such a self-representation permits" (Spivak 244). Two things I want to refute here: first of all, I want to refer to Partha Chatterjee's account in "Whose Imagined Community" that the distance between the two domains "the elite" and the "subaltern" is no longer rigorous, rather there is easy traffic between these two spheres. Thus, Spivak's attachment to the term as the only true category to describe Indian women is no longer valid. Second, although it is true as Partha Chatterjee has also depicted that nineteenth-century middle-class women were used by a new patriarchy as spiritual beings robbed of their sexuality, in the twenty-first-century Indian women can no longer remain concealed under the category of the "subaltern" or "divine mother" but should use "divinity" as a new category, to create a new space.[2] Contrary to Spivak, I suggest a rereading of the image of the "divine Mother" or "goddess-mother" image. The image of the "goddess" I invoke as a concept of infinity, which is distinctly different from the patriarchal concept of it as a scapegoat i.e. as a mother figure making every sacrifice. One more caveat, I am not trying to suggest that the materialist version of feminism or Marxist feminism cannot offer any solution. Instead, I am suggesting that Oriental women can have recourse to the theory of divinity, since the notion of feminine divinity is rooted in Indian culture in spite of all the contradictions embedded in it. I will enter into a more detailed account of this aspect later in this discussion.

What is the problem of the West when it comes to women? Luce Irigaray has argued in the 'Volume-Fluidity,' chapter of *Speculum of the Other Woman*, that woman is identified in terms of negation, i.e., as a non-entity, but ironically it is from her that men draw their resources even though they always fail to acknowledge her. Irigaray comments: "Woman remains this nothing at all, or this all at nothing, in which each (male) one seeks to find the means to replenish the resemblance to self (as) to same" (*Speculum* 227). This is the main lacuna of the West that women's position or subjectivity is not acknowledged at least theoretically in this culture, whereas in the East, woman's place is theoretically or in an apparently contradictory way acknowledged in the culture but hardly heeded. According to the Hindu philosophy, it is thought that the world cannot exist without the co-existence of *Puruṣa* (male) and *Prakṛti* (female), or without the union of *Shiva* and *Shakti*. At the same time it nurtures the cult of *Sati-daha* (burning of the widow on her husband's funeral pyre). In Western phallogocentric culture, woman's position remains unacknow-ledged in religion, in philosophy, and the branch of knowledge called psychoanalysis, each of which places her in a disadvantaged position. Irigaray is castigating those terms of psychoanalysis which deny women access to society, language and culture. Irigaray points out the loophole in Lacanian psychoanalysis[3] which relegates women to the realm of the unconscious and the imaginary

and denies them access to the symbolic which represents
patriarchy and the way culture, religion and language are manifest.
Irigaray is re-reading the Lacanian imaginary by attributing a
status which has not been attributed to it so far in the Western
discourse. Irigaray unravels the imaginary or women's
unconscious in terms of consciousness and Irigaray's theory of
jouissance helps her to elucidate this. The imaginary has always
been associated with the unconscious. But, the problematic lies in
the fact that whereas men's unconscious, or the imaginary is
justified by their access to the symbolic order or language or the
phallus—women's unconscious remains unrepresented. In brief,
women remained men's unconscious in Western psychoanalytical
theories. In "God and Jouissance of the Woman," Lacan almost
ridicules 'good old God,' by identifying both God and Woman as
the Other—he is attributing the position of a second class citizen to
both God and Women. He is describing God as a third party
between man and woman:

> Today, however, my objective is rather to show you precisely, in
> what he exists, this good old God. The mode in which he exists
> may well not please everyone, especially not the theologians
> who, as I have been saying for a long time, are far more capable
> than I am of doing without his existence. Unfortunately, I am not
> quite in the same position because I am dealing with the Other.
> The Other, while it may be alone, must have some relation to
> what appears of the other sex. (*God and the Jouissance of the
> Woman* 140-41)

Lacan clearly distinguishes Him from the theologians, but he
accomplishes more than that. Lacan makes it quite clear that he is
dealing with the Other—or in other words God is positioned as an
other to him, or God is a mode of defining woman as Other. What
is most disturbing is the fact of woman being inscribed as non-
existent—even when Lacan mentions God as Aristotle's supreme
being from which everything originates—he (God) is situated in
the 'opaque place of the jouissance of the Other' again connecting
that other with woman, 'that Other, which if she existed, the
woman might be.' Lacan always expresses his misgiving about the
'existence' of the 'woman,' he is not sure if 'that Other' existed!

Irigaray points out other assumptions of Western phallogocentrism which undermine and deny women's proper place in society and culture. She regrets that the Western theological tradition lacks any female Goddess and does not offer the culture a female trinity: 'mother, daughter, spirit.' If women are not provided with a female Goddess, they are unable even to communicate within themselves.

> the relationship among women is governed either by rivalry for the possession of the 'male organ' or, in homosexuality, by identification with the man; the interest that women may take in the affairs of society is dictated of course only by her longing to have powers equal to those of the male sex, and so on. Woman herself is never at issue in these statements: the feminine is defined as the necessary complement to the operation of male sexuality, and more often, as a negative image that provides male sexuality, with an unfailingly phallic-representation. (*IR* 119)

This is the picture of Western phallogocentric society, of what happens if women live in a culture and society which rules out the role of a female God. Thus, women are driven by the desire to possess and sometimes to engage in competition with other women for the 'male organ,' to identify with a man since she has no access as a female to this male sexual imaginary or in Irigaray's term 'homosexual imaginary,' 'hommo' meaning men in French. The sad thing is that a woman does not desire power on her own, but is motivated 'only by her longing to have powers equal to those of the male sex.' In this society, the image of woman is projected as a negative image, that offers the 'homosexual' or male-dominated world, with a 'phallic self-representation,' where women cannot conceive of themselves as having their own system and language. So, Irigaray offers the argument that this happens, because women do not have a divine, some horizon of accomplishment for their gender, which will liberate them from patriarchy. Irigaray argues, "If women have no God, they are unable either to communicate or commune with one another. They need, we need an infinite if they are to share a little" ("Divine Women" 62). I think what Lacan or psychoanalysis in general overlooks is the naked truth that they are still promoting the role of the Father—what Luce Irigaray tries to do is to rehabilitate the divine. This "divine" which Irigaray writes with a small letter and which Lacan chastises as the 'good old God' serves two roles for Irigaray. First of all, Irigaray is rehabilitating God from the condemnation of psychoanalysis; secondly, she is pointing her finger to Western logocentric culture, which deprives women of having any Goddess.[4] So, Irigaray is defending the concept of the divine first from psychoanalysis and then putting it in the context of women. Whereas, Lacan associates God with supplementary jouissance in women or the absence of God as women's vagina hidden, Irigaray perceives that the concept of God or God is the only being that could save women. Irigaray uses the concept of God to give women whatever they need and whatever is not given to them by the so-called patriarchal system which is always already constructed for women. According to Irigaray, the implication of the term God or the concept of God needs to be realized in two different contexts; in the first place, contrary to psychoanalysis, Irigaray thinks of God as a concept of infinity, as a "horizon of accomplishment"—a way out of the phallus—patriarchy—psychoanalysis—thus, an instrument to help create women a new space in the symbolic order. In "La Mysterique" of the *Speculum of the Other Woman* Irigaray talks about the divine love which could save women which is in a way reminiscent of the Hindu religious love for the divine (cf. Rabindranath Tagore), (*"Tomarei koriachi jivaner dhrubatārā, a sumudre ar kabhu habonako pathahārā,"* 18) meaning[5] that once God is the supreme goal like a fixed star in one's life, one does not get lost. Or (*"Āmar sakol niye base achi, sarbanāser āsaya, āmi tār lagi path cheye achi, pathe jejan bhāsaye,"* 332) meaning that one is waiting with all of her/his wealth (material and spiritual) to meet God. It further means that one is awaiting a danger since God is looked upon as somebody for whom one could sacrifice anything. Thus, the theme of all these songs is the total identification with God in surrender, love and giving.

Later, in talking about the ethics of sexual difference or about the love relationship between men and women Irigaray invokes this kind of love in which one partner does not consume the other, and there is always a residue. She is using the relationship between God and women as prototype for the relationship between men and women. But she also talks about God in pure religious terms—she is critiquing the Western logocentric culture, according to which there is only God, and no goddess. It must be remembered here that there were many European goddesses and Irigaray mentions different Greek goddesses; but the problematic lies in the fact that Goddess cult has been submerged under and supplanted by Christianity.

The other lacuna of Western theology and culture, according to Irigaray, derives automatically from the fact that the culture, which is two thousand years old, presents a male trinity and a virgin mother. She regrets, "a mother of the son of God whose alliance with the father is given little consideration [. . .]. The virgin's relations with the Father always remain in the shadow" ("Divine Women" 62). The result of this is that women's sexuality or corporeality is looked down upon and undermined by this theology, and this does not ascribe any importance to warm, human, corporeal man-woman relationship. In *Marine Lover* Irigaray posits the question: "When a body becomes a barrier that cannot be crossed, something closed off inside its own skin, or place or world, isn't this the work of hatred? Doesn't Christianity forget this?" (183). Irigaray does not accuse Christ but condemns the tradition, which has changed the image of Christ according to its will. This is analogous to the apparent contradictions of Hinduism, which offers the image of the Goddess Kali, the creator and the destructor, the Goddess Durga, the protector, the Goddess Lakshmi, the Goddess of Fortune, and the Goddess Saraswati, the Goddess of Learning. But it is the same theology which restricts woman to her widowhood throughout her life in the name of religion. It also used to force women to ascend to their husband's pyre—the modern version of which is dowry death. So, it seems that every culture nurtures a group of people who monopolize it and make rules to their advantage. This group of people could be defined as wielding patriarchal power over society.

Irigaray offers the theory of jouissance, and the theory of divinity (they overlap) as emancipatory strategies. The theory of jouissance offers women the ability to feel both their bodies and their minds. This gross disrespect for the imaginary and the body which associates it with the feminine by Lacan has been positively rendered by Irigaray in terms of the female jouissance. Phallic jouissance has three attributes, which characterizes it as typically male: it is located in the symbolic or at the intersection of the Real and the symbolic, it has no connection with the body (which has everything to do with the female), and it has the grasp of all the signifiers. Irigaray's definition of female jouissance could be characterized as an attempt to redefine the imaginary or the female imaginary of the Western discourse in terms of the symbolic—or an attempt to define female unconscious in terms of consciousness. According to Irigaray, jouissance has two dimensions—corporeal and spiritual. Her theory of corporeal jouissance advocates that the multiple sexuality of the female body is the site of women's jouissance. Thus, the corporeal aspect of jouissance helps women to valorize the body which has been abnegated by the Western theological tradition. The spiritual aspect of jouissance could be inscribed as "An indefinite overflowing in which many a becoming could be inscribed.... Without any conceivable end. With neither telos or arche" (*IR* 55). It would be possible only if women have their own jouissance which they could feel through different parts of their body—and then connect it to their inner heart, and make journey upward or ascend as necessary for their survival. As I have suggested earlier in my discussion this female jouissance "which would be of the order of the constant and gradual creation of a dimension ranging from the most corporeal to the most celestial"[6] (*IR* 190) seems to be located not in women's unconscious but in the conscious mind or heart. There is another important dimension to this kind of love or jouissance—this love is independent of any child, or independent of procreation—this takes place between the persons of two opposite sexes in which "that ecstasy of ourself in us, that transcendence of the flesh of one to that of the other become ourself in us, at any rate 'in me' as a woman, prior to any child" (*IR* 180)[7]. Thus, another important dimension of this jouissance is to liberate women from being tied to the role of mothers. This joy is independent of motherhood—an emblem of a woman's existence as a woman—in which her lover looks at her for what she is.

Now the question is how this theory of jouissance is going to work for women's liberation both in the West and the East. In the West, especially in North America, even feminists are overwhelmed by Lacanian psychoanalysis and foreground it. Irigaray has not been acknowledged to that extent; she is accused of being an essentialist for devising her theory of the female jouissance which links feminine corporeal jouissance to the divine. Irigaray has been questioned as an essentialist because she attaches such great importance to the female body but fortunately she is not without her supporters. I cannot help mentioning here Naomi Schor's article, "This Essentialism Which Is Not One" which "de-hystericizes" the debate about "essentialism," by suggesting that Irigaray's emphasis on the female body (the multiple sexuality of the female body being the source of pleasure, or her theory of jouissance ranging from the corporeal to the celestial) is based on materialism rather than essentialism, meaning her emphasis is not so much on the physiological, as on the physical. But, my point is that instead of engaging in a debate on essentialism, Western feminists should acknowledge their debt to Irigaray for trying to recuperate the female body and mind from the realm of the Western "imaginary" and the unconscious.

Now when it comes to the East, it seems to me that it has its own tradition of jouissance. Irigarayan theory of jouissance could be interpreted in the light of the modern Indian philosopher Sri Aurobindo's theory of the "supramental consciousness." The female jouissance, which Irigaray defines to be ranging from the corporeal to the celestial, is similar to what Sri Aurobindo defines as *ānanda* and according to him it ranges from the "body-consciousness" to the "higher level of consciousness." Unlike Lacan, Sri Aurobindo does not discriminate against women by suggesting that this flow of *ānanda* ranging from the "body-consciousness" to the "supermind" can take place only in men and women are inferior or have lower level of consciousness and can not have access to *ānanda*. This *ānanda* is similar to the *ānanda* conveyed in the *Upaniṣads*. Also, in the Hindu culture consciousness of the mind is valorized more than the unconscious (cf. Sudhir Kakar, and Ashis Nandy). It is important to mention here the first Indian psychoanalyst, Girindrasekhar Bose practiced psychoanalysis as the science of "the philosophy of Consciousness."[8] Thus, the point is that in India we have this tradition of jouissance—but we need to learn how to practice it for women's liberation. As we entered the twenty-first century, women could claim to have access to this "jouissance" in terms of "*ānanda*" by looking at the tradition of Indian psychoanalysis according to which women have equal claim with men and unlike Western psychoanalysis as taught by Lacan, Indian psychoanalytic practice never associates women with the pure unconscious. Woman is rather the "Adya-Shakti." But, we need to fill the gap between theory and praxis.

Thus, the question is how Irigaray's theory of divinity could work as an emancipatory strategy both in the West and in the East. First of all, the theory of divinity offers a concept of infinity against which women can posit themselves and liberate themselves from the pressure of phallocentrism. Because, if women are not presented with a 'horizon of accomplishment,' they will become embroiled in a fight among themselves. Irigaray argues, "If women have no God, they are unable either to communicate or commune with one another. They need, we need, an infinite if they are to share a little" ("Divine Women" 62). This leads to Irigaray's theory of the 'sexual difference,' which could also be claimed as a part of the theory of divinity. The term 'sexual difference' is not a pleasant term to feminists, especially to the social and materialist feminists who wish to obliterate the term because, according to them, it is associated with patriarchal discourse and gender difference.[9] But, Irigaray keeps the term intact and develops her theory on 'sexual difference,' which points towards the harmonious relationship between man and woman.

> Each sex should be considered in relation to its corresponding ideal, its transcendental. If each sex does not strive to realize its powers, an alliance with or an encounter between the energies of both remains impossible. One always encroaches on the other, without fulfilling its own destiny, without finding the blossoming of its becoming and its fertilization by the other. (*IR* 107)

The concept of divinity is important not only for the emancipation of women but also for the flourishing of the perfect man-woman relationship. Each sex must have an independent connection with the divine, so that each has its own space. The truth is that unless each sex realizes his or her own power, any proper sexual encounter between them remains impossible. What Irigaray means is that the perfect man-woman relationship is based on mutuality,

Why can't we connect through a male God? we are all still daughters...

both on alliance and freedom, in which one partner does not consume the other and one is not reducible to the other. But for this, the first stage is to realize the divine; so that one has a 'horizon of accomplishment' which will help each to realize his or her own power and only then can a perfect relationship evolve. Irigaray advocates that procreation is not that important between man-woman relationship; but what is important is they produce together an energy and ecstasy, 'but an energy produced together and as a result of the irreducible difference of sex.' The third aspect of the Irigarayan theory of divinity touches upon the theme of 'carnal ethics,' which stresses that the relationship between man and woman should be based on both corporeal and spiritual aspects. She argues, "In this way it would no longer be a meeting within a shadow or orbit of a God the Father who alone lays down the law, or the immutable mouthpiece of a single sex" (*IR* 174). Irigaray resents the fact that the female body is not properly respected and believes this respect will be restored once the sexual relationship is established in both its corporeal as well as its spiritual aspects.

That the Western logocentric world will be greatly benefited by the Irigarayan theory of divinity, there is no reservation. She is positing the notion of the divine as a philosophical concept—as a concept of infinity, 'a horizon of accomplishment' which will help women to establish themselves in their own right. Women in the West lack an image of God in the female gender which deprive them of any horizon against which they can measure themselves. Once the West succeeds in conceptualizing women in terms of divinity, the emancipation from the custody of the phallus or the supreme signified will take place. And what about the woman in the East, since the East has the tradition of female goddesses? The irony lies in the fact that although the culture is given with the image of Goddesses, it is not reflected in everyday life; where too many women are still beaten to death; used as an exchange object between families and not given proper value as full human beings. This can partially be attributed to the apparent contradictions in the Hindu religion, which worships the image of Goddesses and at the same time forces women to ascend to their husband's funeral pyre, or lead a life of celibacy after their husband's death, or causes a dowry-death. So, how do we read Irigaray's message in the Indian context? I suggest a re-reading of the Indian concept of the divinity or the goddesses and also of jouissance as *ānanda* or bliss. In this regard, I refer back to the two former chapters: "Rādhā's Jouissance and Jouissance and Kali: Body in Transcendence."

NOTES

1. This problem of marriage is quite a complicated question to be resolved too soon. As postcolonial women we are trying to resolve it in multiple ways. A number of Indian women have entered into interracial marriages and some have been successful. A lot of women have access to the US through marriage, or more specifically through arranged marriages; again some of them are successful, and some are not. A lot of women have come to this country for higher studies being accompanied by their lovers or companions (they eventually get married) and most of them are successful. So, my conclusion is that comparatively women are more successful in marital relationships if they value their education and financial independence, and combine both with marriage, instead of sacrificing their own independence. Again, as I have said earlier, it is far more complicated than could be resolved in a single footnote. For, further reference and discussion in this matter, see the writings of Madhu Kishwar, Ruth Vanita and Taslima Nasreen.

2. It is quite pertinent here to look at Partha Chatterjee's comment on the contiguity of the spheres of the "elite" and the "subaltern" in the current era:

> it is rather a recognition in the elite domain of the very real presence of an arena of subaltern politics over which it must dominate and yet which also had to be negotiated on its own terms for the purposes of producing consent. On the other hand, the domain of subaltern politics has increasingly become familiar with, and even adapted itself to, the institutional forms characteristic of the elite domain. ("Whose Imagined Community"? 13)

In the light of this statement it could be claimed that the time also has come to demystify the former divine-woman-mother image and initiate a new movement along that line, since the old world has collapsed and we are heading for a new universal ideology and space.

3. According to Western Lacanian psychoanalysis, mainly there are two orders—the imaginary and the symbolic. The imaginary order is associated with the unconscious and as such the female or the feminine, whereas, the symbolic order stands for the patriarchal order or the phallus meaning language. In Lacan's world, the Reality cannot take place without language. Unfortunately, this language is associated with patriarchy or the male world, and the imaginary, which is identified with the unconscious, does not have any access to language or the patriarchal order and as such is defined as the female, which is highly damaging to Western women. For further reference, see the article "The Rationality and the Imaginary" in Philosophy in the Feminine by Margaret Whitford and Lacan, a Feminist Introduction by Elizabeth Grosz.

4. Here, I must clarify. By saying that Irigaray talks about the issue of women's divinity because the Western culture does not have any female goddess does not preclude Greek goddesses but it must be remembered that Greek goddesses or European Goddesses have been long extinct in terms of cultural or religious practice.

5. Unless otherwise noted, all translations are my own.

6. My entire book addresses clearly how Irigaray's definition of jouissance ranging from Irigaray's definition of jouissance ranging from the corporeal to the celestial is reminiscent of the Indian philosopher Sri Aurobindo's concept of the "Supermind" or "supramental consciousness"—which talks about a transformation of the body from the descent of a supramental light above. According to this concept, body and mind are intimately connected and for any spiritual transformation to occur, the body or matter will ascend upwards, and the supramental light will descend downwards and through this twofold process the transformation will take place. "A spiritual Ananda (meaning joy, pleasure) can flow into the body and inundate cell and tissue; a luminous materialisation of this higher *Ananda* could of itself bring transformation, a total transformation of the deficient or adverse sensibilities of physical nature" (*The Life Divine* 989).

7. When Irigaray describes this jouissance as, "an engendering associated with the world and the universe" or, "a mere expenditure of fire, of water, of seed, of body and of spirit," it seems identical with the Hindu notion of cosmic bliss or divine Ānanda (meaning in harmony with the universe). The ideal love relationship through which this female jouissance could be expressed would be Rādhā (Indian Goddess) and

Krishna (Indian God) whose relationship is portrayed as outside of a marital relationship. Their pleasure could also be expressed as the divine love. Please, see Chapter 2, "Rādhā's Jouissance" in this regard.

8. In this regard, I would like to allude to Ashis Nandy's article "The Savage Freud: The First Non-Western Psychoanalyst and the Politics of Secret Selves in Colonial India," where he refers to Girindrashekhar Bose as the first Indian psychoanalyst who practiced psychoanalysis as "science as a philosophy of consciousness." Please see the detailed discussion on this in the endnote of Chapter 2, "Rādhā's Jouissance."

9. Here, I cannot help clarify the debate between the gender theorists and the sexual difference theorists. Whereas, the gender theorists talk about neutralizing the female body, the sexual difference theorists emphasize that the female body should be valorized and women's liberation could not take place if the female body is not taken into account in conjunction with the female mind.

Chapter 5

The Ascent and the Descent: Irigaray and Brennan through Indian Philosophy

> Therefore the time grows ripe and the tendency of the world moves towards a new and comprehensive affirmation in thought and in inner and outer experience and to its corollary, a new and rich self-fulfillment in an integral human existence for the individual and the race. (*The Life Divine* 9)

This chapter[1] valorizes the theory of the feminist philosopher Teresa Brennan who tries to connect the discourse of the ego to spirituality. This chapter also intends to show the connection of their theories (both Irigaray and Brennan) vis-à-vis Indian philosophy and psyhoanalysis to locate a new moment in the twenty first century. I reread the term jouissance (initially used by Lacan and then by Irigaray) to accomplish this.

The way Irigaray uses the term jouissance, which encompasses both the body and the mind together, is a unique contribution to feminist philosophy in the West. In the Western phallogocentric culture the issue of bringing spirituality to the female body has been neglected for centuries. But it goes even beyond that—it marks a new moment. I enunciate this through Irigaray's theory of jouissance as *ānanda* (meaning bliss) and "consciousness" in relation to Indian philosophy as transcending Western psychoanalysis. Then I suggest that Teresa Brennan's theory of "energetics" and "original logic" is in harmony with this movement of jouissance as consciousness. Jouissance and the theory of "original logic" as a new form of consciousness or a moment of awakening I depict not only through the medium of ancient Indian philosophy but also through the modern Indian philosopher Sri Aurobindo's[2] philosophy of "supramental consciousness" which is about the descent of "consciousness" in the body—of the union between the psychic and the material.

Irigaray and Brennan

Brennan acknowledges Luce Irigaray's contribution to feminist philosophy and delegitimizes the debate on essentialism surrounding Irigaray. However, she critiques Irigaray for being a utopian. Brennan has reservations about Irigaray's use of the term "economy" which she thinks Irigaray sometimes uses in relation to "physics," and sometimes just to refer to a system. While Irigaray's "economy is not identical with the energetic level, energetic psychodynamics are invoked in her references to physics." Brennan also thinks that Irigaray's complaints about "science" are incorrect because of her false notion of the theory of the fluids. As opposed to Irigaray, Brennan argues that the fluids are as measurable as solids. Therefore, according to Brennan, Irigaray's notion that the theory of the fluids has been neglected by science because fluids constitute "the mark of the indefinable feminine" does not stand. Although Brennan corroborates Irigaray's idea of "crossing boundaries," because, in a way that informs her own project too, she thinks that Irigaray dwells on it inadequately. Even when Irigaray does elaborate, she uses the hypothesis of the physicist Ilya Prigogine, whose theory is problematic. As Brennan tells us, the problem with Prigogine's theory is that it, "hypothesized the existence of non-entropic energy systems which cross boundaries, and which exist alongside the energy whose entropy, by Newtonian law, increases" (Brennan 76). Before resolving this debate about Prigogine's theory, I think it is important and imperative to take a look at his theory of "dissipative structures" which Irigaray used to inscribe female sexuality in relation to "crossing boundaries."

Prigogine alludes to the state of order in chaos or order in a state of non-equilibrium. Prigogine's observations in *Order Out of Chaos* are both scientific and philosophic and indicate his aim to achieve a synthesis between the two. He uses Benard cell or "Benard instability" to illustrate his theory of "dissipative structures." "Benard cells" represent dissipative structures and "are essentially a reflection of the global situation of non-equilibrium producing them" (Prigonine 144). Let me quote in more detail from Prigonine's *Order Out of Chaos* to clarify his thoughts about the "dissipative structures" and how they are produced:

The "Benard instability" is another striking example of the instability of a stationary state giving rise to a phenomenon of spontaneous self-organization. The instability is due to a vertical temperature gradient set up in a horizontal liquid layer. The lower surface of the latter is heated to a given temperature, which is higher than that of the upper surface. As a result of these boundary conditions, a permanent heat-flux is set up, moving from the bottom to the top. When the imposed gradient reaches a threshold value, the fluid's state of rest—the stationary state in which heat is conveyed by conduction alone, without convection—becomes unstable. A convection corresponding to the coherent motion of ensembles of molecules is produced, increasing the rate of heat transfer [. . .] Millions of molecules move coherently, forming hexagonal convection cells of a characteristic size. (142)

What is important for our purpose is to note how the millions of molecules which form "hexagonal convection cells of a characteristic size" are produced and move coherently. What is even more crucial for our understanding is that these uniform molecules are produced through energy exchanges from the outside world, a microscopic convection current invading the whole system and producing this new molecular order spontaneously. And it starts when the fluid's state of rest becomes unstable as the imposed gradient reaches a threshold value. What was important to Irigaray's theory of the feminine is this course of the fluids which can cross thresholds, and produce a new molecular order spontaneously in a non-equilibrium stage. The identification of feminine sexuality is that it is a fluidity which can cross thresholds, and still produce order whereas crossing thresholds could be viewed upon as disorder by a patriarchal system.

By alluding to Prigogine's theory of "dissipative structures" what Irigaray tries to invoke is an order in female sexuality which could be produced in chaos or in a non-equilibrium stage because it consists of fluids, and is therefore non-teleological. Irigaray Brennan argues, is trying to do away with logic altogether, since she does not know any other alternative to oppose the "subject-centered masculine logic." Brennan in spite of her support of Irigaray is a bit harsh on her. Brennan advocates logic for the

origin before the foundation. But, Brennan is also concerned that
Irigaray is being utopian. She comments: "Both especially [Irigary
and Cixous] Cixous invoke an economy of generosity, in which a
maternal or female economy is unlimited in what it draws from or
passes on. There probably is such an economy; but it will not come
into being merely by invoking it as an ideal, or writing as if it
already exits" (Brennan 75). Irigaray accepts the subject-object
distinction insofar that she believes that there is logic. On the
contrary, Brennan believes that there is a logic that comes before
subject-object distinction and the subject-object logic to which it
gives rise to. Those differences aside, Brennan's theory of
energetics and "original logic" and Irigaray's theory of "female
jouissance" can be brought together by Indian philosophy ushering
in a journey into *ānanda* and "consciousness."

Jouissance in the Western and Indian Context
Jouissance in a word is what women feel both with their body and
mind. Irigaray's definition of jouissance opposes the Western
psychoanalytical definition of jouissance, which according to
Lacan is impervious to women or occasionally accessible to them.
Lacan also denigrates the definition of jouissance by alluding to a
kind of "mystical jouissance[3]" that is triggered only by the Statue
of Bernini, which is rather a derogatory definition of jouissance
because it does not encompass the whole implication of jouissance
which has both the elements of "corporeality" and "spirituality."
Alice Jardine's *Gynesis* is extremely useful in delineating the
inadequacy of the Lacanian theory of jouissance. The main
attribute of Irigaray's definition of "jouissance" is that it
contributes to the feminist philosophy of the body—Irigaray
introduces the concept of the "divinity" of the female body which
has been neglected in the Western phallocentric culture for
centuries. The most important contribution of this theory of
jouissance is that it goes beyond psychoanalysis and embraces
other cultures like Indian culture, although Irigaray is not too
explicit about it.[4]

What is most important to notice is Irigaray's emphasis on the
term "celestial" which is grounded in the "corporeal." That the
celestial is located in the corporeal seems never to be noticed by
Western psychoanalysis and this thus becomes the ground for

quarrel between Western psychoanalysis and Irigaray. It is for the same reason that Rosi Braidotti and Margaret Whitford allude to Irigaray's ethics of "sexual difference" as an ontologizing of "sexual difference." The book *Between Psychoanalysis and Feminism* by Teresa Brennan is a useful one in this regard. It is a pity that the Anglo-American and French feminists have to fight "essentialism" because of this denial of the divinity of the female body for centuries. However, I want to claim that this introduction of the concept of "divinity" in the body which Irigaray expresses in different terms as "spiritual jouissance" or "goddesses" is where her theory meets Indian philosophy and its concepts of *ānanda* and consciousness.

Unlike Lacan, Sri Aurobindo is not discriminating against women saying that this flow of *ānanda* ranging from the "body-consciousness" to the "supermind" could take place only in men and women who are inferior or have lower levels of consciousness and cannot have access to *ānanda*. This *ānanda* is similar to the *ānanda* conveyed in the *Upaniṣads*, "*Madhu vātā ṛtāyate, madhu kṣaranti sindhavaḥ*: [. . .] *madhumat pārthivam rajaḥ*" (*Brihadaranyaka Upaniṣad* 318). Also, in Hindu culture, the consciousness of mind is valorized more than the unconscious (cf. Sudhir Kakar, and Ashis Nandy). It is important to mention here the first Indian psychoanalyst Girindrasekhar Bose practiced psychoanalysis as the science of "the philosophy of Consciousness.[5]" I also inscribe jouissance as "consciousness" which in Bengali is *chaitanya* i.e., attaining a realization of the Ultimate Reality or Brahman. According to Hindu culture, this is the ultimate goal of human life. In this sense *ānanda* could also be perceived as part of this process of attaining the consciousness of the Ultimate Reality—because attaining *ānanda* is identical with attaining the realization of the Brahman.[6] One more added dimension to this according to Hindu Tantric philosophy[7] (which dates from the ninth to the sixteenth centuries) is that this Brahman is identical with Kali, the Hindu goddess, or we could say this notion of consciousness unlike the view of it posited by Western psychoanalysis does not have any gender. However, Irigaray's notion of jouissance is similar to this notion of *ānanda*, more so when seen through Sri Aurobindo's philosophy of "supramental consciousness." Grounded in *Upaniṣads*, Sri Aurobindo develops this notion of bringing down *ānanda* or delight or "supreme consciousness" in the body which is sometimes neglected in the interpretation of Indian philosophy. Sri Aurobindo's philosophy of "supramental consciousness" makes it very clear that the transformation of the world is not possible without the descent of the supreme consciousness or the realization of Brahman at the level of the body. The essence of Sri Aurobindo's philosophy of the "supramental consciousness" which talks about the descent of the supreme consciousness in the body supports Irigaray's theory of jouissance and links Irigaray to Brennan via his theory of bringing the material and the spiritual together. It also inaugurates a journey into a new form of consciousness.

Brennan and Her Connection with Indian Philosophy

Is there any connection between Brennan's theory of energy of relationality with the Indian concept of Brahman as the Ultimate Reality? Brennan's theory is more open compared to Freud and Lacan, since unlike Lacan she is not reducing the definition of sexuality to the grid of the phallus and attempts instead to redefine sexuality beginning with the intrauterine relation. She also ties all the modern/postmodern desires for commodity or instant gratification through technology as the expression of gratifying the original hallucinatory desire for the mother expressed in earlier infancy. The child experiences this when he/she or she/he comes out of the mother's womb and his or her needs are not satisfied instantly, versus the intrauterine stage, when the child has to hallucinate to gratify his/her needs. This leads to Brennan's theory of "foundational fantasy." Brennan traces the root of the urge for the instant gratification of materialistic desire to the hallucination, which takes place in the child's mind after the child is separated from the mother at birth. As I said, the hallucination is caused by the delay in the satisfaction of the child's needs in contrast to how the child's needs are instantly fulfilled in the intrauterine state. Brennan also calls this intrauterine phase the "original" state whereas the state after birth when the child has recourse to hallucination for the fulfillment of needs is called "imitation" of the "original."

The essence of this theory is that the infant fantasizes a situation in which it is in control. The only way the infant fantasizes itself to be in control is that it gives priority to the mental over the physical body. All the infant can do is fantasize. It cannot make actually happen, but it can delude itself by fantasy into believing that it controls action and the mother/other is a body without a mind who exists to serve it and make material the fantasy of instant gratification. The fantasy is "foundational" because it gives rise to the belief that human beings of either sex are subjects with the mind while the rest of the world and mothers in it are mindless objects there to serve us. We develop technologies to "make the fantasy come true." Thus, Brennan traces the root of the urge for instant gratification by maternal desire. The point is that Brennan tries to transcend the false materialistic and the fake, artificially produced desires (according to Brennan produced by hallucination after birth and later on expressed in the urgent need for the instant gratification of desire in American life) through a return to the "original" state similar to the mother-child union in the intrauterine state. In contrast to the "foundational fantasy" Brennan argues that the original state is characterized by a logic, a logic we find in the flesh, that is—the body, and in nature. This is a logic of connection. It is harmonious in the same way that the musical scales have logic and this is where Brennan insists that the musical scales have logic and this is where Brennan insists that the alternative to "phallo-logocentrism" is not to do away with logic but to discover the real logic before foundational and subject / object thinking. Her idea of the divine is Spinoza's thinking. God is the logic and harmony in all that exists, both material and psychical at the same time. This divine is connected to the feminine and the maternal because it resists the controlling God, the Super-subject, and the masculine God—who stands outside God's creation.

In Brennan's theory of "original logic" all being is energetically connected to one another in their environment, but they are unusually unaware of this situation because living in subject-object relation they forget this energetic connection. But while the subject is unconscious of the energetic connection between beings, the masculine subject still benefits from the material/psychic energy of the feminine object. Two comments here: first of all, I strongly disagree that Brennan's theory should be read as a returning or recapturing of the intrauterine state; second, I want to re-read or reconfigure Brennan's theory by connecting it to a desire to unite with the non-material, pure phase of innocence, which in Indian philosophy could be interpreted as a desire for the greater life, or even the Ultimate Reality. The nuances that we might define as Indian in Brennan resides in her attempt to go beyond the "foundational fantasy" which rules Western logocentric culture where people are chased or chasing the material world for instant gratification of their desire. This quest for the greater life that is implicit in Brennan's argument on the original logic could be expressed according to Indian Hindu culture as the quest for the Brahman. Lacan's concept of the "ego" without the possibility of transformation (cf. *History After Lacan*) is extremely narrow and both Irigaray and Brennan try to transcend or sublimate this claustrophobic situation of the "ego" through their respective theories. Both theories are about transcending the "ego" to a certain extent and it is in this regard that I read or re-read[8] Brennan's theory of the original logic as a search for the true self or Brahman in Hindu philosophy.

The Hindu philosophical text the *Upaniṣads* (seventh or eighth century B.C.) contains this knowledge of Brahman—which transpired between Guru and his disciples through *sruti*—meaning the knowledge was transmitted from Guru to his disciples through oral conversation. Let me start with the verses from various *Upaniṣads*. In the *Isha Upaniṣad* it has been observed: "*Ishā bāysamidam sarbam jat kiṇcha jagatayām jagat/ten takten bhunjithā mā gridha kasyashid dhanam*" (7). It means that the entire universe is the manifestation of Brahman and nothing can exist without his existence and thus one has to aspire to know this Brahman and when one learns about him one sheds the materialistic desires and develops a kind of detachment to material things. In the *Upaniṣads* Brahman has been conceived, as the inner Soul in all, even in each individual and that is why attaining the knowledge of the soul is identical with attaining the knowledge of Brahman. This I discuss in the light of the *Katho Upaniṣad* which alludes to a long dialogue between Nachiketa and Yama (the King of Death according to Hindu religion and mythology). In the *Katho Upaniṣad* there is a strong invocation to attain the knowledge of the soul or "atmagayana." The famous adage in this *Upaniṣad* is: "*uttisthata jāgrata prapya baran nibodhota / khurasaya dhārā nishita durātaya/durgam pathastat kabayo badantī"* (113). The *sloka* asks an individual to wake up from a stupor and that the path leading to the knowledge of the soul is really difficult and sharp as the razor's edge, because in order to achieve this one has to give up materialistic ambition and desires. This knowledge of the Soul was delivered to Nachiketa by Yama, as Nachiketa requested Him to tell him about *atmagayana* or the knowledge of the soul. What is being emphasized in the *Katho Upaniṣad* or in the entire *Upaniṣads* is the importance of attaining this knowledge of the Soul or Brahman attaining which liberates one from the mundane materialistic desires that Brennan is so concerned regarding the West and the "ego's era." The whole *Upaniṣads* is about the invocation to sublimate the ego; with relation to Brennan's argument it means to go beyond the "ego's era" defined by Lacan or the "foundational fantasy." It is about attaining consciousness about which Irigaray is so insistent—to connect the dark continent of the soul defined by psychoanalysis to the higher consciousness with a loving touch from the divine.

However, I would like to ruminate a little bit more on this knowledge of the Soul or Brahman. In the *Katho Upaniṣad* the account of this Soul has been given in great detail and let me quote one more verse: (*"urdhamulahbakoshakho aşoshatha sanatana / tadeb şukram tadbrahman tadebamritutchhatye/tasminlokah srita sarbe tadu nateyti tkachan. atbai tat"* 141). What this verse conveys is that the *sansar* meaning the household life is comparable to a fig tree, which is perishable—but the root of this fig tree is comparable to the imperishable, eternal Brahman whereas all the branches could be compared to the perishable beings. This Brahman is identical with the Soul that Nachiketa questioned. Attaining this self or supreme knowledge of the soul is of absolute necessity in the Hindu culture. Before finishing this meditation on the *Upaniṣads* and the vignette, I would like to say that for better understanding of its connection to the original logic explicated by Brennan I would like to give two more references from the *Upaniṣads*. The knowledge of the Soul is so precious to one's being that it has been compared with *ānanda* or bliss. In *Taittiriya Upaniṣad* it has been said (*"ānanda brahmeti bajana ānandadhev khalmimāni bhutāni jāyante, ānanden jatani jibanti"* 313) which means *ānanda* is identical with Brahman, the whole universe is born out of *ānanda*, grows in *ānanda* and finally returns to *ānanda*.

In *Brihdarnyaka Upaniṣad* this knowledge of Self or Brahman has been compared to *amrit* the most precious or supreme of anything existing in the universe. In it the hermit Jagmabalkya before going to *banaprastha* (it refers to a life of renunciation at the age of fifty, predicated by Hindu Sashtra) wants to give his wealth to his wife Maitraye when she hurls this crucial question to him, ("*jenāham nāmrita sām kimamham ten kurjām*" 820), what do I do with that through which I cannot attain *amrit* meaning Brahman? Maitreyi thinks that the material wealth is transient and she does not have anything to do with that and she aspires for the supreme knowledge which is the knowledge of Brahman the attainment of which will liberate her from materialistic desires and transient life—*amrit* is identical with the supreme knowledge through which one can conquer death. Teresa Brennan's search for the "original logic" (first experienced in but not limited to the intrauterine state) in order to cut through and override the "foundational fantasy" which gives rise to the "ego's era" could very well be connected to this quest for supreme knowledge of the Self or Brahman which is also identical with attaining *ānanda* or bliss in the way I interpret Irigaray's theory of "jouissance." Once anybody attains this kind of supreme knowledge one goes beyond gross materialistic desires and conquers the transience of life. Brennan theory of "relational energy" talks about reviving this phase of purity by symbolically recapitulating the state of innocence in the mother's womb. By this, she demystifies Lacanian "ego's era" and reaches out to the descent of the "supramental consciousness" or a synthesis of the material with the spiritual, which I will discuss in detail later in this chapter.

Nature in Brennan: Connection with the Indian Sankhaya Philosophy

In formulating her theory of the "foundational fantasy" Brennan draws an interesting analogy between Nature versus technology and the mother's body versus the way she is located in the phallogocentric culture of the West as well as in its psychoanalytic theories. As we have seen, the subject is allowed to move at the cost of the other who is "fixed" as an object, and that other is defined as feminine, whereas the subject that moves is considered masculine. Brennan's unique contribution to feminist philosophy is that, unlike Freud and Lacan, she does not merely configure the formation of masculinity and femininity, but goes much further by envisioning and constructing a phase in which she recalls the "original logic" to destabilize the phallogocentric center of Western culture. In this she is very close to Irigaray and the Indian philosophy of Sankhaya[9] and Tantra. In fact Irigaray's theory of "jouissance" is closer to Indian Tantric philosophy, whereas Brennan's reconfiguration of the theory of the "intrauterine" state, which she uses in various terms to refer to under the aegis of "fleshly logic," or, even nature, is more akin to Sankhaya philosophy.

In Sankhaya philosophy, a great deal of importance has been attached to Nature or *Prakṛti*; at the same time, the concept of complementarity between we could say is the male and the female, or *Puruṣa* and *Prakṛti* has been emphasized. This concept of *Puruṣa—Prakṛti* could be likened to Western psychoanalysis, but unlike Western psychoanalysis it acknowledges the female concept or principle as an independent identity which has the capacity to move the universe. Let me quote from the Sankhaya philosophy as Dr. Radhakrishnan interpreted it:

> *Prakṛti* (usually translated "Nature") is the basis of all objective existence, physical and psychical. As the changing object, *Prakṛti* is the source of the world of becoming. In it all determinate existence is implicitly contained. It is pure potentiality. It is not being but force, a state of tension of the three constituents (*gunas*), *sattava*, *rajas*, and *tamas*. *Prakṛti* is, as it were, a string of three strands. *Sattava* is potential consciousness; *rajas* is the source of activity, and *tamas* is a source of that which resists activity. They produce pleasure, pain, and indifference, respectively. All things as products of *Prakṛti*, consist of the three *gunas* in different proportions. The varied interaction of the *gunas* accounts for the variety of the world. (432)

In Sankhaya philosophy *Prakṛti* or Nature is a force or energy consisting of three different states or principles: one is the principle of inertia (*tamas*) meaning inactivity the way Freud uses it which is different than its interpretation in Physics, the principle of vital motion or energy which is rather unruly. Sri Aurobindo interprets it as the principle of kinesis, and the principle of truth, light, and consciousness (*Sattawic*). It has further been enunciated that when the balance between the three *gunas* is achieved, or when the *Sattawic* state is achieved, the connection with the inactive *Puruṣa* is established. Achieving this state of *Puruṣa* could be likened to achieving Brahman of the *Upaniṣads* or Vedantic philosophy.

But, what I want to emphasize is that although *Prakṛti* has been addressed as "unconscious" in Sankhaya philosophy it is still looked upon as a force or energy consisting of three different principles which is activated by *Puruṣa*. The interesting thing is although *Prakṛti* is activated by *Puruṣa*, *Prakṛti* is active and *Puruṣa* is inactive. It has been said, "The evolution of unconscious *Prakṛti* can take place only through the presence of conscious *Puruṣa*" (432). But, although *Prakṛti* has been inscribed as unconscious, it is further being said in Sankhaya philosophy, "The union of *Puruṣa* and *Prakṛti* is compared to a lame man of good vision mounted on the shoulders of a blind man of sure foot" (424). Thus, it seems quite obvious that *Puruṣa* and *Prakṛti* are interdependent—one cannot function without the other. *Puruṣa* initiates action and *Prakṛti* executes it. *Prakṛti* is not completely unconscious either because, according to the three principles by which it operates, it achieves a state of Sattawa equal to achieving a state of consciousness. Thus, along with Sri Aurobino one could say, "*Prakṛti* presents itself as an inconscient Energy in the material world, but, as the scale of consciousness rises, she reveals herself more and more as a conscious force and we perceive that even her inconscience concealed a secret consciousness" (*The Life Divine* 330). Thus, the difference[10] between Sankhaya philosophy and Western psychoanalysis is that whereas in the former Nature or *Prakṛti* although being conceived as unconscious is an active agent in the universe without which *Puruṣa* cannot function, and as such *Prakṛti* is conceived as complementary to *Puruṣa*, in the latter Nature/*Prakṛti*/woman is neither configured as an active agent in the universe (but rather looked upon eternally as unconscious and inconscience) nor looked upon as complementary to men or the male principle. This is where the Western feminists vehemently disagree; Irigaray offers her theory of jouissance and Brennan offers her theory of energetics and "original logic."

Brennan's theory of energy (which is based on Freud's theories but goes beyond him by reconfiguring his theory of energy) credits Nature or *Prakṛti* and the notion of complementarity between *Puruṣa* and *Prakṛti*, or that is the way I reread Brennan's theory in the light of Sankhaya philosophy. By critiquing Irigaray for her inscription of female sexuality as "non-entropic" Brennan has suggested in *The Interpretation of the Flesh* that masculinity and femininity are constructed simultaneously of inertia and entropy meaning inertia and motion—although inertia must be construed here as inactivity as in its common sense meaning. In that sense Brennan constructed her theory that fixity or inertia is associated with women because men pass it to her whereas they move on as active agents. Here, I want to emphasize the connection between Brennan's theory to the Sankhaya philosophy in relation to the concept of complementarity in which *Puruṣa* cannot function without *Prakṛti* and vice versa. I would like to recall that Brennan's is opposing Freud's theory that the individual is self-contained. If we did experience ourselves as energetically connected, then a perfect society with a proper interactive economy might occur, or in Irigaray's terminology, the era of the ethics of the "sexual difference" would begin. But, in reality, it is different—too many points of obstruction to perpetuate female inertia and masculine entropy. Brennan thinks the balance would be restored if the intrauterine state were replaced in the imagination by a suitable alternative to nostalgia for the mother's womb:

This means there has to be a field of contrast which has the same effects and the same benefits as the flesh, but which is lived after birth. The obvious candidate for this field of contrast is the unbound primary process, the life drive. But what is that, other than nature? To nature overall I have attributed the same process of connection and inherent logic, the same inseparability of thought and substance experienced in utero. (*History After Lacan* 116)

Thus the suitable alternative to the intrauterine state is the life-drive or nature. But as I understand it, by establishing a connection to the life drive one can also establish a link with the more rapid motion of the "original logic." Thus capturing the rapid motion of the life-drive also means connecting oneself to Nature—the Nature or *Prakṛti* of Sankhaya philosophy which is the unconscious but active agent and which is called into action by the inactive *Puruṣa*. Thus, Brenann's theory has the nuance that the psychoanalytic invocation of women with inertia and men with motion could be reversed (or both could be part of inertia and motion) by establishing a connection with the life-drive—and there is also the nuance that Brennan wants to achieve a balance and a complementarity between the male principle and the female principle.

Brennan's concept of striving for the original intrauterine state by connecting with the life-drive or 'the unbound primary process after birth' also calls for another interpretation of this theory in the light of Indian Tantric philosophy. According to this school of Indian philosophy,[11] nature or *Prakṛti* has been given the status of absolute power. In contrast to the Sankhaya philosophy, in which nature is still considered dependent on *Puruṣa*, the Tantric philosophy believes that nature or *Prakṛti* reigns over everything. *Prakṛti* keeps the universe moving because Brahman without *Prakṛti* is static. Regarding to *Prakṛti*, I would also refer to another term "*Mula-prakṛti*" meaning basic nature, which according to the *Mahanirvanatantram* refers to a state where balance has been achieved between different gunas.[12] According to the definition of the *Mahanirvanatantram Mula-prakṛti* stands for the phase in which a balance has been achieved in these three *gunas* or qualities (*Sattawa, Rajah,* and *Tamah*). *Mula-prakṛti* as a balance of different mental and physical states has quite a good status compared to the term "nature" in Western phallogocentric culture. *Shakti* originates from *Prakṛti*, which is also defined as *Mula-Prakṛti*. That *Shakti* or *Adya-Shakti* originates from the *Prakṛti* has been made clear in various places of the *Mahanirvanatantram*. Thus, *Adya-Shakti* which originates from the *Mula-prakṛti* dwelling in Brahman creates the entire world which is the manifestation of the Brahman identical with consciousness and again this manifestation is controlled by *Shakti* who devises this world as manifestation of Brahman or consciousness. The creation of the *Shakti* or the *Adya-Shakti* is construed as the first creation. After that the universe as the manifestation of Brahman devised by *Shakti* is called the Second creation. Next what follows is the creation of *ahankara* meaning ego consisting of three *gunas* (*sattawa, rajah, tamah*), from tamasik guna arises five senses (sound, touch, shape, fluidity and smell) and from sattwic guna arises five sensory organs. After that from the five senses arise five elements: earth, water, fire, air and sky.[13] The *Shakti* or the *Adya-Shakti*, or the feminine power, thus controls the creation of the universe.

In the fourth chapter of the *Mahanirvanatantram* it has been described in great detail how powerful this *Adya-Shakti* or Kali is. It has been suggested that She is the power from which the entire universe has emanated; that is, she is the mother[14] of the entire universe. She has also been addressed as "Adya" meaning original power from which all five senses and all five elements originated. She has also been addressed as creator of Brahman, *Vishnu* and *Maheswar*—that means the Hindu holy trinity,[15] the three male gods also originated from her. This *Shakti* has been described as both subtle and manifest and adored in various ways. She has also been described as the *tama* or the dark power beyond words prior to creation and came to create with Brahman with her transformed energy as *Shakti*. This "tama" or darkness through which she is sometimes described prior to creation did not stay forever as the dark power, but transformed itself into creative energy in conjunction with Brahman. The truth of the matter is that Brahman or *Parambrahman* is just the cause. He is all pervasive and he is static. Although his presence is all-pervasive he is not attached to anything. He is inactive; he does not execute anything and he does not have any authority to do so. The *Shakti* is the supreme creator who is creating the entire universe, sustaining it and destroying it just accepting the desire of Brahman. That she is the executive power or energy has been reiterated in the *Mahanirvanatantram*. The entire universe becomes static without her. One could see in this interpretation of Indian Tantric philosophy an advanced and a modified version of Sankhaya philosophy—in which *Prakṛti* has been given an omnipotent status as of *Shakti*. By bringing in the concept of *Prakṛti* as *Shakti* as inscribed in *Tantric* philosophy, I want to enunciate that Brennan's invocation of nature or the call to establish connection with the 'life-drive' to bring the world-order back could be read in the context of *Shakti* or the invocation of *Shakti*. Although, I would like to add that Irigaray's theory of jouissance is more close to this *Tantric* philosophy than Brennan's. Brennan's theory seems to have more connection with Sankhaya philosophy than with Tantric, because Brennan seems to invoke nature to establish balance in the world between male and female principle, but not to invoke an order which would supercede everything—her theory suggests "crossing-boundaries" but also calls for the assessment of the role the environment plays in it (cf. *History After Lacan*). She would have reservations about calling for a *Shakti* which would rule the universe without any impediment, fixity or inertia (Brennan seems to be more practical)—but Irigaray is more *Tantric* in this way by conquering any thought about fixity or obstruction. Although Irigaray thinks the evolution of the ethics of "sexual difference" would not occur without the involvement of two parties of different sexes, her theory of jouissance gestures towards a course which like *Shakti* in *Tantra* goes beyond everything—invoking an order of Prigogine's "dissipative structure," where Brennan would have second thoughts about obstructions or fixities in the environment.

Psychic versus Social in Brennan and Sri Aurobindo

The unique contribution of Brennan's theory of "relational energy" is its juxtaposition of the social and historical representations with their psychic counterparts.[16] All the feminist philosophers who believe in the ethics of sexual-difference are highly hopeful to reconcile the social and the psychic, the corporeal and the spiritual, and the matter and the spirit. Elizabeth Grosz's *Volatile Bodies* is an attempt to reconcile these two into one framework. Judith Butler's work *The Psychic Life of Power* finally admits the importance of the theory of a psyche along with the theory of power and critiques psychoanalysis for eschewing this task, but unfortunately still foregrounds the social in the development of the psyche. Butler's observation in the introduction of her book about "becoming" illuminates the truth that for the becoming of a being the psychic is dependent on the social, not the other way around— whereas Irigaray's theory of "jouissance" or Brennan's theory of "relational energy" discuss the psychic controlling the social or vice versa—but in Butler the social being seems to have the position of the supreme signified. Butler writes, "That 'becoming' is no simple or continuous affair, but an uneasy practice of repetition and its risks, compelled yet incomplete, wavering on the horizon of social being" (Butler 30). The "psychic" is obviously undermined here in the process of "becoming." Drucilla Cornell's work *The Imaginary Domain* seems to follow the same trajectory which trying to construct a psychic space through her construction of an "imaginary domain" in which one has the right to construct one's own sexual being by exerting one's imagination is extremely limited in its perception. It foregrounds, "the legal guarantee of the social bases of self-respect," as the ground for becoming a person who lacks a psychic dimension. Here, as in Butler, the psychic part of being is neglected.

However, to return to Brennan I would like to note that her theory is grounded in the psychic or the soul and because of this postulates a transformational theory of the social world. In the "Conclusion" of *History After Lacan* she gives a thorough account of her fear as to what would happen if the real being—who lives in spite of the overlay of the narcissistic subject, is not restored through rehabilitating its connection with "nature" or "fleshly logic" or " life-drive":

> The consequence of living in the high-tech built environment is that one almost has to be a subject to repel its deadening effects. As I hope I have shown, these deadening effects are deceptive: the world from which they emanate appears to be a world of more rapid motion, with a rapid pulse that can for a time be taken as energy itself, as it speeds up one's conscious tempo. But the price of this temporary excitement will be paid somewhere. Even if it is not paid by the subject who benefits, the deadening effects of this environment more and more make each and everyone an object. (187)

According to Brennan the Western high-tech environment has started an overall objectification process and there are only two ways out: 'striving for subjectivity through the exploitation of others' (Brennan has deftly depicted this when inscribing the formation of masculinity and femininity, i.e., the way the masculine subject becomes a subject by making woman a fixed entity or object), or positively by seeking to connect oneself to the life-drive. Unfortunately, this process of connecting oneself to the life-drive is not happening. On the contrary, what is occurring is that the paranoia in "sexual difference" is increasing because of the process of objectification process in "ego's era."

What Brennan's theory suggests as a remedy, alliance with nature, and the alliance with the original logic, which I would read through Indian philosophy. Brennan's invocation of the original logic and the life-drive I have explained in relation to the *Upaniṣads* and Sankhaya philosophy. Brennan's stress on the original logic as beyond the traditional oppositions of rationality and romanticism or order and chaos, differentiates her approach from the call to return to mother nature invoked by the Romantic poets. There is more to it. Brennan's theory of "relational energy" synthesizes the spiritual with the material, the psychic with the social, and this makes her theory doubly connected to the modern Indian philosopher Sri Aurobindo's theory of "supramental consciousness." The main contribution of this philosophy is to integrate the material and the spiritual. Sri Aurobindo's philosophy is heavily grounded in Indian philosophical texts like the *Vedas* and *Upaniṣads* but he is developing these texts in his theory of "supramental consciousness" which he also inscribes as Brahman on the material plane or in the body. The significant criteria of the theory of "supramental consciousness" useful in relation to Brennan's theory, is the idea of calling on the spiritual consciousness in the body for the transformation of the world. Sri Aurobindo's theory postulates the transformation of the world through the descent of supreme consciousness on the material plane. What then is this supreme consciousness?

> If the rift in the lid of mind is made, what happens is an opening of vision to something above us or a rising up towards it or a descent of its powers into our being. What we see by the opening of vision is an infinity above us, an eternal Presence or an infinite Existence, an infinity of consciousness, an infinity of bliss—a boundless Self, a boundless Light, a boundless Power, a boundless Ecstasy. It may be that for a long time all that is obtained is the occasional or frequent or constant vision of it and

a longing and aspiration, but without anything further, [. . .] for
the full spiritual transformation more is needed, a permanent
ascension from the lower into the higher consciousness and an
effectual permanent descent of the higher into the lower nature.
(*The Life Divine* 911-12)

The opening of this vision, this boundless ecstasy could be likened
to the *Upaniṣadic* realization of Brahman or the Ultimate Reality
but what Sri Auroindo adds to it are the processes of ascent and
descent.

For the full manifestation of consciousness what is needed is
first an ascension from the lower level of consciousness to the
highest level of it which then should be followed by a descent of
that supreme bliss to the lower nature, or mundane, or corporeal or
material plane. The descent is as important as the ascent. The
Upaniṣads have nuances about this descent but do not amplify the
process and that is the important contribution of Sri Aurobindo's
philosophy of "supra-mental consciousness." To elaborate a bit
more about this process of descent as Sri Aurobindo portrays it in
The Life Divine:

This is the third motion, the descent which is essential for
bringing the permanent ascension, an increasing inflow from
above, an experience of reception and retention of the
descending Spirit or its powers and elements of consciousness [.
. .]. A light descends and touches or envelops or penetrates the
lower being, the mind, the life or the body; or a presence or a
power or a stream of knowledge pours in waves and currents, or
there is a flood of bliss or a sudden ecstasy; the contact with the
superconscient has been established [. . .] the heart and the sense
become subtle, intense, large to embrace all existence, to see
God, to feel and hear and touch the Eternal, to make a deeper
and closer unity of self and the world in a transcendent
realization. (913)

The process of descent is essential to bring Ecstasy down to the
material plane and then stabilize it there. The second most
important characteristic of this descent is that it penetrates the
lower being meaning the unconscious or the inconscient, (it must
be remembered here that in the Hindu philosophy the unconscious

is not associated with women—or, women are not considered as men's unconscious). The descent must take place.[17] The descent is dependent on the connection between the "subconscient" meaning subconscious and the "superconscient" meaning the highest level of consciousness—mind and reason are intermediaries between these two states. Unlike Freud, who thinks that without binding the primary process, the pleasure principle cannot function, Sri Aurobindo's theory of "supramental consciousness" creates synthesis between the primary process and the secondary process. Instead of the binding of the primary process, he establishes a connection between the primary process and the secondary process via his spiritual theory of "supramental consciousness." Critiquing Western psychoanalysis Sri Aurobindo suggests that both "subconscient" and "superconscient" are important but the process has to start at the "superconscient." This means first one has to establish a connection with one's psychic center, achieve ecstasy, intuition or light and then bring it down to the "subconscient." But, the problem with Western psychoanalysis is that it focuses on the "subconscient" and thus stagnates. Instead of tying the primary process, Sri Aurobindo lets it flow uninterrupted and the ego gradually comes to terms with the secondary process. The pleasure principle starts to operate when the proper connection is established between the two processes. Sri Aurobindo writes, "The subconscient and the superconscient are two different formulations of the same All" (*The Life Divine* 65).

Brennan's theory of original logic is a dismantling of the Freudian and the Lacanian theory of the ego, according to which we are locked into the world of the ego. Brennan's theory of energy rereads both Freudian and Lacanian psychoanalysis (cf. Irigaray's theory of jouissance) and looks for that origin or the psychic center which might be traced to the intrauterine nest. But, her theory does not stop there; it is also about bringing the life-drive back to the world for its transformation to oppose the foundational fantasy, to put an end to "ego's era." Analogous to Sri Aurobindo's theory, Brennan's theory also searches for ways to transcend the ego. She tries to resolve the problem with the ego through her theory of energy of going back to the intrauterine nest. This is her way of unwinding the knot between the primary and the secondary processes. But, like Irigaray, she invokes the discourse

She's done it psychically, now she needs to apply it socially

Nature + the Material

of the spirit—which transcends the binaries between matter and spirit. Both Irigaray and Brennan are together in their attempts to find alternatives to Western psychoanalytic practice. Both of their theories have nuances through which they try to resolve this problem with the ego by turning to other cultures and philosophies than the Western ones. In the "Conclusion" of *History After Lacan*:

> Acknowledging one's indebtedness to and dependence on the extraordinary activity of the 'God as Nature' is aligned here with the opposition to power over others in any form; the feminist concern with symbolizing divinity in maternal terms (Irigaray 1984) becomes an imperative that is aligned with the advocacy of tolerance that lends liberal vocabularies their good sense as distinct from their egoism. The intellect is allied with the living spirit, for it is the intellect's task to labour against the fixed points that block thought and the resurrection of the body. The fact that so many movements embody aspects of this alliance, the power of the life-drive evident in all of them, is grounds for real optimism. Together these movements constitute an opposition to the acting out of the fantasy in all its aspects. (194-95)

According to Brennan the psychic or the spiritual or "God as Nature" should not be reduced to the psychic realm. For the transformation of Western patriarchal and materialistic culture, it is also essential to transform the social. But, without a psychic transformation, the social transformation will not take place. It has to start by seeking the root, seeking the origin, seeking the psychic, seeking the spiritual, seeking nature, and transforming the social. The process can start either psychically or socially, but it cannot be completed without both dimensions.

NOTES

1. The chapter originated in response to Teresa Brennan's inquiry about the concept of Brahman in Indian Hindu Philosophy during the summer of 1998. Also note that, all translations from Sanskrit to English are my own

2. Sri Aurobindo (Aurobindo Ghosh, 1872-1950) is one of the modern philosophers of India. I emphasize Sri Aurobindo's name in relation to Indian philosophy quite strongly, because it is through his philosophy of supra-mental consciousness that bringing down *ānanda* or the energy of union with the Ultimate Reality or Brahman to the material plane has been foregrounded. In general, Indian philosophy, or, prior to him, Indian philosophy talks about only *ānanda* which could be attained only through unconscious intuitive processes. His major contribution to Indian philosophy is to bring matter and spirit together and show that it is possible to achieve *ānanda* or the Ultimate Reality on the material plane. I would like to allude to Dr. Radhakrishnan's remark on Sri Aurobindo in this regard:

> Attained by mystical insight and expressed in brilliant literary and rational form, the philosophy of Sri Aurobindo constitutes a point of view which he considers to be original Vedanta but which stands in strong opposition to the Advaita Vedanta of Samkara on several basic issues. (575)

3. It is worthwhile to take into account Lacan's observation about "mystical jouissance" in his article, "God and the Jouissance of The Woman":

> The mystical is by no means that which is not political. It is something serious, which a few people teach us about, and most often women or highly gifted people like Saint John of the Cross [. . .]. You can also put yourself on the side of not-all. There are men who are just as good as women. It does happen. And who therefore feel just as good. Despite, I won't say their phallus, despite what encounters them on that score, they get the idea, they sense that there must be a *jouissance* which goes beyond. That is what we call a mystic. (146-47)

4. Only in Irigary's most recently published book, *Between East and West*, she has become explicit about her reference to Indian culture.

5. In this regard, I would like to refer to Ashis Nandy's article "The Savage Freud: The First Non-Western Psychoanalyst and the Politics of Secret Selves in Colonial India," where he refers to Girindrashekhar Bose as the first Indian psychoanalyst who practiced psychoanalysis as "science as a philosophy of consciousness."

6. The Hindu philosophical text the *Upaniṣads* mainly discusses Brahman—the pure Absolute. Brahman is conceived as both transcendent and immanent. Brahman is conceived as both as the transcendental Self and the Self in the individual selves. The message of the *Upaniṣads* is that once a person attains the knowledge of Brahman or the pure Absolute, one attains Brahman in one's own self.

7. I must mention here that the concept of Brahman of the *Upaniṣads* was developed later by Hindu Tantric philosophy (which dates from ninth to sixteenth centuries). What is significant here is to note that Brahman is conceived as independent of gender in Tantric philosophy. Brahman—the pure Absolute of the Upaniṣadic philosophy has been conceived as both male and female in Tantric philosophy. Although, one must note that the concept of Brahman as both male and female energy was there in the *Upaniṣads* as well, but it was more pronounced in Tantric philosophy.

8. For clarification I would like to suggest that when I read Irigaray's theory of "jouissance" as "consciousness" or "delight" or *ānanda*, I refer to the same Upaniṣadic origin but Brennan's theory is more linked to the quest of the self as opposed to materialistic desire as expressed in It, whereas Irigaray's theory is more related to the Brahman as consciousness and *ānanda* as revealed in the *Upaniṣads*. But, still the underlying agenda is the same—to attain a way out of the Western phallogocentrism, and materialistic desires in search for the transformation. Both the theories are guided by transformational ethics.

9. The Sankhaya philosophy is one of the six schools of Indian philosophy (third century A.D.) According to Sankhaya philosophy, everything in the universe is based on the duality of the 'knowing subject' *Puruṣa* and the 'known subject' *Prakṛti*.

10. I do not want my readers to think that I am too quick to draw an analogy between Western psychoanalysis and Indian philosophy. There is a connection between them in relation to the truth that both branches deal with human "mind." I could further confirm my realization with the

first Indian psychoanalyst Girindra Shekhar Bose's practice of psychoanalysis. He practiced psychoanalysis by connecting it to Indian philosophy (Sankhaya philosophy) according to which achieving between three mental states: *sattawa, rajah,* and *tamah*—(*sattawa* meaning perfection, light and beauty, *rajah* meaning the excessive vital energy, and *tamah* meaning inertia) leads one to attain perfection. The modern Indian philosopher Sri Aurobindo's theory of "supra-mental consciousness" theory also refers to achieving a kind of balance in these three mental states as one of the rules of *sadhana* meaning yoga.

11. Hindu Tantric philosophy has not yet entered the canon of Indian philosophy. Although, I must mention that the modern Indian philosopher Sri Aurobindo tried to raise its status to the canon of philosophy. In this regard, I would like to mention Sri Aurobindo's *The Life Divine, Yogic Sadhan* and *The Foundation of Indian Culture.*

12. The "*gunas*" refer to three mental stages *sattawa, rajah* and *tamah* in one's psychic being according to both the Indian Sankhaya and the Tantric philosophy—with the difference that in Tantric philosophy *Prakṛti* supercedes everything unlike in Sankhaya philosophy. Whereas Sankhaya philosophy believes that there is a balance between *Puruṣa* and *Prakṛti,* Tantric philosophy believes that *Prakṛti* or *Shakti* is behind the creation and its manifestation.

13. It is worth noting here that Irigaray often talked about these five elements in terms of Nature and how important it is for women to establish a connection with these five elements.

14. I have reservations using her as a mother figure as well, since it has been distorted by patriarchy in the Hindu culture. By conceiving this Shakti as the mother, women are brainwashed to sacrifice everything. Mother as a religious figure or the Divine mother is different from the conception of real motherhood. The picture of a real mother is subsumed under the image of the Divine mother and who is expected to do anything and everything, whereas she does not possess the power and strength of the Divine mother. It is more appropriate to establish a connection first with the real mother before calling her the "Divine mother." Both Teresa Brennan and Irigaray's theories are useful in this regard.

15. The power of the *Devi* as the creator of *Brahma, Vishnu, Maheshwar* has been described in the *Devibhagavata Purana* where Brahman rising from *Vishnu* naval started to wonder why *Vishnu* was meditating since he was the creator of the world. When *Brahma* approached *Vishnu*, he explained that he is not the creator but *Devi Bhagavati* (who is identical with Shakti) is the creator and it is She who gave him the power to conquer the demons *MadhuKaitava*. If he had been free he would never have left *baikunthaya*, meaning heaven, and take birth in different forms. Thus, *Brahma, Vishnu,* and *Maheshwar* gathered to think about the creator when they heard the oracle: "The entire universe consists of me (meaning Shakti) and there is nothing eternal without me." Then they heard another oracle, "Be prepared to create." After that a carrier arrived to take them to heaven and they arrived at a place where *Bhagavati* was surrounded by thousands of maids and as soon as they landed they were turned into women and had to spend ten thousand years attending Bhagavati. Finally, when she was happy with their prayers, she transformed them into males and from her own body imparted Mahasaraswati, Mahalakshmi, and Mahakali to them and asked them to create, to sustain and to destroy with the help of these three manifestations of *Shaktis*. Finally, *Brahma, Vishnu* and *Maheswar* realized that there is nothing else except these three forms of *Shaktis*.

16. Michelle Renee Matisons's article "The New Feminist Philosophy of the Body: Haraway, Butler and Brennan" is useful in this regard as it foregrounds Brennan's contribution of bringing the psychic and the social together. She comments, "This theory, developed first in *The Interpretation of the Flesh* (Brennan 1992) and furthered in *History After Lacan* (Brenan 1993) and *Vision in Context* (Brennan 1996), combines analyses of social and historical processes with a detailed account of the psychic dynamics of socialization and individuation" (26).

17. It is important for our purpose to see how Sri Aurobindo describes the processes of the ascent and descent as contrary to Western psychoanalysis:

> I find it difficult, [. . .] to take these psychoanalysts at all seriously—yet perhaps one ought to, for half knowledge is a powerful thing and can be a great obstacle to the coming in front of the true Truth.[. . .]. They look from down up and explain the higher lights by the lower obscurities; but the foundation of these things is above and not below. The *superconscient* and not the *subconscient*, is the true foundation of things. The significance

of the lotus is not to be found by analysing the secrets of the mud from which it grows here; its secret is to be found in the heavenly archetype of the lotus that blooms or ever in the Light above. (*The Adventure of Consciousness* 44).

Part II: Literature

Chapter 6

Jouissance and Ānanda in Joyce[*]

This is the first chapter on the aspect of "jouissance in literature"; in this journey I choose both Western and Indian writers as the book takes a comparative approach in exploring the concept of jouissance not only in theory, but in literature as well. James Joyce's *A Portrait of the Artist as a Young Man* exemplifies both Irigaray's theory of jouissance and the concept of *ānanda* as I will show it in this chapter. *A Portrait of the Artist as a Young Man* embodies the notion of jouissance as both corporeal and celestial, as it is emphasized through Stephen's staunch critique of Catholicism, which I will discuss shortly. More significantly, this novel provides a perfect vehicle through which as a postcolonial writer and as an outsider to view the story from the Indian philosophical theory of *ānanda*, as it inscribes the moments, which represent the supreme form of consciousness achievable through transcendence of ego, which Joyce calls *stasis*.

The novel *A Portrait of the Artist as a Young Man* was published in 1916, around the same time Rabindranath Tagore wrote the lyric play, *The King of the Dark Chamber*. But, what is significant about these two works is that Joyce's novel embodies the search for the supreme moment of consciousness, as does Tagore's *The King of the Dark Chamber*, although the genres are of course, different. Another significant point about Joyce that I want to explore in this chapter is my reading of his work *A Portrait of the Artist as A Young Man*, through the lens of Indian philosophical theory of *ānanda*. According to Indian philosophy, the supreme moment achieved through art or poetry is identical to the supreme moment of consciousness called *ānanda*.

* An earlier version of this chapter was presented during the 1999-2000 seminar (Aesthetics, Politics, and Difference) at the Pembroke Center for Study and Research on Women, Brown University, Providence, RI, USA.

Epiphany

It is quite significant to notice that Joyce's epiphany is his artistic reconstruction which on the one hand defies the value system of the Catholic church, and on the other hand, the artistic process that gives rise to poetry is very spiritual and thus close to the Indian philosophical poetry of the Vedic times and what Sri Aurobindo defines as *The Future Poetry*. Tagore foregrounds it as it is there in Indian culture. Although Joyce ascribes great importance to the role of women, he is overwhelmed and sad about how Christianity treats women, and is preoccupied, like the feminist philosopher Luce Irigaray in voicing his criticism about it. Irigaray's *Marine Lover* inscribes her critique of Christianity and her grievances about it:

> He comes from the Father. To the Father he aspires. Toward the Father he walks and never falters. By the Father alone he fears to be forsaken. By the Father alone he fears to be forsaken. Showing the path to be followed if one is to obtain transfiguration, resurrection, ascension—become the Father's word, and accept agony and crucifixion as passages from incarnation into eternal life.
>
> This is the most common interpretation, and in general the values of sin and redemption it espouses have formed the basis of Christian ethics. This Christic model consecrates an historic stage where man stands between nature and God, flesh and Word, body and speech. Moment in which man constitutes himself in boundless allegiance to the Father's will, and in which attraction of the original mother, wife, sister, mistress disappears, even as enchanting reflections. (165)

The above passage embodies Irigaray's sadness as well as her delegitimization of Christianity. It obviously represents her feminist standpoint about how the Western religious hegemony exerts such a controlling power on women, limiting women to merely being virgin. According to Christianity, a woman should not be engaged in any carnal exchange—because Jesus was born of a virgin mother and that eliminates any possibility of a woman having had a sexual role. As Irigaray further suggests in the same chapter, "The Crucified One," women appear in Christianity only as virgins or repentant sinners. What is unique to notice here is that

Irigaray wrote her first book *Speculum* in 1975, and Joyce wrote his novel in 1914, but there is a striking similarity in the way each perceives Christianity, and it is quite pertinent to note this striking resemblance. Scholars on Joyce have exhaustively written about Joyce's use of epiphany; and women are an essential part of that epiphanic moment. Either, the epiphanic realization is triggered by a woman figure, or the figures appear as the spiritual experiences of epiphany. But, Joyce wants to give the message that spiritual realization as revealed through epiphanic moments are subject to his encounter with women. Women acquire supreme importance in the world of Joyce's art.

Since his childhood, the hero of the novel, Stephen, has had the deep desire to pursue a spiritual life—a desire which occurred to him through epiphany. His first access to the spiritual world of epiphany occurs through his contemplation of the image of Mercedes, a character he read about in a novel. Let us encounter his venture into the world of Mercedes which transports him to a different world:

> He did not want to play. He wanted to meet in the real world the unsubstantial image which his soul so constantly beheld. He did not know where to seek it or how; but a premonition which led him on told him that this image would, without any overt act of his, encounter him. They would meet quietly as if they had known each other and had made their tryst, perhaps at one of the gates or in some more secret place. They would be alone, surrounded by darkness and silence: and in that moment of supreme tenderness he would be transfigured. Weakness and timidity and inexperience would fall from him in that magic moment. (75)

From the perspective of Western culture, this is an experience of epiphany; according to Indian philosophy/culture, here we encounter a person who is seeking the supreme knowledge which is identical with Brahman or the concept of the pure Absolute. First of all, we see that Stephen's soul is searching for something which he calls the unsubstantial image. This unsubstantial image stands for Mercedes, the imaginary character whom he adores and who later turns into other images of women—a constant inspiration for Stephen's writing of poems. In this particular experience he imagines that when he meets this imaginary character, Mercedes, he will be transfigured. So, the aspiration for a spiritual life is very strong in the little boy Stephen's mind. All the epiphanies that Joyce portrays point towards Stephen's spiritual desire—a desire which I define as *ānanda*. In fact, the entire fictional piece is a series of epiphanic experiences through which Stephen increasingly approaches towards ānanda while his aesthetic theory foregrounds his spiritual inclination.

For instance, his epiphanic experience triggered by the clouds is remarkable and could be inscribed as a preamble to his aesthetic theory:

> Disheartened, he raised his eyes towards the slowdrifting clouds, dappled and seaborne. They were voyaging across the deserts of the sky, a host of nomads on the march, voyaging high over Ireland, westward bound [. . .]. He heard a confused music within him as of memories and names which he was almost conscious of but could not capture even for an instant; then the music seemed to recede, to recede, to recede, to recede: and from each receding trail of nebulous music there fell always one long-drawn calling note, piercing like a star the dusk of silence. Again! Again! Again! A voice from beyond the world was calling.
> —Hello, Stephanos!
> —Here comes The Dedalus!
> [. . . . .]
> Yes! Yes! Yes! He would create proudly out of the freedom and power of his soul, as the great artificer whose name he bore, a living thing, new and soaring and beautiful, impalpable, imperishable. (172-74)

The epiphany has not fully occurred yet, but what is crucial to understand his aesthetic theory is the way Stephen ascribes great importance to his name, both parts of it, Stephen and Dedalus point to the intransigence of the artist, a point he finally conveys through his aesthetic theory. Stephen's name is derived from the name of Christian St. Stephen and Ovid's Daedalus and it is quite useful to see the way Robert Scholes traces the allusion related to the name. Robert Scholes says that St. Stephen dedicated his life to a good cause; he tried to awaken the conscience of his race, although he was finally cast out of the city and martyred. Regarding the other name he suggests, "And Stephen Dedalus resembles not only the fabulous artificer and his son Icarus but also the too-clever nephew of Daedalus who was pushed off a high tower by his uncle and turned into a lapwing" (261). Thus, this allusive parallel highlights the theme of Stephen's intransigence from which his aesthetic theory springs. Stephen is clearly a rebel as an artist, especially in his going against the Christian tradition. I have mentioned earlier in my discussion the resemblance of his character's thought to the French feminist Luce Irigaray's critique of Christianity in terms of the abnegation of women. Joyce would inveigh against both Freud and Lacan as he inscribes women as crucial to the theory of epiphany.

In the same epiphanic experience that I am in the process of describing, we see that the climactic epiphanic moment is triggered through the visual experience of a woman. As Stephen takes an oath to him that he will perform the role of the great artificer as an artist, he looks outside for the supreme epiphanic moment and perceives a girl. Follow the aftermath as he sees the girl. The image of the girl becomes absorbed into his soul and he feels ecstatic, "A wild angel had appeared to him, the angel of mortal youth and beauty, an envoy from the fair courts of life, to throw open before him in an instant of ecstasy the gates of all the ways of error and glory. On and on and on and on" (176-77). What is noticeable is the expression *error* which makes this experience not just transcendental but earthly as well. That this ecstatic experience is very much grounded in flesh is clear from the description of the girl:

A girl stood before him in midstream, alone and still, gazing out to sea. She seemed like one whom magic had changed into the likeness of a strange and beautiful sea bird. Her long slender bare legs were delicate as a crane's and pure save where an emerald trail of seaweed has fashioned itself as a sign upon the flesh [. . .]. Her bosom was as a bird's soft and slight, slight and soft as the breast of some darkplumaged dove. (176)

It has also been suggested her face was touched with the wonder of *mortal beauty*. So, her image is very much grounded on earth. Still, not withstanding this earthly experience, her image leads to the transcendental experience of epiphany. He is solely transported to a different world, "some new world, fantastic, dim, uncertain as under sea, traversed by cloudy shapes and beings" (177). The following experience is totally ecstatic and spiritual:

> A world, a glimmer, or a flower? Glimmering and trembling, trembling and unfolding, a breaking light, an opening flower, it spread in endless succession to itself, breaking in full crimson and unfolding and fading to palest rose, leaf by leaf and wave of light by wave of light, flooding all the heavens with its soft flushes, every flush deeper than other. (177)

The symbol i.e., use of a rose is recurrent in this work and here it signifies a spiritual experience—which according to the theory of *ānanda* could signify one of those moments when one reaches the highest level of consciousness. But, what we experience here, as Stephen's epiphanic experience is a preamble to what he narrates later in the fiction in more definitive terms. Here we see a glimpse of that ecstatic experience in which one transcends one's ego and enters the world of divine ecstasy, which Stephen defines later as *stasis*.

What is of utmost importance in this experience of epiphany is the fact that the most spiritual experience is triggered by a woman figure, by its impressive corporeal beauty. As opposed to Christianity Joyce/Stephen ascribes supreme importance to women's body—to the spiritual aspect of the female body. Luce Irigaray has articulated it very well, and Joyce wrote in early part of the twentieth century, prior to Irigaray. Joyce offers his critique of Christianity, which is expressed in his aesthetic theory, as I mentioned earlier that this artist is a rebel and intransigent. Irigaray writes in the *Marine Lover*:

> All that she offers as an abyss of life and jouissance is closed off, like the mouth of hell itself. All the inexhaustible love she conceals for anyone who knows how to approach her is projected into the All Powerful On High. She, a dumb virgin with lips closed, occasionally receives the favor of a word, which she must bring into the world in the shape of a child of God. Mediatrix between Word and flesh, she is the means by which

the male One passes into the other. Receptacle that, faithfully, welcomes and reproduces the will of the Father. Grace that no longer abounds in her womb, even though it is from her womb that she will birth the child. (166)

In the above quotation, Irigaray is virulent about the Christian tradition which does not acknowledge women's spirituality in her corporeal/carnal experience. As she suggests that Virgin Mary is literally and symbolically a mute virgin whose lips are closed, which allude to Western psychoanalytic theory in which women have no access to the symbolic order. As a matter of fact, both Freud and Lacan followed the Christian tradition and formulated their psychoanalytic theory accordingly to deny women access to the symbolic order. Thus, in the quotation Irigaray alludes to the irony that it is from women's womb that the child is born, whereas, the womb is not considered as graceful according to the Christian tradition. However, I must clarify here that Irigaray is supportive of the image of Christ and she thinks that Christian tradition has distorted the message of Christ; rather, she thinks that Christian tradition has distorted the image of Christ. That is the basis of her rereading of Christianity through her theory of the divine—because she firmly believes that women need a divine to create the horizon of accomplishment, which is not given to them by the Christian tradition. In her most recent book *Between East and West*, Irigaray reiterates even more strongly how women in the West can borrow from other cultural traditions.

Thus, Irigaray is in the constant process of re-inscribing Christian tradition, especially as it relates to women, which she does through her psychoanalytical/philosophical writings. Likewise Joyce reconstructs how the Christian tradition relates to women in his *Portrait of the Artist as a Young Man*. Stephen's experience with women at first causes him great agony, which Stephen/Joyce overcomes with his re-reading of the concept of the Virgin Mary. In the fiction, Joyce/Stephen agonizes over the constraints imposed by Christianity which he inveighs against and overcomes by replacing with his own reconstructed ideology. This argument with Christianity's presentation of women we later encounter in Luce Irigaray's theory. Then, in this text, I further interpret Joyce's ideology through the Indian philosophical theory of *ānanda* and complementarity. However, let us look at Joyce's rereading of it in *A Portrait of the Artist as a Young Man*. Stephen describes his imaginary carnal contact with Emma and feels at first repelled by the sense of sin that he faces within his mind, as instilled in him by Christian tradition:

> Shame rose from his smitten heart and flooded his whole being. The image of Emma appeared before him and, under her eyes, the flood of shame rushed forth anew from his heart. If she knew to what his mind had subjected her or how his brute like lust had torn and trampled upon her innocence! Was that boyish love? Was that chivalry? Was that Poetry? (123)

Stephen shudders even at the thought of imaginary physical contact with Emma. It is also interesting to see how the image of Emma is connected to his inspiration of poetry. It is also important to see now how Stephen reconstructs[1] the image of Virgin Mary as a kind person who forgives him and them as well, for the sin of love via carnal exchange, especially in the scene in which Stephen describes his reverie on the Virgin Mary:

> In the wide land under a tender lucid evening sky, a cloud drifting westward amid a pale green sea of heaven, they stood together, children that had erred. Their error had offended deeply God's majesty though it was the error of two children, but it had not offended her *whose beauty is not like earthly beauty, dangerous to look upon, but like the morning star which is its emblem, bright and musical.* The eyes were not offended which she turned upon them nor reproachful. She placed their hands together, hand in hand, and said speaking to their hearts:
> —Take hands, Stephen and Emma. It is a beautiful evening now in heaven. You have erred but you are always my children. It is one heart that loves another heart. Take hands together, my dear children, and you will be happy together, my dear children and your hearts will love each other. (123-24)

Here, Stephen reconstructs the image of a Virgin Mary who gently supports the carnal exchange. Without disapproving Stephen's sexual feeling and imagination about Emma, the holy Virgin rather vows for it by asking them to join their hands and to love each other. One more significant point to notice is Stephen's description of Emma's beauty, which creates harmony rather than disharmony. This inkling of beauty has connection with the *stasis* that he describes later in his definition of beauty and aesthetic theory. However, this imaginary exchange with the Virgin Mary and the reconstruction of her image according to his ideology points towards Stephen/Joyce's aesthetic theory in which women is the entire source of inspiration. And, in a way this bears resemblance to the Indian philosophical concepts of *Puruṣa* (male energy) and *Prakṛti* (female energy), according to which *Puruṣa* or the Conscious-Force and male energy cannot function without *Prakṛti* (the female energy). They are complementary to each other. Not just Stephen/Joyce's perception of women's status in Christianity, which he intends to correct through his writing as an artist, but also his construction of artistic theory goes beyond the West. It is not merely based on Western philosophical theories of Aristotle or St. Thomas Acquinas, but has nuances in it which embody the Indian philosophical concept of *ānanda*.

Concept of Ānanda in Joyce's *A Portrait of the Artist as a Young Man*

Many critics have addressed Joyce's aesthetic theory as revealed in the *A Portrait of the Artist as a Young Man*, but I find Robert Scholes' discussion of it relevant to my discussion. Robert Scholes says that the source of Joyce's aesthetic theory is eclectic, since, it derives from various sources like Scholasticism, Romanticism, Realism, Aestheticism, and Symbolism. In keeping with this view, it is significant to notice the influence of Shelley and Yeats on Joyce's development of aesthetic theory. As Scholes quotes from Shelley's *A Defence of Poetry*, "Poetry is indeed something divine. It is at once the center and circumference of knowledge; it is that which comprehends all science, and that to which all science must be referred" (246). For this study, the critical statement is Shelley's inscription of the source of poetry as divine—in other words, it is a manifestation of the supreme height of consciousness. Sri Aurobindo's book *The Future Poetry* valorizes Shelley's poetry and suggests that poetry is connected to the supreme moment of consciousness, into a discussion which I will enter into in the next section of this chapter. Alluding to the Symbolic movement in literature, Scholes suggests that Yeats' thought influenced Joyce's aesthetic theory as well. In "The Symbolism of Poetry," Yeats said:

> All writers, all artists of any kind, insofar as they have had any philosophical or critical power, perhaps just insofar as they have been deliberate artists at all, have had some philosophy, some criticism of their art; and it has often been this philosophy, or this criticism, that has evoked their most startling inspiration, calling into outer life some portion of the divine life, of the buried reality, which could alone extinguish in the emotions what their philosophy or their criticism would extinguish in the intellect. (253)

The significant point made in this quotation is the valorization of the divine life, which a poet can grasp in his poetry. Most recently Christy Burns in her book *Gestural Politics* has also emphasized the influence of Mallerme on Joyce and the symbolic movement[2] on Joyce. It is remarkable to see how Joyce's text is full of nuances, which cannot only be read as signifying *ānanda* but as representing a certain kind of mystical element which has been defined in the ancient philosophy of the *Vedas* and the *Upaniṣads* and the modern poet Sri Aurobindo's *The Future Poetry* as poetic essence. In *The Future Poetry*, Sri Aurobindo writes:

> The ancient Indian critics defined the essence of poetry as rasa and by that word they meant a concentrated taste, a spiritual essence of emotion, an essential aesthesis, the soul's pleasure in the pure and perfect sources of feeling. The memory of the soul that takes in, broods over and transmutes the mind's thought, feeling and experience, is a large part of the process which comes by this aesthesis, but it is not quite the whole thing; it is rather only a common way by which we get at something that stands behind, the spiritual being in us which has the secret of the universal delight and the eternal beauty of existence. (343)

Both Shelley and Yeats attribute a divine status to the origin of poetry; but, Sri Aurobindo's definition of the Indian classical poetry of the *Vedas* and the *Upaniṣads* having spiritual essence is more conducive to understanding Joyce's definition of the aesthetic process and the meaning of the word *stasis*, which proves to be significant. In Indian philosophy, the word *rasa* means aesthetic pleasure; but *rasa* also alludes to a higher spiritual essence. This means *rasa* does not stand for any ordinary kind of aesthetic pleasure, but rather the kind of aesthetic pleasure which is refined and is connected to the world of spirit or Brahman. In the *Upaniṣads* the word itself has been connected to Brahman; the word is identical with Brahman. Thus, aesthetic pleasure derived from poetry must be connected to the concept of the Absolute or Brahman. In the above quotation by Sri Aurobindo, it is clear that the vagaries of emotion that the soul oversees become transmuted with the final goal to penetrate the veil of thought, feeling and experience and reach that spiritual being which is the source of universal delight. Thus, poetry embodies a spiritual essence of emotion. It is rather unique to find that Joyce as a modernist writer attempts to invoke spirituality in his definition of aesthetic theory which could be interpreted through the Indian philosophical theory of *ānanda*.[3]

Concept of Ānanda in Joyce's *A Portrait of the Artist as a Young Man*

Joyce's *A Portrait of the Artist as a Young Man* is not simply about art or aesthetics, but about attaining supreme *ānanda* or the ultimate reality as well. So, one could say that in Stephen's discussion of aesthetics—(*integretas, consonantia, claritas*), he reveals his philosophy of life, which is to achieve something beyond aesthetics, which I could inscribe as rather non-Western. Joyce's definition of aesthetics I render as jouissance and *ānanda* which encompasses art, beauty, of sublimity, and the female body and which has two dimensions, that of the empirical and of the transcendental—or the material and the spiritual.

Stephen's discussion with the Dean, and his friends Lynch and Cranly clarifies his definition of the aesthetics. That Stephen is an artist is acknowledged by the Dean, as he asks him, "You are an artist, are you not Dedalus? [. . .]. The object of the artist is the creation of the beautiful. What the beautiful is is another question" (189). The Dean inspires him to articulate his artistic theory, which is a striving for the supreme level of consciousness. That he strives for that height is revealed in his conversation with his friend Davin to whom he suggests how important is the birth of the soul, to which he also adds his concern about Ireland. Prior to the articulation of his aesthetic theory, he makes it clear that he hopes to do work toward reform for Ireland in terms of nationality, religion and language. Thus, it reminds us of Stephen's role as an intransigent artist, and the reason he chose the name Dedalus.

Stephen or Joyce's definition of aesthetics first comes forward through the redefinition of Aristotle's theory of pity and terror: "Pity is the feeling which arrests the mind in the presence of whatsoever is grave and constant in human sufferings and unites it with the human sufferer. Terror is the feeling which arrests the mind in the presence of whatsoever is grave and constant in human sufferings and unites it with the secret cause" (204). It could be suggested that Stephen's definition of "terror" is identical with his definition of "sublimity." According to this definition "pity" and "terror" both arrest the mind in the presence of something grave in human suffering with the difference being that pity stays at the level of the human sufferer and terror sublimates the suffering and translates it to a secret cause. So, if we think in terms of a Kantian definition here, we could say that "pity" is identical with the perception of beauty and terror with the Kantian definition of sublimity. What is more unique than this redefinition of catharsis is his distinction between kinetic and esthetic emotion:

> The feelings excited by improper art are kinetic, desire or loathing. Desire urges us to possess, to go to something; loathing urges us to abandon, to go from something. These are kinetic emotions. The arts which excite them, pornographical or didactic, are therefore improper arts. The esthetic emotion (I use the general term) is therefore static. The mind is arrested and raised above desire and loathing. (208)

This suggests rise above "desire." The arts, which invoke desire and loathing, he categorizes as improper art and further suggests that pornography and didactic arts belong to this category. According to him, aesthetic emotion is static, the mind transcends the emotions of desire and loathing in aesthetic perception. In his discussion with Lynch, Stephen clarifies the status of aesthetic emotion. He also equates *stasis* with the *rhythm of beauty*. This definition of art meets the definition of the future poetry defined by Sri Aurobindo. In his book *The Future Poetry* Indian aesthetic art or poetry is not only related to the superficial or surface emotions of love and hate, but according to the Indian definition of aesthetics, art should be presented as being beyond those surface emotions. Put within the concepts introduced within this chapter, art should represent *ānanda* or jouissance each one of which is at one and the same time, empirical and transcendental. In his definition of art, Joyce foregrounds that poise or *stasis* which is beyond any vital agitation. This *stasis* is identical with the state achieved *ānanda*—a state beyond the ego, which one achieves as one transcends it. This state is achieved when one transcends ego and attains Brahman—or the Absolute. Joyce's aesthetic theory has a universal appeal and embodies what I convey in this entire book through the concept of *ānanda*. In *The Future Poetry* Sri Aurobindo's definition of this kind of poetry or art, which contains spiritual essence, is not limited to ancient Indian concept of poetry as represented by the *Upaniṣads* or the *Vedas*. Rather, it embraces poetry of the West as well and he attributes the same status to romantic poetry, specifically to Shelley, and from a philosophical stance, foregrounds Plato who valorizes this divine essence. Sri Aurobindo cautions that what is considered modern poetry is sometimes far removed from the spiritual essence to which he alludes. Modern poetry sometimes becomes too embroiled with what Sri Aurobindo calls vital emotion—with the lower mental state—and does not convey the purified emotion presented through what Joyce calls *stasis*. Here, it is pertinent to look at the comment made by the famous modern Indian poet and singer Dilip Kumar's Roy on Sri Aurobindo's aestheticism in his article, "Sri Aurobindo as an Aesthete":

James H. Cousins, in his New Ways in English Literature, has described Sri Aurobindo as "the philosopher as poet." It is really seen that a philosopher presents his philosophy in sheer poetry. We can, of course, speak of Lucretius, the philosopher, who, in his De Rerum Natura, has successfully proved himself as a poet. In India we get the great philosophical poems like the Gita and the Upanishads, but they are taken more as philosophy than poetry. As other examples of poet-philosophers we can refer to

Vaishnava poets, obviously not excluding the poet Rabindranath
Tagore. Their songs center round God and Love Divine, but
looms large in them is the human significance, leaving behind
the spiritual significance as merely esoteric. But a rare, yet
unique case of the philosopher poet we find Sri Aurobindo. His
intuitive experience of spiritual truths finds a poetic expression
in ideas or thoughts which are marked by luminosity, clarity and
force. He has expressed the spiritual truths, not through all-too-
human symbols and allegories and images, but in their true form,
in the form in which he has seen and realized them. (92)

Dilip Kumar Roy is correct when he highlights that the Vaishnava
poets, (one of their works *Gita Govinda* which I discuss *The King
of the Dark Chamber* discussed in Chapter 2, Radha's Jouissance,
and Tagore's lyric play[4] in Chapter 7) are poet-philosophers. Roy
is not totally correct in his evaluation when he says that these poet-
philosophers valorize human significance and relegate the divine.
On the contrary, especially in Tagore's poetry and lyrical play in
which the divine essence of poetry is very much foregrounded,
because, it deals with the manifestation of Brahman and *ānanda*
through the dissolution of the ego. However, there is no doubt
about the fact that Sri Aurobindo is a philosopher-poet who tries to
reconstruct the divine essence of poetry following ancient texts
like the *Vedas* and the *Upaniṣads*. In *The Future Poetry* he strives
to recapture the divine essence of aesthetic emotion expressed in
the ancient works. In the *Vedas*, the poet has been addressed as a
visionary or the seer who sees the truth. Dilip Kumar Roy
discusses in the same article how in the *Vedas*, the word "heaven"
or "Dyus" stands for the divine Mind. In the same article, "Sri
Aurobindo as an Aesthete," he further describes this mind as, "a
luminous mind receiving faithfully the deeper vibrations of the
Truth, and out of its profound consciousness, expresses them in a
form of beauty, in a golden form, as it were, which is true to them,
i.e., in a perfect body comprising the right thought and the right
word" (96). Roy highlights that the poet has to be the seer
possessing a luminous mind which receives luminous vibrations of
the Truth and then renders it in a beautiful form. Roy also
reemphasizes that truth is aesthetic, and should represent divine
essence. In other words, *stasis* is identical with divine. Finally, it

illumines that Sri Aurobindo as an aesthete equates poetic delight with divine essence.

According to Sri Aurobindo, poetry or art belongs to that highest level of consciousness. In *The Future Poetry*, he tries to retrieve the tradition of philosophical poetry represented in the *Vedas* and the *Upaniṣads*:

> The mental and vital interest, pleasure, pain of thought, life, action is not the source of poetic delight and beauty and can be turned into that deeper thing only when they have sunk into the soul and been transmuted in the soul's radiant memory into spiritual experience—that perhaps was what the Greeks meant when they made Mnemosyne the eternal mother of the muses; the passions can only change into poetic matter when they have been spiritualised in the same bright sources and have undergone the purification, the katharsis spoken by the Greek critic; the life values are only poetic when they have come out heightened and changed into soul values. The poetic delight and beauty are born of a deeper rapture and not of the surface mind's excited interest and enjoyment of life and existence. (342)

Sri Aurobindo clearly distinguishes between mental and vital interest and poetic delight which is spiritual. In alluding to poetic delight, which is a manifestation of Brahman, he uses the Greek word *katharsis* metaphorically to allude to what Joyce calls *stasis*—which Sri Aurobindo refers to as soul values. He clarifies that the life values are only poetic when they are distilled and transformed into soul values which grapple with the highest form of consciousness or Brahman. Thus, what Sri Aurobindo re-inscribes from the *Upaniṣads* portray how poetry or any other form of art should manifest that divine essence which one can achieve only by transcending all mental and vital emotions associated with the ego. He finds the root of this not only in ancient and modern Indian poetry, but also, in Greek poetry, especially in Plato and in the romantic poet Shelley as he articulates in his book *The Future Poetry*. The aesthetic theory that Joyce offers upholds the vision of *The Future Poetry*, in which art should always present poise and *stasis*, and not any turbulence of the vital mind. He is disappointed with modern poetry, because he thinks that modern poetry represents the vital rather than the spiritual essence. With this thought in mind, it is quite relevant to look at the modern Indian Bengali poet[5] Jagadish Chandra Das' poem from his book, *Their Songs and Whispers*, "The Impersonal First-Person":

Self-same this I
Was water,
And was the sky
And remained anon
The earth in water to reflect
Limitless the sky.
The same I
That could be, and indeed was, in so many
Fullest forms
In air and sky, in water and high,
Remain now in dimensionless deformed.
Yet on the bedrock of the Promise perfect
Wait in ambush encased in human frame
For me to transcend,
The Divine to become. (32)

The poem embodies the sign of what Sri Aurobindo defines as future poetry, the spiritual essence. The poet talks about his identification with the different elements of nature—water, sky, air, and earth which refer back again to the concept of Brahman, because, according to ancient Indian Hindu philosophy, the entire world is a manifestation of the Brahman or the Absolute. The poet wants to identify with the Brahman which is present in every object on earth. Finally, the poet aspires to become totally unified with Brahman. Thus, in representing the spiritual essence the poem carries the sign of *The Future Poetry*. This particular poem which was written in 1972, could even be claimed to be postmodern if we take Lyotard's time frame. Thus, one could suggest that the future poetry is regenerated in this poem which contains the spiritual essence of ancient Indian poetry. The emotion expressed here is highly refined in nature. In another important poem by Das,[6] note the transcendental element, "One by One I Catch the Stars," which is immanent as well:

One by One I catch the stars
And I bring them to touch my body one by one:

They all turn into birds and fly away.

The stars glow like fire-flies
They come and settle all over my body:
Indeed my body is made of countless stars.

At long last I have found out:
I exist no longer,
Filled with stars, am myself a star. (182)

These first three stanzas of the poem reveal the height of spiritual essence. The hiatus between the stars and the human body or the divide between the starry heaven/the transcendental plane and the human body/the material plane is totally obviated here. Rather, the transcendental plane and the material planes are unified in this poem. The poem represents what Joyce calls *stasis*, which here is identical to *ānanda*. The poem represents that supreme moment that goes beyond vital emotion and can only be achieved through the collapse of the ego.

It is quite intriguing to see the spiritual essence of the future poetry as defined by Sri Aurobindo being manifest in Joyce's concept of aesthetic theory. Sri Aurobindo predicted the future of poetry in his *The Future Poetry* and it was first published as a series of essays in *Arya.*[7] What is most important is that both Joyce and Sri Aurobindo value and identify spiritual essence or *stasis* as the goal of aesthetic theory. Thus, many modern writers' works underscore a spiritual desire that intersects the world of matter and spirit. All the litterateurs that I discuss in the section, *Jouissance in Literature*, both modern and postcolonial, embody the notion of jouissance as consciousness.

Joyce's aesthetic theory is grounded in Aquinas, but I reiterate throughout this chapter that it goes much beyond Acquinas' philosophy in invoking a theory of consciousness that curiously in its strivings, intersects with the goals of Indian philosophy. It equates the supreme moment of beauty with the supreme moment of consciousness that one achieves when one conquers all vital emotion. This Joyce calls *stasis*, but has also been defined by Acquinas in his theory of *integritas, consonantia* and *claritas*. This theory is also based on the synthesis between the empirical and the transcendental world. In developing his theory Joyce as Stephen uses the example of a simple basket. Stephen suggests, "In order to see that basket [. . .] your mind first of all separates the basket from the rest of the visible universe which is not the basket. The first phase of apprehension is a bounding line drawn about the object to be apprehended" (214). In enunciating this aesthetic theory what Joyce emphasizes here is concentration and meditation. In order to perceive   the   basket,   a   simple   object,   one   needs   full concentration—cognitive skill plus something else—which one can describe as a meditative stance. The Hindu philosophical text, the *Geetā* alludes to this meditative poise which one needs to accomplish anything. But, as the name *integritas* itself signifies, it also refers to the wholeness of a thing, as Joyce writes about it, "You apprehend it as *one* thing. You see it as *one* whole. You apprehend its wholeness. That is *integritas*" (214). What is significant is the repeated emphasis on the term, one or wholeness. The implication of the term *integritas*/oneness/wholeness is not limited to Acquinas, but, from an Eastern stance, invokes the concept of Brahman or the Pure Absolute of the Hindu Upaniṣadic philosophy as has already been mentioned. According to the *Upaniṣads*, the entire world is the manifestation of the Brahman or the Pure Absolute. Thus, Joyce's emphasis on wholeness alludes to the same kind of integrity in which there is no divide between the object and its source—in other words, between immanence and transcendence. This becomes clearer as we look into a more detailed analysis of Joyce's aesthetic theory.

The next important criterion of an aesthetic image is *consonantia*—the balance between the parts—the rhythm of the structure. It is described by Stephen/Joyce in the following way: "In other words the synthesis of immediate perception is followed by the analysis of apprehension" (212). Once the object is comprehended as a whole or as one thing, one needs to comprehend the basic harmony and concord established between the parts. All the parts need to be balanced. The next important, or perhaps the most important, step in the perception of an aesthetic image is *claritas*.

This supreme quality is felt by the artist when the esthetic image is first conceived in his imagination. The mind in that mysterious instant Shelley likened beautifully to a fading coal. The instant wherein that supreme quality of beauty, the clear radiance of the esthetic image is apprehended luminously by the mind which has been arrested by its wholeness and fascinated by its harmony is the luminous silent stasis of esthetic pleasure, a spiritual state very much like to that cardiac condition which the Italian physiologist Luigi Galvani, using a phrase almost as beautiful as Shelley's, called the enchantment of the heart. (215)

Joyce defines *claritas* as the supreme quality, he clearly delineates it as a spiritual state, imbued with the "luminous silent stasis of esthetic pleasure." His reference to *claritas*, as "the supreme quality of beauty," and "the clear radiance of the esthetic image, are significant." This supreme quality of beauty is comprehended by the mind; it has been captured not just by the oneness of the thing or by the harmony of it, but, ultimately transcends the turbulence of vital egotistic emotion and reaches a spiritual moment which Joyce calls *stasis*, and which I call *ānanda* as conceived in Indian philosophy. Through Aristotle's rereading of the theory of pity and terror related to catharsis and through his reading of Acquinas' theory, Joyce conveys his aesthetic philosophy which is the supreme state of beauty or spiritual *stasis*. It captures the moment that Sri Aurobindo defines as the spiritual essence of poetry. Furthermore, Joyce's definition of aesthetic theory could also be applied to interpret the modern Indian poet Das' poems which embody that supreme moment of the unification with the Brahman through the transcendence of ego. Joyce repeatedly asserts how important it is to achieve the state beyond kinetic pleasure—kinetic pleasure standing for the vital emotion associated with the ego. However, it would be quite pertinent to look at another observation from Sri Aurobindo's *The Future Poetry*, to shed more light on Joyce's aesthetic concept of *claritas*. Sri Aurobindo thus writes in the chapter, "The Soul of Poetic Delight and Beauty":

This finer soul of poetic delight throws itself out on the physical mind and being, takes up its experiences and turns them by its own innate and peculiar power into things of beauty, fuses into itself the experiences of the life soul and transmutes to beauty their power and passion in the surge of its poetic ecstasy, takes

up all life and form into the reflective thought-mind and changes
them in the beauty and rapture of thought discovering and
embodying new values of soul and Nature and existence. (344)

In this one long sentence, Sri Aurobindo clarifies how all the
turbulence of the vital emotion needs to be tamed and conquered to
use them for poetic/aesthetic beauty. He also asserts that the world
of beauty, which is identical with the highest form of
consciousness, could be equated with the world of love. In other
words, there is no divide between the world of consciousness and
the world of love—whether love between the partners, or love in
general which is not tied to vital emotion centered around ego. A
world of love could be identical with the world of aesthetic
sensibility and with the world of the highest level of consciousness—since, the essential criterion is same—the transcendence of
one's ego or vital emotion. The last chapter in this section clarifies
it further as to how human love could be both spiritual and
corporeal with no divide between the two. Joyce's *A Portrait of the
Artist as a Young Man* advocates through innuendos his
philosophy that in his aesthetic theory the role of woman is
essential. The aesthetic theory, which leads to the world of *stasis*
or spirituality reveals itself on earth through the embodiment of
poetry which is inspired by the image of a woman throughout
Stephen /Joyce's literary career.

If we consider *integritas*, and *consonantia* as empirical steps in
the realization of an aesthetic image—we could certainly define
claritas as transcendental. Stephen/Joyce confesses that at first he
thought that this "claritas" that Aquinas talks about is purely
transcendental. Stephen confesses, "It would lead you to believe
that he had in mind symbolism or idealism, the supreme quality of
beauty being a light from some other world, the idea of which the
matter is but the shadow, the reality of which it is but the symbol"
(213). But, gradually Stephen configured that the radiance of
which Aquinas speaks is the "the scholastic *quidditas*, the
whatness of a thing." Thus, it is both scholastic *quidditas* and
whatness of a thing. The scholastic *quidditas* refer to the spiritual
stasis achieved in aesthetic experience, whereas the whatness of a
thing simply signifies the manifestation of it on earth—the validity
of the descent of the spirit into the body. This supreme quality is

the first experienced by the artist when the aesthetic image is first formed in the imagination. Thus, there are two major steps in achieving aesthetic pleasure. He describes this aesthetic pleasure as a "luminous silent stasis," "a spiritual state" which he further calls "the enchantment of the heart." That this aesthetic pleasure is grounded in the empirical world is further expressed by his act of connecting "the enchantment of heart" to the image of a woman he views by the sea:

> While his soul had passed from ecstasy to languor where had she been? Might it be, in the mysterious ways of spiritual life, that her soul at those same moments had been conscious of his homage.
> A glow of desire kindled again his soul and fired and fulfilled all his body. Conscious of his desire she was waking from odorous sleep, the temptress of his nakedness yielded to him, radiant, warm, odorous, and lavish limbed, enfolded him like a shining cloud, enfolded him like water with a liquid life: and like a vapour or mystery, flowed forth over his brain. (223)

One could posit that Joyce's artistic theory intersects with Irigaray's theory of the female jouissance in which corporeality or corporeal love related to women's body has been redeemed or ascribed a spiritual significance. Furthermore, it inspires art/poetry in Stephen/Joyce. Most of the epiphanic moments occur through the image of this woman. Delineating about women figures in Joyce's villanelle, Robert Scholes relates it to the standard literary discourse in the Middle Ages in which scholastic and humanistic ideas were synthesized and flourished in works like Dante's *Divine Comedy* and Spenser's *Faerie Queene*. Scholes also thinks that Joyce was familiar with Sir Walter Pater's *Studies in the History of the Renaissance* and influenced by the concept of the artist trained in Christian schools need to reconcile these theories with the pagan ideas of art. Scholes further links this to the influences of poets like Yeats, Boyd and Swinburne. He draws the conclusion that Joyce must have read Yeats' comment about the Leanhaun Shee in *Fairy and Folk Tales of the Irish Peasantry*. Yeats makes the comment that Leanhaun Shee seeks the love of human beings—that she is a Gaelic Muse who, "she gives inspiration to those she persecutes"

(259). Scholes alludes to other sources as well like Blake's "The
Mental Traveller," and Keats' "La Belle Dame Sans Merci," which
point to a paradoxical concept of femininity in which the female
figure is represented as a creative-destructive force. However,
Schoels' interpretation clarifies partially Joyce's use of women
figures as part of villanelle and epiphany. Joyce ascribes far more
importance to women figures he uses as inspiration for his
villanelle and epiphany. It is far more complex than Scholes'
speculation about it. It seems as I argued earlier, Joyce offers his
staunch critique of Christianity by combining the sexual and the
spiritual in the women figures in his writing. He wants to disavow
the paradox of Christianity that in order to be celestial a woman-
figure has to be virgin—she is denied the right of carnal exchange
in order to be divine. Joyce tries to liberate women figures from
this kind of oppressive boundary. Therefore, women figures
assume such supreme importance in the world of aesthetics; the
presence of woman is concomitant to the writing of his poetry.

One might argue that Joyce's passion for a woman figure
creates a kind of paradox in his aesthetic world, because, his theory
of *stasis* inscribes a moment beyond any vital emotion. In
redefining Aristotle's definition of pity and terror, he alludes to the
same theory of *stasis*—which I have compared to *ānanda*, as the
moment when one conquers one's ego. Thus, the connection
between *stasis* and Joyce's passion for women could be reconciled
through the help of Irigaray's theory of jouissance, which
encompasses corporeality with spirituality. If *stasis* is understood
as the supreme moment of consciousness, then, that particular
moment inscribes a nexus in which one can inhibit corporeally
after liberating one's ego and after attaining *stasis*. *Stasis* must not
be understood as a blank state or the nirvana of Buddhist
philosophy, which purports the concept of escape from the world
through extinction. Rather, Joyce's theory of *stasis* can be thought
of as invoking Sri Aurobindo's theory of "supramental
consciousness," in which the Supermind consciousness needs to
descend to an earthly plane and into the body, for the entire
evolution of consciousness to occur. Thus, Joyce's theory of *stasis*
is not oppositional to the association of women in the theory. On
the contrary, women figures inspire both his epiphanic experiences
and writing. It is quite pertinent here to say that Joyce's portrayal

of women as agents of light and inspiration could be thought of as intersecting with Indian philosophy, which valorizes both the concept of complementarity and the feminine power itself. As the embodiment of power, I would refer back to my chapter, "Jouissance and Kali," of the previous section and for the discussion of complementarity, I would refer both to the chapters on Tagore and Chitra Banerjee. Women figures could also be looked upon as *Prakṛti* of Indian Hindu philosophy who works in tandem with *Puruṣa*. *Puruṣa* represents the Conscious-Soul who is inactive without *Prakṛti* or nature. *Puruṣa* stands for the male energy and *Prakṛti* stands for the female energy; they complement each other and one cannot function without the other. Joyce's world of aesthetics operates the same way: the artist as the Conscious-Soul cannot function without Nature or inspiration of women. Joyce's *A Portrait of the Artist as a Young Man* is extremely rich in its philosophical implications in the delineation of jouissance.

NOTES

1. It would be worthwhile to look at the comment by Christine Froula in her book entitled, *Modernism's Body, Sex, Culture and Joyce*:

> In analyzing voices that seem at once to descend from on high and to erupt from psychic depths, Stephen recasts the religious sublime as what we might call a transcendence downward. He dismantles the repression that dissimulates forbidden desires into religious impulses—and in doing so, the mystified opposition between the sacred and the profane—by exposing the psychic processes of the unconscious which knows no negation. (36)

The flaw in Froula's argument is that her interpretation is limited to the Freudian interpretation of the unconscious. Joyce's *A Portrait of the Artist as a Young Man*, however, embodies a higher level of consciousness which goes beyond Freudian theory of the unconscious.

2. Please, see the following observation from Christy L. Burns' *Gestural Politics*:

> Joyce's oscillation between the transcendence of materiality, in Stephen's development in *Portrait*, and his own repeated return to verbal embodiment may have arisen from Joyce's early interest in the writings of Stephen Mallerme. Indeed Stephen's formulation of *consonantia*, in which the perception will "pass from point to point," echoes not only Coleridge but also seems to take up Arthur Symons' summary of Mallerme: "the poet, who has seen the thing from the beginning, still sees the relation of point to point" [. . .]. Ellman and others have noted that Joyce copied down Symons' translation of one passage in *The Symbolist Movement in Literature*, suggesting that Joyce's main familiarity with Mallarme was heavily, if not exclusively, mediated by Symons' interpretation. (30)

3. It is reminiscent of Teresa Brennan's comment in that since the Romantic era there has been this search for the spiritual world which gets revived again in the current century, although it must not be construed as a new age kind of thing, because, it is too simplistic.

4. Tagore is a modern poet, but his poetry highlights the Vaishnavite transcendental emotion. Roy highlights the names of the poets, who he thinks represent what Sri Aurobindo calls the characteristics of the future poetry, "spiritual essence," which reaches the highest level of consciousness. Although Vaishnava poets wrote in the twelfth century and Tagore wrote his poems in the twentieth century, their poetry is imbued with "spiritual essence."

5. This particular poem is from the poet Jagadish Chandra Das' book, *Their Songs and Whispers*. It is a book representing poetry with spiritual essence, or what Joyce calls *stasis*, and Sri Aurobindo calls "the future poetry."

6. This poem has been translated from Bengali to both English and French. This particular poem created a great impact among the devotees of Sri Aurobindo. The great disciple of Sri Aurobindo, Nolini Kanta Gupta, also known as a poet, translated this poem from Bengali to English, and included in his the book entitled, *Light of Life*, Vol. V. The poet Prithwindra Mukherjee in his collection entitled, *Anthologie de la poesie bengalie*, has also translated the poem in French in 1991. The

poem is a perfect embodiment of Sri Aurobindo calls, the spiritual essence in his *The Future Poetry*.

7. A journal edited and published by Sri Aurobindo from 1917 till 1920. It got published as a book entitled *The Future Poetry* in 1953.

Chapter 7

Ego and Its Transcendence in Tagore's *The King of the Dark Chamber*

The modern Indian poet Rabindranath Tagore's lyric play *The King of the Dark Chamber* explores the idea of the transcendence of the ego. The Queen Sudarshana finds it difficult to believe the truth that the King is humble. Sudarshana goes through different phases in terms of her journey from ego to obtaining the spiritual truth. The main theme of the story is portrayed in the song of the mad friend:

> Yet I roam in search of the golden stag, though I never catch him in these wilds! Oh, I roam and wander through woods and fields and nameless lands like a restless vagabond, never caring to turn my back. (44)

The song in the beginning of the play foreshadows the theme that the entire play is a search for the supreme truth and the difficulty in achieving the supreme level of consciousness. The other important and interesting character in the play is that of the Grandfather, who plays the role of a choric voice always assuring the humbleness and the nobility of the King who has conquered his ego. When the Queen Sudarshana wants to bow down to him, he says he never accepts anybody's obeisance and his relationship with everyone is that of "comradeship." Thus, he delegitimizes any kind of power relation and points to the main message of the play which has been more strongly manifest in his song:

> I am waiting with my all in the hope of
> Losing everything
> I am waiting at the roadside for him
> Who turns one out into the open Road,

[. . . . .]
I am waiting with my all in the hope
Of losing everything. (190-91)

What is significant here is the refrain, "losing everything," which means losing all mundane things which usually make people egoistic. He reiterates the truth that by losing all material things, he will be able to connect more to the divine and the King symbolizes that divine. Repeatedly, he asserts that the King represents inner glory and inner beauty and that is why he made the Queen also devoid of all ornaments. He says, "And that beauty has today taken off its veil and cloak of pride and vanity!" By the end of the play everybody involved has gone through the process of transformation from ego to the transcendence of ego. Surangama, the maid of honor, told the story of her life to Sudarshana of how she was freed from her ego through the intervention of the King who rescued her from her father's gambling den, which again denotes false material greed. The trumped-up King also surrenders quite early in the play. The play ends on a note of surrender to the supreme through the complete dissolution of the ego.

The drama opens in the dark chamber: "Light, light! Will the lamp never be lighted in this chamber?" This darkness is symbolic of the ego. Sudarshana asks, "But why should this room be kept dark?" The dark room represents the dark side of Sudarshana's level of consciousness. It represents the dark side of her psyche. Surangama (the assistant of the Queen) represents the voice of the King. His role could also be interpreted as the conscious force invoking Sudarshana or awakening her to "jouissance" or consciousness. Surangama thus invokes her, "Because, otherwise you would know neither light nor darkness" (46). And, observe the following comment, "This room is placed deep down, in the very heart of the earth. The King has built this room specially for your sake" (46). In this chapter, I want to show that the Queen Sudarshana achieves her moment of jouissance in terms of consciousness at the end of the play and the entire play, is in fact, a search for that supreme moment.

It is quite interesting to note that this lyric play was published in 1910, prior to the publication of Freud's *Ego and the Id*, which validates the fact that the concept of the unconscious was present in Indian philosophy/psychoanalysis from ancient times. I have discussed in the introductory chapter, "Jouissance As Ānanda (Bliss)," and in the second chapter, "Body in Transcendence: Jouissance and Kali," the history of consciousness in Indian philosophy. According to Vedanta philosophy there are three states of mind: *sattwa, raja,* and *tama.* The *sattwic* state alludes to the highest level of consciousness, the *rajasic* state alludes to the vital plane and the *tamasic* state is associated with the lowest level of consciousness, or inertia. The concept of the unconscious is present in Indian philosophy not necessarily as inertia, but, as a psychic plane which has access to intuition as Sudhir Kakar,[1] the great Indian psychoanalyst discusses it in his book. In the ancient Indian philosophical text, the *Upaniṣads* the unconscious is not associated or construed as is the Western unconscious, but, as that state of mind which has access to the intuitive plane of the mind. But, according to Indian Upaniṣadic philosophy the ego is associated with the unconscious. In other words, the unconscious is associated with the ego. Let me clarify here in details. According to Indian philosophy, as I just suggested, the unconscious or the Western unconscious is associated with the intuitive plane of mind; thus, unconscious has a positive connotation. The equivalent of the Western unconscious is the ego, in Indian philosophy. Thus, what is referred to in Vedanta philosophy as the *tamasic* state is caused by the problem of the "ego." What Tagore portrays in the play is the attainment of consciousness of the Queen and several other egoistic characters through the dissolution of their ego.

To elaborate on the theory of the consciousness through the dissolution of the ego, it is imperative to discuss the modern Indian philosopher Sri Aurobindo's philosophy of "supramental consciousness." Sri Aurobindo and Rabindranath Tagore are almost contemporary and Sri Aurobindo's philosophy of "supramental consciousness" is highly conducive to understanding of Tagore's lyric play *The King of the Dark Chamber.* It is also important to mention here that Sri Aurobindo's philosophy of "supramental consciousness" is grounded in the ancient Indian philosophical text of the *Upaniṣads.* Sri Aurobindo's theory of "supramental consciousness" through the dissolution of the ego is conducive to the understanding of the functioning of ego in the play. In the chapter entitled, "The Ego and the Dualities" in *The Life Divine*, Sri Aurobindo emphasizes the importance of the dissolution of the ego:

> We have the dissolution of this egoistic construction by the self-opening of the individual to the universe and to God as the means of that supreme fulfillment to which egoistic life is only a prelude even as animal life was only a prelude to the human. We have the realization of the all in the individual by the transformation of the limited ego into a conscious center of the divine unity and freedom as the term at which the fulfillment arrives. And we have the outflowing of the infinite and absolute Existence, Truth, Good and Delight of being on the Many in the world as the divine result towards which the cycles of our evolution move. (59)

What Sri Aurobindo explains here is how fulfillment can take place through the dissolution of the ego; ego works as a stumbling block and as soon as one learns how to overcome that littleness, one achieves fulfillment. In fact, my book is an elaboration on that theory as to how one can achieve "jouissance" or "consciousness" as one comes to terms with both one's inner and outer being through the shedding of one's ego. But, how can one become connected to that divine center as Sri Aurobindo enunciates that? In explaining further the limitation of the ego, Sri Aurobindo suggests in "The Ego and the Dualities," that, if one does not meditate on the world of the spirit or the divine, ("Absolute Existence, Truth, Good and Delight of Being"), then transcendence will be achievable though extinction and nirvana. It will not be manifest on the material plane.[2] In order to show how the transcendence is achievable in the material plane, he offers his theory of "supramental consciousness."

Let me analyze the Queen's moment of awakening from her inconscience to jouissance through her series of encounters with her husband the King who until the last moment of the resolution of the play does not reveal his face to the Queen. Instead, he always meets her in the dark chamber and describes himself as the King of the dark chamber. Why is the King associated with darkness? And, why does he refuse to meet the Queen in the light? Rabindranath Tagore in this play *The King of the Dark Chamber*, deals with the different levels of human psyche. In the play, there is constant emphasis on "darkness." It is in the title of the play, the Queen always meets the King in the dark chamber, their meeting place is always the dark chamber and the King also describes himself as dark. But, at the end of the play the Queen is welcomed into the world of light by the King himself. What then is the significance of this journey from darkness into light?   Before seeking the answer, we should probe further into Sri Aurobindo's theory of "supramental consciousness."

According to Sri Aurobindo, the mind has several planes: in ascending order after mind, is the Higher mind, then the Illumined mind, and then Intuition, (also considered as a plane of mind). After this there is Over mind and finally the Supermind which ushers in the descent of the "supramental consciousness." Each level of mind possesses a different level of consciousness in this ascending order. In the Higher mind, which transcends to a great extent the pulling of the half-light or half-consciousness, its activity is dominated by thought. It is a first step towards the Supermind and it prepares the mind for the transformation of consciousness. After this one achieves the Illumined Mind which is, "A Mind no longer of higher Thought but of spiritual light." The next is Intuition, a plane of the mind which is not only a step higher but also one that advances the senses. This stage is part of the Supramental light, but it is also a stage in which the spiritual evolution is still in progress. It is at this point that the transformation has begun, but it has not achieved stability, because one's highest level of consciousness or intuition is blocked from the inconscience.[3] The next plane, the Overmind, helps one to conquer one's ego; in this phase one's psychic being starts to establish a connection with the Cosmic self. Now the ego enters a process of dissolution, but this is still not adequate to obtain the total psychic transformation and the achievement of a Supramental level of consciousness. Instead, what is needed is the descent of the Supermind.[4] To quote from Sri Aurobindo's chapter, "The Ascent Towards Supermind," in *The Life Divine*, a book which emphasizes the importance of the consciousness of the Supermind and total transformation of one's being:

it (Overmind) can unite individual mind with cosmic mind on its
highest plane, equate individual self with cosmic self and give to
the nature an action of universality; but it cannot lead Mind
beyond itself, and in this world of original Inconscience it cannot
dynamise the Transcendence; for it is the Supermind alone that is
the supreme self-determining truth action and the direct power of
manifestation of that Transcendence. (953 V.2)

The Overmind has its limitations even though it is at this stage that
the dissolution of the ego begins to take shape. The theory of the
Supermind also addresses the problems and resistance each step of
the plane of consciousness faces in order to go to the next plane of
consciousness. At each step there is a stumbling block and Sri
Aurobindo thus addresses them in the same chapter. As he has just
observed above that the Overmind does not have the power to help
overcome its original inconscience, he reiterates by saying: "In the
lower grades of the ascension the new assumption, the integration
into a higher principle of consciousness, remains incomplete"
(932). Therefore, what is needed is the journey from mind to the
Supermind consciousness. Sri Aurobindo uses the words the ascent
and the descent to indicate the completion of the spiritual process
for the achievement of "ānanda" or "fulfillment." Thus, as
described above, the mind makes an ascent ultimately to the
Supramental plane by journeying upwards via the stages of higher
mind, illumined mind, intuition and overmind. When the ascent
takes places, and the inconscience is fully conquered, the
Supramental light starts descending into the material plane and into
the body. It effectuates a complete transformation of the ignorance,
the inconscience and the ego. On the one hand, human beings need
to strive to overcome inconscience, and the ego through the
spiritual journey from Higher mind to the Supermind; and
concurrently, the other necessary condition for the transformation
is the descent of the Supramental light into the material plane and
into the body. But, at every step in the ascent there is great
resistance from the ego, which is finally overcome by the strength
of the Supermind.

Thus, in Tagore's The King of the Dark Chamber, the dark
chamber could be interpreted as inconscience itself or inconscience

personified. Sudarshana is allowed to meet the King in the dark chamber in her three encounters because it symbolizes the state of her mind. Applying Sri Aurobindo's theory I would suggest that Sudarshana's mind has undertaken the journey into the Supramental plane and if she had not have done so, then the King would not have led her through the journey. The King could be inscribed as the representative of the mission of "supramental consciousness," who does not reveal himself in the light as long as Sudarshana is confined to the world of inconscience and unable to enter the world of fulfillment and in Sri Aurobindo's words, the world of "supramental consciousness." In the first encounter with the King, he tells Sudarshana that Sudarshana is his second self. By saying this the King assures everybody that she is his accomplice in the journey of consciousness. He also communicates to her that she is not the ordinary individual she considers her to be. Sudarshana is not convinced and she thus expresses her anxiety: "No, no—it is impossible; there is a barrier betwixt us two; [. . .] I want to find you where I see trees and animals, birds, and stars and the earth." In the light of this conversation, it is clear that although the King accepts Sudarshana in his heart, there is a barrier in her psyche. She has to go through the process of the transformation of herself in order to be united with the King. Since Sudarshana wants to meet the King in the light, the King offers to meet her in the festival of the full moon of the spring. It is significant to note the way he refers to the full moon festival: "The pleasure gardens are in their full-bloom. You will join in my festivities there" (62). The meaning of pleasure could be rendered as *ānanda*, as it does not allude to just simple pleasure, but fulfillment through the dissolution of the ego. Also, it is interesting to note that Tagore uses choric songs to highlight the theme of the play:

But the time of their surrender will come,
their flight hither and thither
will be ended when
the music of enchantment will pursue
them and pierce their hearts.
Alas, the wild birds would fly to the
Wilderness. (64)

By alluding to birds Tagore highlights the theme of surrender. The flight of the birds actually emphasizes the importance of the surrender of the human ego to transcendence or the divine. In the next few acts we shall see that Sudarshana is in the pleasure garden in the full moon festival present. In this full moon festival Kings from different countries as well as the common people of the country (who serve the role of the choric character) are invited. The pleasure garden symbolically stands for the place in which the evolution of Sudarshana's consciousness begins.

The King of the dark chamber has a special role to play apart from awakening Sudarshana into consciousness; the King keeps himself inaccessible and invisible to his people. By doing so he serves a symbolic purpose—to convey the message to his people that anybody can rule in the kingdom, provided that person has the highest level of consciousness. But, not everyone has such supreme form of consciousness to understand his message; therefore the Queen journeys through evil to reach him. Her mind is so preoccupied with her own egotistical consciousness that she mistakes the trumped-up King as the real King, her husband, because, the fraudulent King has a fair complexion and is outwardly handsome. In this play, the word beauty has a special connotation; inner beauty or inner worth is presented as superior to external beauty which is considered misleading, and thus, negative. Therefore, Queen Sudarshana's attraction to and fascination with the false King signifies her nescience[5] and that downward pull to her lower mind/inconscience, which is still very strong in her mind. The journey has just started. The choric characters play a significant role by reiterating the theme of the play which is to completely surrender one's ego to consciousness:

> We have nothing, indeed we have nothing at all!
> We sing merely fol de rol de rol! (68)

Joy seems to spring from nothingness. In contrast the Queen Sudarshana is brimming with excitement and possessed with restlessness as she herself expresses: "My heart is all a-quiver and restless tonight [. . .]. The white, silver light of the full moon is flooding the heavens and brimming over on every side [. . .]. It seizes on me like a yearning, like a mantling intoxication" (87).

Sudarshana is obviously in an ecstatic state of mind: but how does she find her King since she has assured him, "I shall know you; I shall recognize you. I shall find you out among a million men. I cannot be mistaken" (60).

In reality we perceive that she is beguiled by the apparent beauty of the false King and is so sure that he is the real King, that she sends him flowers. The false King gives a pearl necklace to Rohini, the Queen's assistant who carries flowers to the false King. The Queen is so upset that she wants to snatch the necklace from Rohini. However, her disillusionment commences as finds out that the necklace did not come from the real King. As a matter of fact, the person who she thought was the real King is in reality an accomplice of the King of a different country called Kanchi and the King of Kanchi who instigated the false King to set fire to the pleasure gardens and the fire has now reached her palace.

The compunction is realized as she cries, "No King! He is not the King? Then, O thou God of fire, burn me, reduce me to ashes! I shall throw myself into thy hands, O thou great purifier; burn to ashes my shame, my longing, my desire" (112). The question is if the Queen's disillusionment has truly begun and does she really start her journey towards her fulfillment by finding out who the real King is.

Here, the question might also be raised if yielding to the King stands for the phallus or the Lacanian symbolic order! According to Indian philosophy/psychoanalysis, the perfect male-female relationship can flourish when the relationship has been established between a man and a woman through the silencing of their egos. Irigaray has elaborated on this through her theory of "sexual difference," in her books *Speculum, Marine Lover, An Ethics of Sexual Difference*. I will allude to my earlier chapters in the book when I explain how according to Irigaray the ethics of "sexual difference" could be achieved when one partner does not reduce one to the other. The relationship is based on mutuality and alliance. Luce Irigaray's views are advanced further in her most recent book *To Be Two*,[6] in which she refers to yoga, silence and Buddhist philosophy and presents her nuance that the perfect male-female relationship could be established through silence. She is not explicit about what happens when one conquers one's ego, but the nuance is there about the outcome of it. This, I advance through the discussion of Sri Aurobindo's theory which, based on ancient Indian philosophy, asserts that through the dissolution of one's ego, it is possible to achieve the true psychic relationship between male and female partners which is manifest in the material plane as well. Let me come back to the resolution of the play as Sudarshana truly discovers the King in the dark chamber in the pleasure gardens and shows how the relationship between them is established.

It is quite significant that the Queen Sudarshana meets the King again in the dark chamber, although the King arranged the meeting place as the pleasure gardens. We perceive that the Queen flees from the pleasure gardens, because, they are on fire and she encounters the King inside the palace in the dark room one more time. But, the journey from the ego to consciousness involves successive stages and it is a difficult journey. Therefore, we see the wavering in Sudarshana's mind. Although, she feels that she should be purified as the fire plays a symbolic role not just in reference to pleasure gardens, but also in its signification as a purifying agent. As soon as the King's face is revealed in the sparkle of flame and she sees that the King is dark and not as fair and handsome as the King of Kanchi, she feels repelled and reacts in a negative manner. The conversation and the encounter between the King and Sudarshana are extremely crucial and significant here. Sudarshana's mind is steeped in her little ego and she bursts out in her agony as she sees the King's face in the flashing light of the fire:

> Terrible,—oh, it was terrible! I am afraid even to think of it again. Black, black—oh, thou art black like the everlasting night! The blaze of the fire fell on your features—you looked like the awful night when a comet swings fearfully into our ken—oh, then I closed my eyes—I could not look on you any more. Black as the threatening storm cloud, black as the shoreless sea with the spectral red tint of twilight on its tumultuous waves. (116)

Notice the reiterated emphasis on the words black or blackness. The expressions used by the Queen to describe the King are, "everlasting night," "black as the threatening storm cloud," and "black as the shoreless sea." All these images allude to something dark on a grand scale. I would like to render the dark appearance of the King in the Queen's mind as the reflection of Sudarshana's mind itself. It is not the King who is dark, but it is the Queen's state of consciousness, which perceives him as dark, because her mind is still in the phase of inconscience, which has also been defined by Sri Aurobindo as nescience, or ignorance. I have suggested earlier in my discussion of Sri Aurobindo's philosophical theory of "supramental consciousness" that in the ascending order in the journey from the mind to the Supermind, one faces many setbacks including a regression into inconscience until the mind is totally redeemed by the Supermind consciousness. Regarding this inconscience Sri Aurobindo observes in *The Life Divine*:

> The essential difficulty comes from the fact that the substance of our normal being is moulded out of the Inconscience. Our ignorance is a growth of knowledge in a substance of being which is nescient; the consciousness it develops, the knowledge it establishes are always dogged, penetrated, enveloped by this nescience. It is this substance of nescience that has to be transformed into a substance of superconscience, a substance in which consciousness and spiritual awareness are always there even when they are not active, not expressed, not put into form of knowledge. (960-61)

The observation reinforces the fact that the inconscience needs to be fully redeemed by spirituality ushered in by the Supermind consciousness; until that state is completely achieved, one can easily slide regress into ignorance, nescience and ego. Queen Sudarshana experiences a number of psychic upheavals prior to the moment of entering the world of light. It is significant that until the end of the play the encounter between the King and the Queen takes place in the dark chamber. In act eight, the King gave the opportunity to the Queen and she went as far as exploring that she has not been successful in detecting the real King. What more, as the King's face is revealed to the Queen in the light flashing from the flames, Sudarshana is horrified, since, she is unable to associate the King with darkness. On the one hand, this could be interpreted as done so above as the dark state of Sudarshana's psyche which is still in the state of nescience and not fully recovered by the descent of Supramental light or consciousness. At another level, it could be interpreted as evincing that inner beauty is more valuable than external beauty, because, external beauty relates to false ego and inner beauty is associated with an inner level of consciousness. Thus, Sudarshana perceives the King as ugly and black as long as she is unable to see the fundamental distinction between inner beauty and external beauty. Act VIII could be considered as the climax of the play. The Queen leaves the King as she is not ready to face the truth, although she is perturbed that the King did not force her to stay with him.

Let us examine the mourning and the agony in Sudarshana's character. She mourns her alienation from the King in a way which only expresses her egoistic concerns:

Did I lose my all to sweep the dust, to sweat and slave in this dismal hole? Why do the torches of mourning not flare up for me all over the world? Why does not the earth quake and tremble? Is my fall but the unobserved dropping of the puny bean-flower? Is it not more like the fall of a glowing star, whose fiery blazons bursts the heavens asunder? (132)

Sudarshana's mind is steeped in her ego to such an extent that even in her fall she is far more concerned about her material rather than her spiritual fall. She compares her fall to the descent of a glowing star, but is unable to configure the root cause of that fall. It is quite pertinent here to introduce the character of Surangama who is her maid of honor, a symbolic character who herself has gone through the process of the dissolution of ego and whose role is to inspire the Queen to take the right direction. In the beginning of the play, we notice that the King himself appoints Surangama to help the Queen to find him—or, in other words, to lead her to the right path of consciousness. So, we see as we approach the end of the play that the Queen exchanges all her ideas with Surangama who constantly provides the Queen with the right advice. Meanwhile, what happens is the Queen has left her husband's palace and has gone to her father's house. Her father is the King of Kanyakubja (another province). Her father is indisposed with her for this violation and what is more, all the Kings who came to join her father's party for the moonlight festival in the garden of pleasure being invited by her husband, now follow her to her father's country. They join in league to win her from her father's palace and the battle is led by the King of Kanchi who is always trying to get the Queen in trouble. He has already done so by setting fire to her husband's palace and also, trying to allure through his accomplice Suvarna, who is extremely handsome, and who the Queen mistook as the real King. The plot of this episode is concocted by the King of Kanchi, the evil King who chases merely after mundane pleasure, and one must remember that Tagore criticizes the greed for material pleasure as well, since, that also submerges one into false ego and this false ego is repeatedly criticized in Indian philosophy as *rajasik* pleasure, as I mentioned briefly in my earlier discussion. Thus, in a way one could suggest that the King of Kanchi is the ego personified in the play by alluring the Queen to the wrong path. So, the question is how is the Queen finally redeemed from her ego?

The King helps her through Surangama, her maid of honor, who is a soul who has been redeemed from her ego by the King, as she recounts her story at the beginning of the play. As Sudarshana moves into her father's palace (although she is not given access to the main palace) the realization of her mistake arises as she talks with Surangama. It is significant to see the Queen's constant reference to the dark chamber in her husband's palace in which she always meets the King. She describes how she used to stand at her window in the evening, "out of that blank darkness of our lampless meeting-place used to stream forth strains and songs and melodies, dancing and vibrating in endless succession and overflowing profusion, like the passionate exuberance of a ceaseless fountain" (150-51). What is important for us to note is that darkness is invested with great potential; moreover darkness has a strong connection with the light. As Surangama observes in relation to darkness, "O deep and sweet darkness! The profound and mystic darkness whose servant I was!" (151). Even according to Sri Aurobindo, the journey to the Supramental world of light starts with the mind in nescience/ignorance/darkness.

Both Tagore and Sri Aurobindo put forth the message that the darkness has great potential, because darkness is unavoidable. Sri Aurobindo reiterates the truth that many times one falls back into inconscience—but, eventually one has to make the journey to that highest plane through the transcendence of ego. It is also important for us to notice that the King never forces Sudarshana to do anything; rather she arranges circumstances in such a way that Sudarshana is led toward the right path through her trials and tribulations. Her final trial comes as she is asked to meet all the prince-suitors who have been fighting to win her as their bride. The situation jolts her into imploring the King her husband who she has left:

> This body of mine has received a stain—I shall make a sacrifice of it today in the dust of the hall, before all these princes! But shall I never be able to tell you that I know of no stain of faithlessness within the hidden chambers of my heart? That dark chamber where you would come to meet me lies cold and empty within my bosom today—but O my Lord! None has opened its doors, none has entered it but you, O King! Will you never come again to open those doors? Then, let death come, for it is dark like yourself, and its features are beautiful as yours. It is you—it is yourself, O King! (161)

Sudarshana's transformation has begun. Finally, she articulates that her soul has been touched only by the King, and she understands the importance of the dark chamber and the meaning of darkness. She understands the truth that apparent grandeur is delusional. She compares the King with death[7]—which she now envisions as dark and beautiful. Now, as the drama proceeds we perceive her as totally dedicating herself to the King. She also realizes that it is the King himself who ultimately saves her from ignominy and defeats all the other Kings. However, it is a symbolic play and we duly note that the Queen has to surrender herself totally to the King in order to achieve enlightenment.

In the process, she surrenders her ego and pride and walks as an ordinary individual to meet the King. Although the King defeats all the other Kings, he does not come personally to take Sudarshana with him. Rather, the King wants Sudarshana to consent to go to the King on her own, which can happen only when she has transcended her ego. Let us heed the way Sudarshana confesses the defeat and transcends her own ego: "What a relief, Surangama, what freedom!   It is my defeat that brought me freedom. Oh, what an iron pride was mine! Nothing could move it or soften it" (192). Another significant observation made by her is crucial to the understanding of the transformation of her character:

> As long as a sense of offended pride remained within me, I could not help thinking that he had left me for good; but when I flung my dignity and pride to the winds and came out on the open streets, then it seemed to me that he too had come out: I have been finding him since the moment I was on the road. I have no misgivings now. All this suffering that I have gone through for his sake, the very bitterness of all this is giving me his company. (195)

Sudarshana's level of consciousness could very well be analyzed here via Sri Aurobindo's overmind consciousness. According to Indian philosophy, through transcendence of one's ego one feels identified with the rest of the universe. That is when the transformation occurs in one's psychic being, and when one overcomes one's ego consciousness, one then enters the world of light in which one is not preoccupied with one's mere self-interests, but, looks at the world itself in a different light and creates a bond with the world by identifying with everyone else in it. Sri Aurobindo has alluded to this phase of being as the Overmind phase of consciousness, in which one establishes a connection with one's cosmic self. Sri Aurobindo thus observes:

> But with a strong influence or full action of the Overmind a very integral sense of governance, a complete supporting or over-ruling presence and direction of the cosmic self or the Ishwara can come in and become normal; or a special center may be revealed or created overtopping and dominating the physical instrument, individual in fact of *existence*, but impersonal in feeling and recognized by a free cognition as something instrumental to the action of a Transcendent and universal being. (951)

What is significant is the emphasis on the term "impersonal" and "the cosmic self," which one gets connected to as one's psychic being enters the Overmind level of consciousness. Sudarshana's state of mind could be inscribed as attaining that Overmind level of consciousness in which her ego consciousness wants to merge with the cosmic self. We see her finally re-embracing life and seeking the King, both of which could be symbolically interpreted as her search for the universal or the cosmic self.

Let us look now at the last act of the play (XX) which takes place in the dark chamber of the King's palace in which Sudarshana is united with the King by literally journeying to the King's palace on foot, a gesture which symbolizes her desire to merge her material self with her cosmic self. The conversation between the Queen Sudarshana and the King is crucial to the understanding of the play. The Queen does not want to be honored by the King anymore, because she has derived contentment through the dissolution of her egoistic self. Sudarshana has completely surrendered herself to the King and she implores the King by saying, "I am the servant of your feet—I only seek the privilege of serving you" (204). The relationship between the King and the Queen is not a power relationship but is based on the symbolic connection achieved through the transcendence of ego and needs to be understood in that light. This observation could be interpreted on multiple levels. At one level, it indicates the union with the divine—which is a pervasive theme in Tagore's songs, as I have discussed in great detail in Chapter 2. Thus, the union with the King needs to be seen in a symbolic light, not literally. The relationship between the King and the Queen could also be interpreted through Indian Sankhaya philosophy as the relationship between *Puruṣa* and *Prakṛti*. According to this theory, *Puruṣa*, the male energy is the Conscious power of the universe and *Prakṛti* is the female energy which dynamizes the energy of *Puruṣa*; these two forces are complementary to each other. I will enter into the detailed discussion of this in the next section of this chapter. But, here I simply want to highlight the point that the relation between the King and Sudarshana is one of love and alliance which could be achieved through the realization of the self through the transcendence of her ego.

Let us also look at Sudarshana's observation that the fever of her longing has left her now. She does not judge the King by external appearance, but, instead, by inner beauty or worth, because she has come to the realization that what matters most is the knowledge of the sense of fulfillment rather than being tempted to chase the external manifestation of grandeur. However, from the King and Queen's intimate conversation, what becomes clear is that their inner (corporeal and spiritual) union has taken place:

King
That which can be comparable with me lies within yourself.
Sudarshana
If this be so, then that too is beyond comparison. Your love lives
In me—you are mirrored in that love
And you see your face reflected in me;
Nothing of this mine, it is all yours,
O lord! (205)

Both of them allude to the truth that their union has taken place at the psychic level. The King reiterates the truth that whatever is comparable with him lies within herself and likewise the Queen comments that his love resides within herself and she sees him reflected in that love. The underlying message is that both their psychic levels of consciousness are now on the same plane—a plane that is the highest plane of consciousness, since, Sudarshana is liberated from her egoistic self. At the end of the play we perceive that Sudarshana enters the world of light from the dark chamber:

King
I open the doors of this dark room today—the game is finished here! Come, come with me now, come outside—*into the light!* (205)

It is interesting how Tagore and Sri Aurobindo both have emphasized the philosophy of the transcendence of ego in their own ways. It is also significant to see the way both of them focus on a conception of light that is grounded in the ancient Indian philosophical text, *Upaniṣads*. In the ancient Hindu text, the *Isha*

Upaniṣads, it has been observed in a *sloka* that the face of truth is covered by gold plate. The golden plate stands for material wealth and external beauty. The invocation of the sloka is to dismantle and open the disk, so that the truth could be fully revealed. This manifestation of the truth has been compared with the sunlight. The *sloka* invokes the light to be revealed to be as bright as the sunlight which uncovers the truth. We see the influence of this sloka in Tagore's lyric play and Sri Aurobindo uses this concept in his philosophy of "supramental consciousness." Sri Aurobindo foregrounds the truth that in order to achieve the highest / Supramental plane of consciousness, one has to have a descent of Supramental light into the body.[8]

This chapter does not specifically address the theme of the body—as to how the light could be manifest in the body or in the material plane, but, it is engaged in the discussion of the supreme form of consciousness in which ego sense is completely dissolved and Sri Aurobindo talks about it in the following way:

> A Supramental change of the whole substance of the being and therefore necessarily of all its characters, powers, movements takes place when the involved Supermind in Nature emerges to meet and join with the Supramental light and power descending from Supernature. (962)

What Sri Aurobindo defines as Supramental change, Tagore inscribes as the dissolution of the ego. A complete transformation of the being takes place when the mind in its ascent has already reached the Supramental plane and joins itself in that Supramental light which starts descending on it. The phrase Supramental light does not need to be taken literally. Rather, it refers to the highest form of consciousness or spiritual power as developed in the philosophy of Sri Aurobindo. Both Sri Aurobindo and Tagore strive to reach that highest plane of consciousness and transformation of ego in their writing. In Tagore's lyric play the moment the peak of consciousness has been reached by the character of the Queen, she enters the world of light—her connection with the dark chamber is closed. But, as long as that moment does not occur when her consciousness reaches that highest peak, she remains confined and pushed back to the dark chamber. The transformation of Sudarshana's character occurs in successive stages, almost similar to the way Sri Aurobindo's theory of Supermind works, in which the mind evolves in ascending order from the higher mind to the Supermind via other levels of mind. Since her psyche goes through several planes of mind/consciousness, her encounters with the King take place always in the dark chamber—possibly almost to symbolize that entry into the world of light cannot take place until one's whole being responds to change and development.

In this section, I want to further interpret the relationship between Sudarshana, the Queen and the King through the concepts of *Puruṣa* (male energy or Brahman) and *Prakṛti* (female energy or Shakti) as enunciated in Indian Sankhya philosophy. I want to clarify the truth that their relationship is based on complementarity, rather than on power. The King does not signify patriarchy or the phallus, rather the King represents what is called *Puruṣa* in Indian philosophy. *Puruṣa* stands for Brahman. What is this Brahman? Brahman represents the concept of the pure absolute and conscious power which is also identified as male energy. On the other hand, *Prakṛti*, refers to creative energy and is identified as the female energy without which *Puruṣa* or the concept of Brahman remains static. The literal meaning of the word *Puruṣa* is male and Sri Aurobindo further elaborates and defines *Puruṣa* as Brahman and *Ishwara*. According to the *Upaniṣads*, Brahman is the conscious power that sustains the universe; it is not just the conscious power or the Absolute "but Brahman is at the same time the omnipresent Reality in which all that is relative exists as its forms or its movements" (*The Life Divine* 324). That is, according to the *Upaniṣads*, every single object in the universe is the manifestation of Brahman; Brahman holds the entire universe within it. Not only every object in the universe is the embodiment of *Brahman*, but also *Brahman* resides in every human soul, "*Brahman* is the Absolute, the transcendent and incommunicable, the Supracosmic Existence that sustains the cosmos, the Cosmic Self that upholds all beings, but It is too the self of each individual" (*The Life Divine* 324). One thing must be made clear here is that Brahman is identical with *Puruṣa*. Thus, *Puruṣa* could be construed as one aspect of Brahman—the aspect that is defined as the Conscious

Being. *Puruṣa* is thus defined by Sri Aurobindo, "The Conscious being, *Puruṣa*, is the self as originator, witness, support and lord and enjoyer of the forms and works of Nature" (*The Life Divine* 348). Now, it remains to be seen whether *Puruṣa*, the Conscious Being, the manifestation of *Brahman*, remains incomplete without *Prakṛti* or Nature. The literal meaning of *Prakṛti* in Indian philosophy and in a variety of Indian vernaculars is Nature. What this means is that *Puruṣa,* or the Conscious Being, cannot function without the help of *Prakṛti,* or Nature. *Prakṛti* executes everything; it is the driving and mobilizing energy and power without which *Puruṣa* is inactive.

The other intriguing aspect of the relation between *Puruṣa* and *Prakṛti* is that although *Puruṣa* is called the Conscious Being and *Prakṛti* is called Nature, Nature can have a negative connotation both in Western and Indian culture. The workings of this Nature, according to Indian Sankhaya philosophy are expected to be in harmony with the Conscious Being, or *Puruṣa.* Thus, *Prakṛti* or Nature is not inert or subsumed in darkness. *Prakṛti* has the potential to move from darkness to light. The lacunae in Lacanian Western psychoanalysis that women are associated solely with the unconscious with no hope of redemption through any form of spiritual jouissance, is overridden by Indian philosophy / psychoanalysis. According to Indian philosophy, *Prakṛti* (which is always female) has the power to keep the universe moving perfectly if it is in proper liaison with *Puruṣa.* Here, it is most appropriate to consult Sri Aurobindo's observation in this regard on Indian Sankhaya philosophy:

> Prakriti presents itself as an Inconscient Energy in the material world, but, as the scale of consciousness rises she reveals herself more and more as a conscious force and we perceive that even her inconscience concealed a secret consciousness; [. . .] even in its passivity its consent is necessary to the action of Prakriti and this relation shows sufficiently that the two are not alien to each other. The duality is a position taken up, a double status accepted for the operation of the self-manifestation of the being; but there is no eternal and fundamental separateness and dualism of Being and its Consciousness-Force, of the Soul and Nature. (*The Life Divine* 350)

The point is that *Puruṣa* is inactive and powerless without *Prakṛti*. The observation also reinforces the importance of this duality and the importance of the power of complementarity between male and female energy. As has been explained in the above passage by Sri Aurobindo the duality is a position needed for the evolution of the self-manifestation of the being. But, there is no fundamental dualism between *Puruṣa* and *Prakṛti*; they are complementary to each other. The other most significant aspect about *Prakṛti* is that within her is embedded a secret consciousness—her inconscience is rooted in consciousness.

Thus, from this philosophical perspective when one looks at the play *The King of the Dark Chamber*, one can perceive that the relationship between the King and the Queen could very well be explained as a relationship between *Puruṣa* and *Prakṛti*. The King symbolically stands for *Puruṣa*—the Conscious Being who watches over the Queen, who in her own right represents *Prakṛti*. The King as *Puruṣa* remains hidden, behind the curtain whereas *Prakṛti*, posing as the Queen, makes all the mistakes. But, as the level of her consciousness rises, the Queen is finally redeemed and establishes a perfect connection with the King, or *Puruṣa*, as he becomes the light emanating out of the dark chamber. In other words, the dark chamber is the place; here, the King invisible until the last moment when he comes to light as Sudarshana transcends her ego. What is significant to note here is that the King does not enter the world of light alone, or reveal his identity alone in the world of light; rather, he does together with Sudarshana. He awaits that supreme moment when Sudarshana as *Prakṛti*, rises to the highest level of consciousness through the dissolution of her ego and inconscience and is capable of entering the world of light. Thus, this symbolic meaning of the play rules out any doubt that the King represents a phallus or patriarchy. That the King totally identifies himself with the Queen is apparent in the opening of the play when the King suggests that the Queen is his second self. Note the conversation between them at the beginning of the play:

Sudarshana
Am I so wonderful, so beautiful?
When I hear you speak so, my heart
swells with gladness and pride. But

how can I believe the wonderful things
you tell me? I cannot find them in
myself!

King

Your own mirror will not reflect
Them—it lessens you, limits you, makes
you look small and insignificant. But
could you see yourself mirrored in my
own mind, how grand would you
appear! In my own heart you are no longer
the daily individual which
you think you are—you are verily my
second self. (58-59)

The King clarifies his relationship with the Queen Sudarshana at the beginning of the play—she dwells inside his own self as his second self—there is no division between the two. It matches with the relation *Puruṣa* has with *Prakṛti*—in which *Puruṣa* is insignificant without *Prakṛti* and cannot play any role without her. The Queen cannot see herself in the mirror of her own self; instead, she views herself in the mirror of the King's self to know herself. This point also clarifies one more blind spot that their relation is not based on power, but on love. The King has already acknowledged the Queen as his equal by allowing her to dwell within his self—the only gap that they have between them is that they have been created by the ego in which the Queen's consciousness is steeped. Thus, the Queen symbolically stands for *Prakṛti* who has the power to achieve the highest form of consciousness—but to do so *Prakṛti* needs to be inspired by *Puruṣa*, or the Conscious-Being. Once the Queen finds an incentive from the King, her process of self-manifestation starts and through the union between the two the union takes place between the Conscious-Being and Nature. Thus, it is very appropriate to see the relationship between the King and the Queen symbolically in the light of Sankhaya philosophy which aids us in reading the play correctly. It also emphasizes the message of the Indian Sankhya philosophy that male and female relationship must be based on complementarity. Moreover, there is a harmony in the cosmic order which could be best preserved through the balanced relationship between the two which could be attained through the transcendence of ego. The question might be raised about the ego status of the King, the answer to which is that the King symbolically represents that level of consciousness in which the ego has been completely overcome. In other words, the King represents *Puruṣa*, or the Conscious-Being, and the Queen represents, *Prakṛti*, who works in close relationship with the King to achieve a state in which there is harmony between them. This harmony could be likened to that harmonious relationship between men and women which is advocated by Irigaray's theory of "sexual difference."

The discussion will however, remain incomplete without an analysis of Irigaray's theory and its connection to the concept of consciousness, and the manner in which Tagore applies it in this play. Irigaray's theory of "sexual difference" foregrounds the concept of "wonder," which she takes from Descartes and re-reads in order to posit what she calls the perfect man-woman relationship. Irigaray interprets "wonder" as an emotion which helps both partners to look at one another as though for the first time. The issue of "wonder" is crucial for the perfect relationship to flourish, because, there will always be a sense of novelty, amour and respect for each other, in which neither will reduce the other to the status of a nonentity. I have discussed this in great detail in my introductory chapter in the section called, "Can Wonder Displace the Ego," in which I say that wonder helps transcend the ego of both of the partners and achieve harmony. Also, one must note that Irigaray's latest book *To be Two* discusses achieving a harmonious relationship through silence and yoga. Irigaray does not talk about Hindu philosophy[9] of transcendence of ego, but, her theory of "sexual difference," is grounded in Buddhist philosophy and silence of the yogic process. Irigaray observes thus in *To be Two*:

> And yet to say it in this way is not enough. I would go to the extent of saying that silence is basic for the loving relationship between the genders, which historically has yet to be thought because it rests at the level of nature, of the drives, of instinct, but because it maintains itself in difference, a difference that cannot be expressed. This silence which exists between the subjectivity of man and woman must not be overcome either in words or in representations, but must be protected, cultivated,

generated, also historically, so that it becomes more refined and shared. (62)

What Tagore expresses in *The King of the Dark Chamber* as the transcendence of ego achieved through the evolution of the Queen's consciousness in close harmony with the King's, could be likened to Irigaray's theory of silence and yoga. What she wants partners to achieve through silence is achieved in a way in the King-Queen relationship, although the implication goes further in Tagore's play because the play has a few more levels of philosophical underpinnings (Sri Aurobindo's philosophy and Sankhaya philosophy) beneath it.

The transformation of the ego in other characters of the play also contributes to the main theme of the story. There are other characters like the character of the King of Kanchi, Surangama, and the Grandfather and a few choric characters, which point towards this goal. The King of Kanchi, the great accomplice who inspired the trumped-up King to set fire in the pleasure garden has relinquished his vocation as a King and is a mere pedestrian now at his own will. He wanted to fight the King of the dark chamber, the real King. But, finally the King of Kanchi realizes that what he has thus far been doing is wrong:

> *Kanchi*
> But how long more will he elude me like this? When nothing could make me acknowledge him as my King, he came all of a sudden like a terrific tempest—God knows from where—and scattered my men and horses and banners in one wild tumult: but now, when I am seeking the ends of the earth to pay him my humble homage, he is nowhere to be seen. (189)

This observation underlies his urge to pay his homage to the real King. Earlier in the play we noted that everybody is looking for the King, but, the King hides himself from his people. There are two meanings we could draw from this behavior: one is by hiding himself the King wants to give power to his people, and this shows the King as someone who does not desire absolute power, but, as someone who is beyond ego and very humble instead. Now the King of Kanchi has known the true nature of the real King who is really a King of consciousness, because, he acquitted all the Kings of the guilt of trying to fight to win Sudarshana. The real King's nobleness and the humbleness of character opened his eyes to acknowledge the true worth of kinghood—to be a King in consciousness, and not in terms of power.

NOTES

1. See my discussion on this topic in Chapter 3, "Body in Transcendence: Jouissance and Kali."

2. It would be interesting to look at the commentaries of the Indian philosopher Shankara (eighth century A.D.) on the Indian philosophic text the *Upaniṣads*. His philosophy is known as Adaivta Vedanta which preaches that Brahman or the concept of the Pure Absolute is the only reality, and the entire world is an illusion or *maya*. It has strong similarity with the Buddhist philosophy, which also advocates the notion of withdrawal from the world which ultimately leads to nirvana.

3. Inconscience is the word used by Sri Aurobindo, as one of the key expressions of his philosophy of "supramental consciousness." By inconscience he refers to the state of mind which is a repository of evil emotion, which one could also call the ego.

4. This is Sri Aurobindo's way of defining the highest level of consciousness. One has to understand the meaning of this word in the light of his Supramental philosophy.

5. The word "nescience" has a special meaning in Sri Aurobindo's philosophy of "supramental consciousness." It alludes to not just ignorance, but to problems of the ego, more specifically.

6. Please see in this regard Irigaray's most recent book, *Between East and West*. Let me offer a quote here from the book:

Nevertheless the practice of yoga continually brings me back to this obvious fact, as do certain texts or commentaries of Indian tradition. In this way Mircea Eliade often presents the culture of India as a culture that has succeeded in retaining Asiatic aboriginal elements alongside later patriarchal contributions. There is therefore, in India, room for spiritualization of the masculine and of the feminine. Moreover, it is one of the only traditions where women goddesses and divine loving couples are still venerated. (65)

7. Rabindranath Tagore often compares death as something great. What it means is that in order to achieve something really great in life, often, one has to go through great hardship. In its intensity the hardship is even comparable to death. It is reminiscent of William Blake's *Songs of Innocence and Songs of Experience.*

8. I will enter into the detailed discussion of the descent of the Supramental light into the body in my next chapter which completely is devoted to the discussion of the spiritual transcendence of the body through Supramental light as I discuss this theoretical aspect through Chitra Banerjee Divakaruni's *The Mistress of Spices.* In this regard, I would also like to refer to the French philosopher Satprem's book, *The Mind of the Cells* and please note the following observation from this book:

> When a change has to be carried out, it is done not by an external and artificial means, but by an inner operation, BY AN OPERATION OF CONSCIOUSNESS which gives a form or an appearance to the substance. Life creates its own forms [. . .]. The absurdity here is all the artificial means that have to be used: any idiot has more power if he has more means to acquire the necessary artifices. Whereas in the supramental world, the more you are conscious and in relation with the truth of things, the more authority your will has over substance. (70)

9. Only in her most recent book *Between East and West,* Luce Irigaray refers to Hindu philosophy and her admiration for it.

Chapter 8

Is Jouissance Writing or Love?

But if I cannot affect myself in that sparkling night of my jouissance, you imprison me in the closure of your gaze. I am an object for your desire. I no longer desire. If I am deprived of that invisible touching again and again, nothing moves me any longer. Drawn out of myself. Exiled from my intuition. At best, turned inwards to some inner gaze. Making it even more penetrating? (*Elemental Passions* 44)

This chapter, the third in the literature section, by focusing more on jouissance from the Western psychoanalytic point of view becomes a slight aberration. Here, I undertake to interpret Clarice Lispector's novel *The Stream of Life* by exploring the being of a woman, her jouissance—which is connected to her unconscious, her body, and thereby her writing. Jouissance as consciousness is expressed here through writing; in a way it has connection with Joyce's aesthetic theory with the difference that the artist in Joyce's novel is more articulate, whereas Lispector's heroine shows instability which Cixous[1] positively renders as passion. The heroine strives to achieve the supreme level of consciousness through her writing, writing that emanates from her body—writing that encompasses both the body and the spirit. This chapter also engages in discussion of Lispector's other novel, *An Apprenticeship or The Book of Delights*, to represent how fulfillment can be achieved through love. It corroborates my thesis in this chapter, which is also a recurrent theme throughout the book that jouissance/consciousness could be achieved in the material plane and in the body. This latter novel proves that jouissance as love could be experienced in both corporeal and spiritual planes; and the fulfillment could be achieved through a perfect relationship of love as well.

Jouissance as Unconscious

Irigaray's theory of jouissance is a great tool to interpret Lispector's novel, *The Stream of Life*, since it valorizes women's unconscious and strives to redefine women's unconscious/ imaginary in term of the symbolic and consciousness. While Anna Rosalind Jones acknowledges the presence of jouissance as a tool for feminist vocalization towards the path of emancipation, she unnecessarily and quite unjustly hurls charges against Cixous and Irigaray: "How can one libidinal voice—or the two vulval lips so startlingly presented by Irigaray speak for all women" (*Writing the Body* 255)? Maggi Berg's article, "Irigaray and Her Feminist Critics" is written in defense of Irigaray by refuting the charges made by Ann Rosalind Jones. Quite staunchly Berg argues that "When Jones castigates the French for attempting to write the body, it is she who makes of it an essentialist position, by reading it within a framework of humanistic assumptions about the individual" (*Irigaray and Her Feminist Critics* 68). Maggie Berg clarifies that the problem with Jones's interpretation is that of positing the unconscious as "something innate and a priori—the strangely static origin of women's subjective identity." But, Berg tells us that the French are not at all interested in Jones's unconscious and Irigaray would reverse Jones's order. Berg further argues that for Irigaray 'the unconscious is not a priori,' not the determining cause but the result of women's subjective experience. To support this, Margaret Whitford writes, "For Irigaray, the unconscious is a 'reservoir of a yet-to-come,' a creative and regenerative source" (*The Irigaray Reader* 73).

Jane Gallop advocates that Irigaray posits the "possibility of a language that can reflect woman's natural specificity." She further expounds that Irigaray has been criticized by some for this "naturalistic belief in a real unmediated body available outside the symbolic order." Jane Gallop suggests that according to phallo-morphic logic the female genital has been defined as a clitoris, that is, 'phallic-same,' or has been described as vagina, 'phallic-opposite.' I do not think that Irigaray was thinking of the female body as outside of the symbolic order. Rather, her challenge is to establish the female body or to access the female body inside the symbolic order by acknowledging her sexual organs, and not reducing her to a vagina. Gallop suggests, "Irigaray seems to be advocating a female sexuality that replaces the anxious either-or with a pleasurable both: vagina and clitoris. But Irigaray ultimately chooses not both but neither, and the sparks of her genital poetics rather comes to light on the lips" (Gallop 81). Rather, Irigaray's poetics of the body is not confined to the female labia but is extended through the whole body and as a matter of fact the multiple sexuality of the female body is the site of her jouissance. In psychoanalytic discourse, or more specifically, according to Freud, women cannot have any jouissance of their own—they suffer from penis envy. There is no turning back of a daughter to a mother for its Oedipal phase, or the little girl is considered a little man—as if women are condemned not to have any sexuality of their own. But, Irigaray ecstatically talks about women's jouissance in their bodies—in the multiple parts of a woman's body which goes far beyond the stereotypical Western interpretation of the female body, but at the same time does not go beyond the symbolic order: it is a female body trying to make its place along a male phallic body in terms of sexual difference.

The Stream of Life embodies Irigaray's theory to a great extent by rendering the heroine's unconscious through writing as consciousness, and also reaching the supreme level of consciousness towards the end of the book through writing. In rendering the unconscious as consciousness the novel traces the unconscious in various ways, in terms of aphasia and pain as well. But, what gets valorized eventually is the victory in the way the heroine reaches the height of consciousness through her writing. Her body is very much involved in her writing, and this asserts the other aspect of the theory of jouissance, that of corporeality—the corporeality is the source of writing. The unconscious pours forth in the corporeality, and then the corporeality transmits itself into writing and finally, the corporeality reaches the supreme moment of consciousness, which strives to descend on the body/material plane.

Jouissance and Femininity

The Stream of Life is about a woman who, not given a name by the author, tries to express herself through various ways: mainly through her pleasure of writing, sometimes painting. At the end of the novel, she achieves beatitude through her writing. So, the basic premise of the book is that fulfillment could be achieved through writing—or jouissance as consciousness could be obtained through writing as the heroine does in this novella. She is in love with her writing and her bodily jouissance is expressed through this love which is writing. The book opens with the groan of a newly-born woman; woman in the stage of evolving, emerging, becoming something else. Marta Peixoto has overemphasized this element of pain in Lispector's novel: "The female sublime aspects of the novella may indeed put some readers off as self-indulgent and solipsistic: cries of vulnerability alternate with a haughty superiority" (Peixoto 71); or "The oscillation between exaltation and dejection follows no discernibly logical pattern, but is simply a rhythmic alternation like the in and out of breathing (a physiological process that the narrator often invokes)" (71). I partially agree with Peixto's comment because the novel is permeated with a great deal of restlessness and the heroine seems to change her function/role too quickly. Even at the end of the novel, when the heroine describes grace, at that supreme moment of attaining grace she switches to the linguistic discussion of the word, "beatitude." Although Peixoto critiques Cixous for her identification with Lispector as if she were a "Cixousian twin," Cixous's interpretation of juxtaposition of the elements of pain and joy in Lispector's novel seems to be more plausible to me, as she said, "Clarice never forgets that there is no paradise without hell" (Cixous 42). This mixture of exhilaration with pain has also been expressed as a 'shout of diabolical happiness'; happiness is associated with a certain amount of violence, since women have been choked, repressed, stifled for centuries. The pain of the heroine could be best rendered as a reflection of her agony when the unconscious binds the path to consciousness from which both Lispector and Irigaray strive to liberate women.

Jouissance and Writing

One could really start reading *The Stream Life* from any point—even in the end, in the middle, or in the beginning—and one would feel the same way. There is no perfect grammatical or syntactical structure, but there is an overwhelming feeling of infinity in which all the passion of the heroine going somewhere without introducing any sense of teleology. I mainly interpret this book in terms of female writing originating from women's innate feeling of their unconscious, their body and as such their own sexuality. The writing that Irigaray talks about as feminine writing and connected to women's jouissance is linked to touch or tactile sensations. Irigaray describes it in "Power of Discourse," as the "style" which "does not privilege sight; instead, it takes each figure back to its source, which is among other things tactile." She is in fact rereading Merleau-Ponty's theory according to which the visible and the tactile are mutually dependent. In *Lived Bodies*, Elizabeth Grosz discusses how in opposition to Merleau-Ponty, Irigaray claims that the visible is dependent on the tangible, but the tangible is independent of the visible and could have its autonomous existence. According to Irigaray, the visual is the 'domain in which lack is to be located'; it is the visual "which designates female genitals as missing, an order which is incompatible with the plenitude, enfolding and infinite complexity of the tactile and the tangible" (Grosz 106). The tactile or the tangible which has the potential for infinite jouissance is related to the concept of the mucus and fluidity and this concept of fluidity is the mark of feminine writing or feminine style.[2] In "Power of Discourse," Irigaray writes: "To put it another way: there would no longer be either a right side or a wrong side of discourse, or even of texts, but each passing from one to the other would make audible and comprehensible even what resists the recto-verso structure that shores up common sense" (127). That means feminine writing does not need to follow any recto-verso structure. It is not linear. According to this interpretation, one could start reading the discourse at any point. Therefore, one could start from the end.

In *The Stream of Life* what she writes is new to her. Her true word has remained untouched until now because the limitations of a patriarchal society have denied women access to language. But the moment has come when the word is becoming her fourth dimension; the word which she plans to invent through her 'auto-eroticism,' 'diffuse-sexuality,' or jouissance. She is trying to give shape to the excess which has been defined as nothing. In the beginning of the same paragraph, she is talking about the pleasure in writing [presumably to her lover] 'completely whole' and conveys her feeling of pleasure in 'being' and communicates that her pleasure [with him presumably] is abstract. The pleasure she derives from her lover is abstract or she wants to derive it at the abstract level because otherwise there is a chance that she would be relegated to phallogocentric jouissance. She seems so determined to explore her own writing that her passion for writing supersedes her passion for her lover. She expresses a kind of detachment from her human lover—who signifies phallus. In *Elemental Passions* Irigaray has expounded how women could be shut out:

> Have you shut me within the sun? To gaze at me through screens? You have positioned me in the site of jouissance. I can burn, be consumed, illuminate you [. . .] but I cannot play with fire. Unless perhaps in your gaze? But do you not take me then in the economy of your natural light? Have I not already been taken from the sun's irradiation? (*Elemental Passions* 43)

Therefore, the narrator in jouissance is safeguarding the pleasure she derives from her jouissance, by keeping her pleasure at the abstract level, out of her lover's reach.

According to Irigaray, jouissance is an expression of women's unconscious, 'a reservoir-yet-to-come,' a creative and regenerative force which has been relegated by patriarchy (psychoanalysis) to the imaginary order as being feminine. But, through her theory of jouissance, Irigaray recuperates the feminine, the unconscious and the imaginary to the symbolic order. The narrator retrieves her unconscious through her writing, as she explores it through her jouissance. From the mode of writing she switches into painting, and conveys that she paints her pictures with her entire body, and on the canvas she achieves a synthesis or bridges a gap between her incorporeal and corporeal existences. Her incorporeal existence could be rendered in Irigarayan terms as a vacancy or 'a gap in form' and she returns to the canvas, returning to another edge where she feels her corporeal self by retouching herself with the help of nothing.

Resistance to Jouissance and Writing
The narrator expresses her agony over her writing that her writing is 'coarse' and 'order less' and her friend might insist that she should stick to painting but her new realization is that she has a

need for words, that is, language. And she boldly articulates, "the word is going to be her fourth dimension." It is constituted of round lines penetrating each other in their black strokes which resemble writing per se. But she attributes the color of her 'black strokes' as being associated with the past, when women were repressed. Then she explains the nature of her writing with the epithets that it is 'round,' 'complicated' and 'tepid' and she tries to impart tactile sensation in her writing by offering the analogy that it is 'frigid like fresh instants' or like 'stream water trembling always on its own.' Her question is if what she has painted could be transferred into words which, according to her, is identical to a 'mute word,' yet 'implicit in musical sound.' She depicts her feeling that when she listens to music it creates and imparts vibration in her body—she craves for a kind of corporeality. And hence her realization is that she wants "the vibrant substratum of the word repeated in a Gregorian chant." Chanting will create vibration in her body—and she wants to create corporeal existence for words[3]. Her articulation is that it is difficult to express every feeling in words and she knows this through her experience in painting and 'pronouncing syllables blind of meaning,' through her libidinal expression. She wants to create bodily meaning in words. She transmits her libidinal energy in language saying that what is invented through language or within language is pure vibration, "without meaning except that of each bubbling syllable." Lispector's undescribed character is somebody whose domain is that of discursive words but who lacks the straightforward expression of her painting. She constantly talks about the lacuna or inadequacy of language because women have been unrepresented in male or patriarchal discourse and for the feminine libido the best expression seems to be that of painting, "When I write I can't create as I do in painting." But she has come up with a new mode of writing—that is, writing with her body.

Aphasia: Block to Jouissance

Aphasia is a phase in the realization of jouissance and so we see the narrator moving between aphasia and jouissansic pleasure. At times, she depicts her current phase of jouissance—its pleasure boldly by articulating that there is no harm done in departing from logic. She writes, "I am dealing with primal matter. I'm after

what's behind thought. It's useless to try to classify me: I simply
slip away not leaving" (*The Stream* 7). She has transcended all the
categories of patriarchal order and they can no longer pin her
down. She is on the verge of unfolding her new identity. She
articulates that she is in a new and true state, very curious about
herself, and this state is so 'attractive,' and personal that it defies
her ability to paint or write about this state. But at times, she is
fraught with aphasia, even though she is overwhelmed with her
pleasure. She writes, "It's a state of contact with the surrounding
energy, and I tremble. A kind of crazy, crazy harmony. I know that
my look must be the look of a primitive person who surrenders
completely to the world" (7). She seems to be in touch with her
cosmic energy (cf. Lawrence).   Maggi Berg's article, "Irigaray
and Her Feminist Critics" helps us to understand the term 'aphasia'
in the feminine context:

> Her (Irigaray's) prose is based on the speech of the hysterical
> woman, which is a double-edged discourse: evidence at once of
> the effects of repression and resistance to it. The hysteric
> converts repressed desire into another language, another syntax.
> The major symptom of hysteria is 'aphasia' or loss of the power
> of speech. The similarity between Irigaray's text and the
> discourse of Anna O (Freud's and Breuer's first case study) are
> remarkable. The loss of mastery over discourse is, says Irigaray
> 'a symptom of historical repression' (S 135). She goes back (in a
> kind of 'talking cure') over her relationship with her 'fathers' the
> philosophers in order to discover the historical origins of her
> hysteria. (71)

Hence, we see the narrator of *The Stream of Life*, occasionally
being caught in a state of aphasia. She delves into words as if she
were painting shadow. She alludes to silence several times, "I
delve into words as if I were painting not just an object but its
shadow. I don't want to ask why, one can eternally ask why and
remain eternally without an answer." And then "Listen to me,
listen to the silence. Capture this thing that escapes me, and I
nonetheless live off of it and am on the surface of brilliant
darkness." She constantly alludes to 'silence' and 'darkness'—if
this is the expression of repression, it is followed by her resistance
to it. Her moment of darkness is followed by her moment of

illumination: "I slowly enter writing, just as I have entered painting." Her world is comprised of a 'tangled world of vines'; syllables are of honeysuckle colors, and words she describes as the "threshold of an ancestral cavern which is the uterus of the world" and she configures herself to be born through their space or passage. The world of writing has been described as the gateway of an ancestral cavern which is again conceived as the uterus of the world and the writer wants to be born through her writing. Note the word 'uterus'—and the concept of birth through writing.

Images on Aphasia as Resistance to Jouissance as Writing

The book abounds in metaphor and the metaphors that I am discussing here allude to the narrator's phases of mind as she goes through her experiences of jouissance. The narrator of *The Stream of Life* alludes to 'caves' and she narrates that her painting of caves is identical with her 'submersion' into the ear:

> And if many times I paint caves it's because they are my submersion into the earth, dark but clouded with clarity, and I, nature's blood—extravagant and dangerous caves, Earth's talisman, where stalactites, fossils, and stones come together and where creatures crazy through their own evil nature seek refuge. (*The Stream* 8)

This is a stage of hibernation or could be described as an aphasic stage of existence for the unnamed character who is resisting patriarchal discourse.   Her aphasia is followed by her exuberant phase of jouissance. She depicts that everything is 'heavy with dreams' when she paints a cave but out of this is generated 'the clatter of dozens of unfettered horses to trample the shadows with dry hooves' and from this friction is born 'rejoicing' or 'jouissance' which liberates itself in 'sparks.' In various ways we notice her expressing her jouissance, "in this now-instant I'm enveloped by a drifting desire, diffuse with wonder and thousands of sun reflections in the water" (*The Stream* 10). Again, she is using the metaphor of water, "My state is that of a garden with running water." The metaphor of water is conducive to understand feminine jouissance and I think Lispector deliberately uses this metaphor here.[4] The narrator also offers the metaphor of 'snarled roots' to convey carnal energy transmitted to writing. She tells us that she is writing with rage and energy by tearing out the snarled roots of a colossal tree and she compares those roots with the "voluminous nude bodies of strong women wrapped in serpents and carnal desires of realization" (13). She is filled with 'carnal desires of realization' for her writing, because it originates from her multiple sexual organs.

Writing and Pleasure

Now the question remains as to what does Lispector's heroine accomplish in writing, or writing with jouissance? Has she been able to express herself completely in her writing, through her corporeal jouissance, feeling the multiple sexuality of her body? We can validate that there is a strong erotic connection between her writing and jouissance as corporeal pleasure. She renders it in terms of a new kind of writing. This she defines as 'improvising,' "I improvise in the same way they improvise in jazz, I improvise in front of the audience" (15). Then, she describes this technique or the process of improvising. She expresses it in terms of 'secret desires,' and says that with the words she achieves a 'confused, orgiastic beauty' (16). "I shiver with pleasure in the midst of the innovation of using words that form intense underbrush!" (16). She shivers with her pleasure of jouissance in the midst of creating words. "I struggle to conquer more fully the freedom that I have of sensations and thoughts without any utilitarian meaning" (16). She is describing her pleasure of using words as the freedom of such proportions that it could scandalize a savage. Her freedom is without any perceptible frontiers. Her pleasure in delving into language seems to be akin to sexual pleasure. She tells us that she surrounds herself with 'carnivorous plants' and 'legendary creatures,' all permeated with the 'coarse, awkward light of a mythical sex.' What becomes evident is a sort of primitive quality and sexuality attached to this character. She tells her audience that she is organic and to ornament her, leaves and branches are sprouting out of her hair. This is a highly erotic analogy. Again she reiterates her assertion about her writing that what she transmits in her writing is not a message of ideas but rather an instinctive voluptuousness of what is hidden in nature. She talks about painting profusely and my interpretation is that painting could also be explained as a kind of expressive aphasia or feminine discourse coming out of her spontaneous reaction of jouissance.

Spiritual Jouissance

The book also reflects the spiritual jouissance as the narrator moves from the corporeal to the celestial level.[5] Another way to describe the concept of spiritual jouissance is through Irigaray's theory of the divine. The theory of spiritual jouissance allows to women "the horizon of accomplishment," leading to their ascent. In Lispector's *The Stream of Life*, one notes this ascent—ascent to the highest plane of consciousness, which she manifests then through her writing, as I discuss later in the section. Thus, *ānanda*/consciousness here manifests it in writing. But, unlike Joyce's *A Portrait of the Artist as A Young Man*, this novella does not inscribe the divine nuances or "spiritual essence" in writing. The suffering of the named heroine seems sometimes too pronounced as opposed to Joyce's Stephen.

Lispector/her unnamed heroine suggests that she will create a new meaning with her jouissance—with the celestial dimension of her jouissance and she will generate an ethereal light around her. The narrator has just remarked that the world has no desirable order, and she has only the order of her breathing and she lets herself flow. Her reference to breath and air clearly indicates that Lispector/her unnamed heroine, ponders about the benefits of yogic exercise through breathing. The heroine is gradually attaining a transcendental plane. She feels her consciousness is as light as air. Air also belongs to the five elements according to Hindu philosophy—the five elements which control the universe. She describes her experience in the following way, "The air is the non-plane where everything will exist. What I'm writing is the music of the air" (28). This ethereal or celestial dimension which she brings into writing abolishes time, "What I'm writing to you is not to be read—it's to be." She has conceived of the angelic beings blowing their trumpets into timelessness: "The first flower is born in the air. The ground that is earth is formed. The rest is air and the rest is slow fire in perpetual mutation. Does the word 'perpetual' not exist because time does not exist? But the rumble exists. And my existence begins to exist" (28).

The first flower could be interpreted as an expression of the celestial form of jouissance. 'The ground that is earth' is formed from the corporeal aspect of jouissance. 'The air' and 'the slow fire in perpetual mutation' could be interpreted as her feminine jouissance inscribing her new identity. Not only the first flower is born in air, but also the earth is formed. The reference to both earth and air has the nuance of the unification of heaven and earth or the descent of spirituality on earth. What becomes interestingly evident in this text is the mutation from the celestial to the corporeal and vice versa. The next passage explicates the celestial dimension of jouissance into her writing:

> What I write you has no beginning; it's a continuation. From the words of the song, a song that is mine and yours, there arises a halo that transcends the lines [. . .] do you feel it? My experience comes from the fact that I've already been able to paint the halo of things. The halo is more important than the things and than the words. (37)

Here, writing is connected here to transcendence—which she defines as a halo, and suggests that the transcendental source of writing is more important than the writing itself. In a way, it could be related to the experience that Joyce/Stephen experienced as an artist. But, Lispector's style is different and her enunciation of the artistic process is permeated with hysterical sensation which is ecstasy which rapidly evaporates as she progresses to the next section of her writing.

As we proceed more into the book we notice Lispector's writing becoming highly transcendental as in the above mentioned passage in which she tells us about her experience that from the words of the songs there rises a halo which transcends the lines and this halo she interprets as the inner essence of words and things. It is true that initially, in her journey into the transcendental plane of jouissance she is at times caught with her aphasic pain, but she regains her confidence after a moment of pain. Toward the end of the book her experience of spirituality becomes more definitive:

> The state of grace I refer to isn't used for anything. It's as if it came only so one would know that it really exists and that the

world exists. In that state, beyond the tranquil happiness that irradiates from people and things, there's a clarity that I call lightness only because in grace everything is so light [. . .].
And there's a sense of physical well-being that's comparable nothing else. The body is transformed into a gift. And one feels it's a gift because one is experiencing, directly from the source, the suddenly unquestionable gift of miraculously and materially existing. (72)

This is a description of the descent of grace in the body. The state of grace is described as of "tranquil happiness," which is then described in terms of lightness—of an ethereal sensation. The state described here could be likened to the state of supreme consciousness or *ānanda* which is achieved through the dissolution of one's ego, and which in Joyce's writing is referred to as stasis. Thus, although throughout the book one encounters what Cixous calls, "diabolical happiness," or rise and fall of passion, at the end there is an innuendo about this psychic ascent which is followed by the descent onto the material plane. The body is portrayed as being metamorphosed into a gift and in Hindu philosophy the body is considered as sacred as a temple. Lispector/the unnamed heroine also explains that it is elevated to a gift the moment it feels connected to transcendence. But, always she comes back to language and her writing:

I wanted to make that happiness eternal through the objectification of the word. Immediately afterward, I went to the dictionary to look up the word. Immediately afterward, I went to the dictionary to look up the word "beatitude," which I detest as a word, and I saw that it means pleasure of the soul. It speaks of tranquil happiness—I however would call it transport or levitation. I also don't like the way the dictionary definition reads: "a state of someone absorbed in mystical contemplation." That's not it. I wasn't meditating at all, there was no religiousness in me. I had just finished my coffee and I was simply living, sitting there with a cigarette burning down in the ashtray. (73)

It is intriguing to see the way the heroine differentiates the two states—the state of religiosity and the state of transport or levitation. The words "transport" and "levitation" allude to the ascending state of consciousness, which occurs when one transcends the problem of ego. Here, the heroine aspires to achieve that level of consciousness through her writing, and she is keen to separate it from any kind of religiosity. She shuns the word "mystical," she shuns the expression "beatitude," but she adheres to "levitation," which means the ascent of consciousness. The passage also asserts that the feeling of transport could be manifest on the material plane. She assures it in two different ways; she has asserted in the passage that she wants to make the feeling eternal through the embodiment of it in proper words. Thus, language acquires supreme importance here; on the other hand, she validates that the sense of levitation occurs to her when she drinks coffee and smokes a cigarette, implying the importance of levitation/ascent in the mundane life.

The question remains to ask if the jouissance is achieved here as consciousness, or, if the heroine attains a supreme level of consciousness through the transcendence of her ego. Lispector's novel raises that ontological/philosophical question, and solves it on the plane of language. The heroine undergoes various voyeuristic experiences, and all the images she uses, for example, the image of the "halo" alludes to the world beyond ego. What we see here is the heroine's agony and striving to conquer her ego and the pains of the world inflicted on her by patriarchy, however, the exact sublimation of pain comes at the end of the book. It could be inscribed as a journey from Lacan to Irigaray.

Is Love Corporeal or Transcendental?

I read Lispector's novel, *An Apprenticeship or The Book of Delights* through the Irigarayan theory of the 'carnal ethics' which advocates that the relationship between partners of two opposite sexes should be based both on corporeality and spirituality, and that female jouissance ranges from the corporeal to the celestial. Love should be based on both corporeality and spirituality—it should be both immanent and transcendent. But, Lispector's heroine attains her divinity through her contact with an impersonal divine, prior to her union with her lover. Divinity could be attained through the perfect relationship between man and woman. In this book, there are only two characters, Lori and Ulysses and they reach divinity through their corporeal relationship. Lori has to go through several phases of experiences to realize that the mysticality or the impersonal divine that she is yearning for can be attained through a corporeal relationship with Ulysses. The story of Lori and Ulysses has strong similarity with Banerjee Divakaruni's *The Mistress of Spices*.

Irigaray observes that, "The two genealogies must be divinized in each of the two sexes and for the two sexes: mother and father, woman and man, for it to be possible for female and male lovers to love each other" (*IR* 186). So, in this book what Lori is undergoing is a process of divinization—exploring her own spiritual potentiality which has been denied to women by Western phallogocentrism. Lori like G. H. in *Passion According to G.H.* and the unnamable character in *The Stream of Life*, is groping with a mystical yearning but unlike others Lori's journey goes one step further; she does not stop yearning for an impersonal divine, therefore, her character is inexplicable or partially inexplicable if read through Irigaray's theory of the 'La Mysterique.' Her character is totally explicable if approached through Irigaray's theory of 'carnal ethics' or 'sexual ethics' which talks about achieving divinity in the body. At first, Lori like the unnamed character of *The Stream of Life*, and G. H. thinks in terms of the animal life and the impersonal divine which liberates her from the patriarchal pressure: "For a moment, then, she rejected her own humanity and experienced the silent soul of animal life" (*An Apprenticeship* 25). It seems that her fear for the world, or in other words her fear of the patriarchal world pushes her to the animal kingdom. She conceives of herself as 'a diffuse mass of instinct,' and 'a trembling radiation of peace and strife.' She switches her imaginative identity between the animal kingdom and the human world and prefers the animal world, because, she feels that God is easily accessible through the concept of 'not understanding,' "was a concept so vast that it surpassed any understanding, which was always so limited. But not understanding did not have any boundaries and led to the infinite, to God" (*An Apprenticeship*). But Lori's perception of the world is not limited to this mystical realization which critics have interpreted as the combination of the mystical and the existential quest. Lori goes one step further in her realization of the divine which helps her to realize the divine in her body and not merely in the realm of mysticality:

> At times she would regress and surrender with a complete lack of responsibility to the desire to be possessed by Ulysses without any ties, as she had done with the others. But she could fail in this too. She had become used to the ways of the big city now, but the danger lay in the fact that she also had a strong agrarian heritage in her blood going back for generations. And knowing that this heritage could suddenly make her want more, she said to herself, "No, I don't want to be just me for the sake of having my own identity. What I want is the tight bond between me and the unstable, yet sweet-smelling earth." What she called earth had now become the synonym for Ulysses, so much did she love the land of her ancestors. (*An Apprenticeship* 24)

The underlying implication of the statement is that Lori has started to realize the importance of a corporeal relationship. In this passage, she has expressed her desire to 'be possessed by Ulysses,' and also to have a tight bond between her and the 'sweet-smelling' earth which she equates with the existence of Ulysses.

Like Lispector's other female protagonists, Lori goes through the process of wandering until she knows the truth about herself and the world and the way fulfillment comes to her. Thus, we see her interrogating herself about 'existence,' "What kind of pain was it? That of existence? That of belonging to some unknown thing? That of having been born?" But in all her thoughts, Ulysses remains at the back of her mind. In spite of Ulysses's understanding of her she suffers from a kind of trauma that he might abandon her—which is a fear instilled into her by patriarchy. On the contrary, Ulysses helps her to realize the importance of the 'body': "Oh, Lori, can't you recapture, even vaguely, the carnal pleasure that you must have felt in being, in existing, at least in the cradle? Or even some other time in your life whenever or for whatever reason?" (*An Apprenticeship* 37). The pain that prevents Lori from accepting Ulysses fully is the pressure of patriarchy which her pain symbolically represents. In her process of divinization she tries to emancipate herself through her resort to the impersonal divine. But, in the process of realization she comes to know the importance of Ulysses's existence in her life:

At that memory, which she visualized again, she thought that from now on that was all she would want from God: to rest her breast on His and not say a word. But if that were possible, it would happen only after death. As long as she was alive she would have to pray which she no longer wanted. Or else speak with human beings who answered her and perhaps represented God. Especially Ulysses. (*An Apprenticeship* 41)

What is happening here is that Lori is being subjected to the pain of repression inflicted on her by the phallus, and whenever she is subject to this kind of pain, she takes refuge in the divine; but the development that we perceive in Lori's character is that now the divine is being replaced or being represented by an ordinary human being like Ulysses. Lori knows the reality that since mere mysticality is not going to rescue her from the pain, she has to establish contact with human beings who answered her and 'perhaps represented God' and she articulates that that special person could be Ulysses.

The entire section is called 'Luminescence' and we see Lori going through the successive stages of experiences in her realization of the divine. One idiosyncratic feature of Lispector's female protagonists is that they go through the same experience in a recurrent manner until they reach their final realization and we notice the same pattern in Lori's character. Lori goes through her experience of pain and realizes in a recurrent manner that the divine is to be realized in the real, in corporeal life and she finds the corporeal divine in Ulysses but withdraws again because she suspects that she cannot bear this happiness. Below, shortly, I will discuss certain passages that will exemplify the above. Lori gradually denies the existence of the conventional God: 'Up until now her God had been of this world, but He was no longer' (*An Apprenticeship* 42). Now she moves from that kind of divinity to the realization of 'Nothingness.' She also universalizes her pain by identifying with other women, "At that moment she was merely one woman among many and not an individual. And she was preparing herself as if for an eternal march, toward Nothingness. What was nothing was really everything" (*An Apprenticeship* 43).

Her realization of the divine is followed by her encounter with
Ulysses in which they share the feeling of their existence.

> The fact is that she herself existed and this surprised her. Even
> though Ulysses might not hear her she said very softly, "I'm
> existing."
> [. . . . .]
> He looked at her carefully and for a moment discovered a
> familiar woman's face. He was surprised and then he understood
> Lori: he was existing.
> They remained silent as if the two of them had just met for the
> first time. They were existing.
> "I am, too," Ulysses said softly.
> They both knew that this was a big step forward in their
> apprenticeship. And there was no danger of exhausting this
> feeling or fear of losing it because being was infinite, as infinite
> as the wave in the ocean. (*An Apprenticeship* 37)

This realization of corporeal existence which is so important to
their relationship is culminated by Lori's observation that her
extreme individuality might clash with the impersonal world, but
her tie with Ulysses will remain. That means she admits to herself
the importance of their corporeal relationship: "Some day the
supremely impersonal world will be opposed to my extreme
individuality as a person, but we will be one" (*An Apprenticeship*
47). But again she withdraws from her realization that she had
about the importance of corporeal existence. She starts dreading
earthly love. She interrogates herself: "'But how mortal I am. How
earthly love penetrates me' [. . .] What am I to do with this
strange, keen sense of peace that is already beginning to hurt me,
like the great silence of space?" Finally, it is Ulysses who helps
her achieve her final realization of the feeling of divinity in
corporeality.

This section discusses how the Irigarayan theory of female
jouisance or 'carnal ethics' helps one to read this book from the
vantage of mutuality; how these two characters, Lori and Ulysses,
attain their spiritual fulfillment through corporeality and how both
of them are needed for this and cannot attain it alone. I have
discussed so far the divinization process of Lori but she needs
Ulysses to achieve the spirituality that she is yearning—spirituality

in the body; only this achievement liberates her from the pressure of patriarchy. Ulysses helps her to realize the importance of her body which is obviously not devoid of its spirituality: "With me you can bare your soul even in silence. One day I will bare my soul completely and we will never run out of things to say because the soul is infinite. And besides that, we have two bodies that will give us joyous, silent and deep pleasure. Lori blushes to Ulysses' surprise and delight" (*An Apprenticeship* 63).

Ulysses is talking about both corporeal and spiritual pleasure; he inspires Lori to open her soul to him because the soul has infinite potentiality and that will bind them forever. But he does not neglect the body: "And besides that, we have two bodies that will give us joyous, silent and deep pleasure." The most important part is Ulysses's articulation: "We must believe in blood as an important part of life" (*An Apprenticeship* 68). Gradually, we see Lori going through a process of transformation; starting to feel the sensual pleasure, although Lori has her reservations because she has had disappointments, "Because the search for pleasure, those times when she had tried it, had tasted like polluted water"(*An Apprenticeship* 73). So, she thinks for a while that 'legitimate suffering' was preferable to 'forced pleasure.' But here is an example of how she starts enjoying sensual pleasure:

No, she was not referring to the fire, she was referring to her feelings. What she was feeling would never last; it would end and never return again. She seized the moment, then, and her inner fire consumed her. But the fire in front of her burned gently, burned and blazed. Then, as everything was going to end, in her vivid imagination she grabbed the man's free hand. And still in her imagination, as she took that hand in hers, she burned gently all over, she burned and blazed. (*An Apprenticeship* 74)

Lori is burning with passion. In her imagination, she is holding Ulysses's hand and she is burning with passion all over. At other places she articulates that she does not know how to define that thing that is consuming her or "to what she was consuming greedily except that of passion." But the problematic is that Lori cannot accept this pleasure initially and goes through a process of recurrent pain before she can finally accept it. Immediately after her experience of pleasure we notice Lori feels the pleasure has hurt her so much that she would rather feel her usual pain. She comments to herself, "The union with Ulysses that had been and was her desire had become unbearably good." But sadly enough she feels that she is not in a position to enjoy a man. She feels like a wounded Jaguar shot with an arrow and it is Ulysses who relieves her of this pain by pulling out the arrow and through him she reaches the state of grace in which she finally realizes the divinity of her body. Soon she finds herself in a state of grace and it descended upon her to let her know that she truly existed. Suddenly, she feels that her body is becoming a gift, and she feels a sense of physical well-being. Thus, she felt, "And she sensed that it was a gift because, through some direct source, she was experiencing the unmistakable joy of existing materially" (*An Apprenticeship* 98). Grace for Lori consists in the joy of existing materially, or corporeally. It is followed by her realization that the state of grace that she had attained was not saintly but that of an ordinary person, because it is 'common,' 'human,' and 'recognizable.' It is not impervious to a common human being's perception:

> Then slowly she came out of that state. But it was not as if she had been in a trance, for there had been no trance. She slowly came back with the sigh of one who has experienced the world as it is. It was a sigh of longing also, for having already given a body and a soul, the earth and the heavens, she wanted it all the more. But it was useless to wish—it came only spontaneously. (*An Apprenticeship* 98)

So, only through the state of grace which is not a state of trance but a state of vigilant realization does Lori have access to both her body and soul, 'the earth and the heavens' and realizes the importance of both corporeality and spirituality.

The last section discusses the attainment of spirituality in the body through the corporeal union between Lori and Ulysses which also has a spiritual dimension. Lori does not falter any more and attains that stable state of mind which helps her or both of them to attain spirituality in the body, and thereby the perfect union between two persons of the opposite sex. For a moment Lori suffers from the patriarchal fear to which she was subjected by her father who tried to transform her, 'from child to Pieta, the mother of men.' So, when Ulysses kneels before her, she is afraid for a moment that he is relegating her back to the role of a mother. But soon she realizes that with Ulysses it is different. Immediately after this they join in their corporeal union: "And so, greedily, joylessly, they made love a second time. And as that was not enough, as they had waited so long, almost immediately they possessed one another again, this time with solemn, silent joy. She felt herself becoming weightless like a figure in painting by Chagall." (*An Apprenticeship* 110)

The description of their union indicates that Lori and Ulysses really have entered the fluid universe crossing the solid exteriors of their bodies. Lori has the supreme realization that it is knowledge 'so vast and peaceful' that she is transported to a different world. "And it was a synthesis also, as it encompassed at the same time everything great and small [. . .]. She was as complete as God" (*An Apprenticeship* 110). She wants to communicate this to Ulysses and summoning her strength articulates to him, "It's because I love you." She hears Ulysses' frank admission, "'The truth is, Lori, that deep inside I've searched my whole life for divine rapture. I had never thought that, instead, I would discover the divinity of the body.'"[6] This is a very crucial observation because it exemplifies clearly the Irigarayan theory of 'carnal ethics' that divinity could be reached in the body. The body, especially the female body does not need to be chastised.

> She wanted nothing more than exactly what was happening to her: to be a woman lying in the dark next to a man who was asleep. She wondered for a moment if death would interfere in the concrete pleasure of being alive. And the answer was that not even the idea of death could disturb the endless darkness where everything throbbed thickly, heavily, blissfully. (*An Apprenticeship* 111)

Lori also reaches a spiritual height through a corporeal union which even seems to conquer death,[7] and could not disturb the endless darkness 'where everything throbbed thickly, heavily, blissfully.' The union is very close to what Irigaray has described as the relation of 'sexual difference' which is based on both alliance and freedom. Lori and Ulysses possess one another completely, but at the same time maintain their own identity. The most climactic expression is when Ulysses tells Lori that he is now a superman, and Lori, a superwoman and what more that they are 'potential Gods.' This is followed by Ulysses' interpretation that he is not talking about God in the literal sense; he is talking about God in terms of corporeal existence. He tells Lori that she has finally learned how to exist, "Sex and love aren't forbidden to you anymore. You've finally learned how to exist. And this causes the release of many other liberties, which is a threat to your social class" (*An Apprenticeship* 115). It is interesting to see that Ulysses can understand how Lori is situated in the logocentric society and realizes how their union both at the corporeal and the spiritual level is going to liberate her from patriarchy, and could even be a threat to patriarchy. But that does not deter him from his union with Lori; " 'We both know that we're at the threshold of an open door to a better life. This is the entrance'" (*An Apprenticeship* 113).

NOTES

1. Helene Cixous was enamored of Lispector's works and thus comments on *The Stream of Life,* (*Agua viva*):

> To read *Agua viva* requires a double task. On the one hand, one can follow themes. There are themes in *Agua Viva.* There is no harm done by respecting a certain order while remembering that the text is completely organic. One has to follow all that is of the order of truth, of genesis, of fatality. There are thousands of little themes that are of importance. On the other hand, one can follow that which brings pleasure. The text is full of springs. If one has pleasure, it shows that there is something in common between the reader and Clarice, something of a certain type of libidinal structure [. . .]. There is a perpetual phenomenon of overflowing in the text. *Agua viva* deserves that one dare to let oneself

overflow but that, at the same time, one not be afraid to border it. (xiii)

2. Please, see Elizabeth Grosz's observation on Irigaray's style of writing in her *Lived Bodies*, "The tactile is related by Irigaray to the concept of the mucus, which always marks the passage from inside to outside, which accompanies and lubricates the mutual touching of the body's parts and regions. The mucus is neither the subjective touching of the toucher nor the objectivity of the touched but the indeterminacy of any distance between them" (107). Lispector's *The Stream of Life* embodies this fluid feature in it's writing, in its corporeality, and in its spirituality.

3. In Hindu culture, "chanting," has a great importance. By "chanting" a mantra one can reach liberation (*moksha)* from the terrestrial world, and also one can create an ambience to protect oneself from the outside world. Also, *sabda* meaning sound is linked to Brahman, the Ultimate Reality, meaning furthermore that whatever one says should be in harmony with the Ultimate Reality. In *The Stream of Life*, the narrator attempts to reach the Ultimate Reality or the knowledge of Brahman and *ānanda* through language.

4. Water in terms of fluidity is quite important to Irigaray too. Please note Elizabeth Grosz's observation in this regards, "metaphoric of fluids, emblematic of femininity in *This Sex Which is Not One* (1985) and *Marine Lover* (1991), signifies not only the "formlessness" of feminine jouissance but more particularly the amniotic element that houses the child in the mother's body and continues to be a "watermark" etched on the child's body" (Grosz 104).

5. In elucidating "spiritual jouissance," I would like to refer to my dissertation entitled, "Jouissance and Divinity: Reading Lawrence and Lispector through Irigaray." In chapter 2, "Lispector and the Irigarayan Divine," I suggest the following elaborating on the theory of the divine:

> Although the theory of the divine is manifest in a different way in Clarice Lispector's writings, the basic assumptions are similar. Like Irigaray, Lispector also conceives of God leading her to infinity—in terms of emancipation. Lispector's project is no less empowered with the feminist philosophy of 'space out of patriarchy' than Irigaray's. Critics tend to suggest that Lispector's writings reflect phenomenological tension, or existential struggle in trying to grasp the world. Fitz says:

> In the fiction of Clarice Lispector, the ultimate intent of
> effect of this constant phenomenological tension
> between a consciousness and the/world of objects it
> perceives is to allow her protagonists to get beyond
> themselves, to escape momentarily [. . .] from the
> psychological prisons in which their conventionally used
> language and their 'naturalistic' social existences place
> them. (Fitz 38)

Thus, Fitz argues that Lispector's fictions are permeated with
phenomenological tension between protagonists and the 'world
of objects,' it observes. My reading of Lispector suggests that
her female protagonists are trying hard to get out of the prison of
patriarchy and reach the realization of the impersonal divine
which leads them to the path of freedom, by directing their
minds to infinity [. . .]. Lispector is a theorist too in laying out
her own philosophy of the divine as an emancipatory strategy
and I plan to discuss that and claim her as a theorist. (42-43)

6. In the interpretation of the novel, *An Apprenticeship or the Book of
Delights*, I emphasize the concept of the divinity of the body only
through the perspective of Irigaray's theory. But the book stretches it
further via Indian philosophy of *ānanda*, but in this chapter my
discussion on the concept of the divinity of the body remain limited to
Irigaray's theoretical interpretation only. I will ask the readers to read the
last chapter of my book concurrently with this one in order to understand
fully the implication of the concept of the divinity of the body in the light
of Sri Aurobindo's theory and the concept of *ānanda*.

7. Here, I would like to refer to Sri Aurobindo's hyper-epic the *Savitri*,
specifically, to the "Epilogue," "Return to Earth." The *Savitri*
emphasizes how in the cultivation of the theory of Supramental
consciousness, death could be conquered as well. For further discussion
on this, I will refer to the last chapter of my book. I repeat here, although,
I have not gone into the discussion of Supramental consciousness in this
chapter, I will refer my readers to a quote by the French philosopher
Satprem, from his book entitled, *The Mind of the Cells*:

> the body comes out of "that" [the other state], it feels it's going
> to dissolve the next minute, it feels "that" is the only thing
> holding it together. For a long time you feel that if the ego were
> to disappear, the being would disappear, but that's not true! The

difficult thing is that the ordinary laws of life are no longer true. So then, there is the whole old habit, and there is the new thing to be learned. It's as if the cells, the organization that makes a form we call human and which holds all this together, as if this had to learn that it can persist without the sense of a separate individuality, whereas for thousands of years it has been used to separate existence only because of the ego—without the ego, it continues [. . .] through another law which the body doesn't yet know, but [. . .] which is beyond its understanding. It isn't a will, I don't know, it's [. . .] something: a manner of being. (44)

The above passage discusses the transformation of the body through the descent of the "supramental consciousness." Lispector's *An Apprenticeship* touches this theme, but it is more fully revealed in Divakaruni's *The Mistress of Spices*, where the triple transformation of the body is shown in one life.

Chapter 9

Love on the Spiritual and the Corporeal Planes in
The Mistress of Spices

The last chapter of my book focuses on that aspect of the theme of the body, which deals with jouissance as consciousness or fulfillment when it occurs in the body/on the material plane. The chapter is closely connected to Chapter 3, "Jouissance and Kali: Body in Transcendence." But, whereas in Chapter 3, the theme of love is not a primary concern, this chapter foregrounds the aspect of fulfillment achieved through love and complementarity which is rooted in both corporeal and spiritual fulfillment. Furthermore, in this chapter, I use Irigaray's theory of corporeal and spiritual jouissance as expounded primarily in *Speculum*; and Sri Aurobindo's theory of "supramental consciousness," in which spirituality must be brought to the material/corporeal plane as it has been stated in *The Life Divine* and in his hyper-epic[1] the *Savitri*.

In a way, this chapter deconstructs Gayatri Chakrovorty Spivak's critique of the "native informant." Contrary to that, the chapter shows that Chitra Banerjee Divakaruni's *The Mistress of Spices* creates a world through magical realism in order to construct something more than just merely a postcolonial narrative of hybridity. In doing so, Divakaruni presents significant facets of Indian cultural/philosophical heritage in the form of postcoloniality, because, the heroine is Indian whereas, the hero is American. This juxtaposition affects their other level of existence in which both of them have spiritual identities, and through which they connect spiritually by the end as well.

Before proceeding, I want to reinforce that contrary to what Spivak suggests as a critique of postcoloniality, I would believe that post-coloniality could be used as a positive strategy to bridge cultural hiatus—to create discursive space for cross-cultural dialogue, as I am embarking on here in my book. In her book, *A Critique of Postcolonial Reason*, in the section called "History," Spivak quotes some example from Hindu Mythology,[2] which I strongly consider as inappropriate. Using her own terminology "catachresis," I will say that she is doing the same thing with Hindu mythology—she is cathecting her own desire to sublate it and in the process perpetrates "catachresis." I am aware of the fact that India is secular and one does not need to represent India in terms of Hinduism only, but, one should not forget that in Indian Hindu culture—psychoanalysis, philosophy and religion merge. What Spivak attempts to do is to narrow the focus and portray negative examples. I think it is high time to restore some of the Indian Hindu cultural heritage and foreground the positive aspect of its philosophy in terms of transcendence of the ego and spirituality, as discussed not only in ancient Indian texts, but, in the modern Indian philosopher Sri Aurobindo's collection, and in the modern Indian poet Tagore's writings as well as in the postcolonial fiction *The Mistress of Spices*. I strive here to reconstruct a cultural heritage of India based on its conception on spirituality and transcendence of the ego and how fulfillment can be achieved through it. Just as these beliefs are being attempted by feminist philosophers like Irigaray, and Brennan in the West, and the Afro-American scholar Paget Henry, in his book *Caliban's Reason*.

The Mistress of Spices posits that spiritual fulfillment can happen on earth if one achieves proper level of consciousness through the collapse of one's ego. It also conveys the message that the relationship of love is not only very important, but that its fulfillment cannot be attained without the descent of the consciousness into the body. In my discussion of "Jouissance and Kali: Body in Transcendence," I speak in great detail about the importance of the corporeal aspect of jouissance, about its abnegation in Western psychoanalysis and culture, and about the valorization of the female body by Irigaray. Then I render Irigaray's theory via Indian philosophical/psychoanalytical theory and highlighted the significance of having the female body which is considered spiritual—the body when it attains spiritual status or when the spirit descends into the body or the female body—and how the transformation of consciousness can occur. Since I use the term *female body* it might raise some concern whether the male body is excluded from this paradigm in Irigaray's theory of jouissance or in the Indian philosophical texts that I discuss in Chapter 2. I want to emphasize here that the Irigarayan theoretical framework always talks about the complementary relationship between men and women, and so does Indian philosophy. Therefore, the postcolonial novelist Chitra Banerjee Divakaruni's *The Mistress of Spices* embodies many of these theoretical notions; the novel strives to catch the realm beyond the ego. It also attempts to represent the world of complementarity as the perfect form to achieve consciousness and maintain the balance in the universe. That is Divakaruni presents these realms through the portrayal of two worlds—one magical and one terrestrial. I want to elaborate on *The Mistress of Spices* as embodying Irigaray's ethics of love, Teresa Brennan's theory of "energetics" and Sri Aurobindo's philosophical theory of "supramental consciousness" in a framework of postcolonial magical work.

Magical Realism versus Postmodern/Postcolonial

Who is this mistress of spices?   The mistress of spices is an ethereal character, who has undergone the transformation of her body and the name as well in one incarnation. The changing of names is not supra terrestrial as is the transformation of her body. In the beginning of the novel, she is introduced as someone who has a prophetic quality and occult power. Her initial name was Nayantara, given by her parents after her birth. Because she has great prophetic power and can predict many people's destiny in the village, her fame got spread to many different villages and she was kidnapped by pirates for her prophetic power. The pirates gave her the name Bhagayavati—which means one who conquers every-thing. But, the story of the changing of her name does not end there. Because, she escapes from the pirates and is rescued by the snakes who take her to a magical island where she is given the name Tilottama from the magical lady called the first Mother. The name persists until near the very end of the story, when she reaches the moment of fulfillment and is renamed Maya by her companion Raven. The construction of the story allows us to perceive many connections with the magical realism—a postmodernist trend used by Borges, Allende, Cortazar and Rusdie. The fiction has qualities

of magical realism and deals with the philosophical and ontological questions of fulfillment.

As Brian McHale suggests, since postmodernist fiction deals
with ontological questions and the question of being, one could
claim that Divakaruni's novel has postmodernist nuances. I would
like to take this further and analyze this novel rather as a
postcolonial fiction in which we see numerous nuances of Indian
philosophy of consciousness and fulfillment—a characteristic
which also shows its connection to the theory of jouissance. It is
very appropriate here to bring in the observation of Linda
Hutcheon in this regard, because of the controversy that
postmodernism and postcolonialism do not share the same ideals.
While I agree with Hutcheon that postmodernism and
postcolonialism do share similar ideologies, with the difference
that in postcolonialist discourse the resistance to the grand
narratives and the foundation is more direct and pronounced. There
is a more genuine urge to reconstruct the author's own cultural
ideology. In "Circling the Downspout of Empire" Hutcheon posits:

> The formal technique of "magical realism" (with its
> characteristic mixing of the fantastic and the realist) has been
> singled out by many critics as one of the points of conjunction of
> post-modernism and post-colonialism. As Stephen Slemon has
> argued, until recently it has been used to apply to Third World
> literatures, especially Latin American (see Dash 1974) and
> Caribbean, but now is used more broadly in other post-colonial
> and culturally marginalized contexts to signal works which
> encode within themselves some "resistance to the massive
> imperial center and its totalizing systems" (Slemon 1988a: 10;
> also 1987) [. . .]. Thus, it becomes part of the dialogue with
> history that both postmodernism and postcolonialism undertake.
> After modernism's ahistorical rejection of the burden of the past,
> postmodern art has sought self-consciously (and often
> parodically) to reconstruct its relationship to what came before;
> similarly, after that imposition of an imperial culture and that
> truncated indigenous history which colonialism has meant to
> many nations, postcolonial literatures are also negotiating (often
> parodically) the once tyrannical weight of colonial history in
> conjunction with the revalued local past. (*Ariel* 20(4), 1989)

It reaffirms my own argument that both the literary movements—postmodernism, and postcolonialism rose from similar causes. Hutcheon suggests that unlike modernism which rejected history, both of the other movements were intensely preoccupied with history in an anti-foundational way. Thus, both movements are not only anti-foundational, but also intersect with each other. Hutcheon's argument also foregrounds the notion that magical realism is a technique which has been used as a strategy by both postmodern and postcolonial writers. Therefore, we can conclude that the magical realism we encounter in *The Mistress of Spices* is part of the rhetorical strategy of postcolonial fiction. *The Mistress of Spices* tries to reconstruct a world through the synthesis of magic and reality, a world which is grounded in Indian philosophical theory of the past—which I explain through Sri Aurobindo's theory of "supramental consciousness"—which in itself, a reconstruction of the ancient Indian philosophical text the *Upaniṣads*. Thus, the novel embodies my theory of "jouissance" as consciousness in a unique way.

Descent of Consciousness in the Body: Shankara and Sri Aurobindo

In this chapter, I emphasize the concept of the descent of the consciousness into the body and onto the material plane as articulated in *The Mistress of Spices*. To elaborate, I return to Sri Aurobindo's *The Life Divine* in conjunction with his hyper-epic the *Savitri*. The question I want to take up here is why is the descent so important?   To answer leads us to the Indian philosophers Shankara and Buddha who believed in total negation. Shankara, the Indian philosopher (eighth century A.D.) believed that Brahman or the concept of the absolute presents the only reality and the rest is false and an illusion. He uses the word Maya to represent his concept of illusion. Shankar's philosophy is known as the Advaita Vedanta which advocates that it is not possible to achieve the supreme knowledge of Brahman in this mundane world, because the mundane world is seen as an illusion by our ordinary intellect. The knowledge of Brahman is beyond the grasp of ordinary human mind; therefore, there is a divorce between the terrestrial world and the world of Brahman. The terrestrial world is the world of illusion and the world of Brahman is out of the reach of ordinary human intellect. In his commentary on the *Kena Upaniṣad* Shankara observes:

> The one is: Brahman cannot be comprehended by common knowledge, as he is infinite, and whoever defines him accordingly, has only an inadequate knowledge of him; for the knowledge of the senses or the mind is always finite; it is therefore by a knowledge which is not a knowledge in the common sense of the word, that he must be apprehended [. ..].Therefore man, while united with his body, does not fully comprehend Brahman; he approaches merely nearer and nearer to this aim, without wholly attaining it, and the sense of the passage "those comprehend Brahman, who do not know him" would be, that those who are aware, that they cannot comprehend Brahman by intellect, know him as well as he may be comprehended by man. Either explanation accords with the spirit of the *Upaniṣad*s; for they teach, that a knowledge of Brahman is possible, as well that Brahman cannot be fully comprehended by man; and according to them there is not even a contradiction in the admission of both views; for they maintain, than an adequate knowledge of Brahman is only gained at the time when the intellect, which comprehends Brahman in a finite way, has ceased to exist. (17-18)

The entire observation reiterates how the knowledge of Brahman could not be obtained through ordinary senses. The last line staunchly argues that in order to gain the knowledge of Brahman, the ordinary intellect has to cease to exist. Once the action of the ordinary intellect stops, the knowledge of the infinite or Brahman could be obtained. Buddha likewise believed that freedom from the wheel of rebirth will take place through extinction and nirvana. Buddha emphasized nirvana and not on building any kind of earthly paradise. Hence, there is a divorce between the world of spirit and the world of matter. In contrast, Hindu Vedanta philosophy (in the *Upaniṣads*) advocates the notion that the whole world is a manifestation of Brahman and it is possible to feel the absolute or Brahman in every object in the universe. The *Upaniṣads* underscore the message that the entire universe is a manifestation of Brahman and that it is possible to feel Brahman and to achieve the supreme level of consciousness in the body. The modern Indian philosopher Sri Aurobindo qualifies this belief and offers his theory of supramental consciousness which elaborates on the original theory of the *Upaniṣad* and suggests that consciousness can really descend both into the body and onto the material plane. Sri Aurobindo says in the *Life Divine*, "Our subliminal self is not, like our surface physical being, an outcome of the energy of the Inconscient; it is a meeting place of the consciousness that emerges from below by evolution and the consciousness that has descended from above for Involution" (425). What is significant here is the emphasis on the terms descent from above and involution; the word involution does not stand for regression but points towards the impact caused by the descent of the consciousness into the body.[3]

Again, the concept of descent is critical to our discussion. Unlike Shankara and Buddha, Sri Aurobindo believed and foregrounded the message embedded in the Upaniṣadic philosophy that one does not need to escape the material or the mundane world, but that rather, spirituality is achievable in this world and on the material plane, and in one's body. In his philosophy of "supramental consciousness" the message he wants to convey is that all humans should strive to achieve spiritual perfection in their earthly lives. As he enunciates in the abovementioned quotation, the Divine descends into the body and onto the material plane. Unlike the Western psychoanalyst Freud, Sri Aurobindo does not believe that ego is the supreme agency, but posits instead that ego could be overridden by spirituality. Interestingly, Lacan goes one step ahead and believes in the concept of the sublime, but does not remain convinced that one could reach that sublime or the highest level of consciousness in earthly life. In a way, he is like Shankara who speculated that there is a world of Brahman/Absolute, and that it is the only truth in the universe; everything else is an illusion. What Shankara calls Brahman/Absolute is expressed as the Real (Lacan's term). But both Lacan and Shankara think that it is impossible to achieve that sublime or the Absolute in the terrestrial world. The fundamental difference between them resides in the fact that Shankara believes one can achieve Brahman/Absolute if one leaves *sansar* or the material world and goes to the woods to worship Brahman. That is, one has to live like a mendicant. In contrast, Lacan denies that one cannot achieve the sublime; the

Real (Lacan's term to signify the sublime) is out there, but none can access it. In reaction to that the sociologist *cum* psychoanalyst-philosopher Teresa Brennan writes both in her books *History After Lacan* and in *Exhausting Modernity* that what is imperative is to offer a theory of energetics through which one can revive the spiritual connection in the material world. It is also here that her theory of energetics intersects with both Irigaray's theory and the theory of Sri Aurobindo. I have discussed Brennan's theory exhaustively in Chapter 5 of this book and it would still be useful to review it at this point. Thus, in the West as well, in the writings of feminist psychoanalyst philosophers like Brennan and Irigaray there is a desire to bring the world of spirit into the body and into the material.

The theory of the descent of the spirituality or the highest level of consciousness into the body or onto the material plane needs to be understood from the vantage of the man-woman relationship or the relationship of love. In Sri Aurobindo's theory of "supramental consciousness" love reigns supreme—it is a special kind of love similar to Irigaray's ethics of love or carnal ethics, which I discussed in some of the previous chapters and will return to later in the discussion. The lacuna in Shankara's philosophy is that it suggests about shunning the world to achieve fulfillment. Sri Aurobindo stretches his theory of "supramental consciousness" further and in the *Savitri* to portray how spirituality can enter to the material plane or in the corporeal body through the character of Savitri, the heroine and Satyavan, the hero—who is brought back to earth alive through Savitri's power of spirituality. In doing so, an additional message is that spiritual movement could be advanced so far as to conquer death and usher in the transformation of the body beyond death. In the *Savitri*, Savitri, the daughter of King Aswapati falls in love with Satyavan, the son of King Dyumatsen, who is destined to die within a year's time if Savitri marries Satyavan. Because King Dyumatsen was banished to the forest, Savitri meets Satyavan there. When Savitri asks her father's permission to marry Satyavan, the king sends for Narad, the fortune-teller of the gods to predict whether this marriage will bode well. Narad prognosticates that Savitiri will be a widow in a year's time. But, Savitri marries Satyavan against her father's will and when death comes to Satyavan, she conquers death through her spiritual power. Savitri speaks thus in the epilogue entitled, "Return to earth":

> All now is changed, yet all is still the same.
> Lo, we have looked upon the face of God,
> Our life has opened with divinity.
> We have borne identity with the Supreme
> And known his meaning in our mortal lives
> [. . . . .]
> Thy body is my body's counterpart
> Whose every limb my answering limb desires,
> Whose heart is key to all my heartbeats—this
> I am and thou to me, O Satyavan.
> Our wedded walk through life begins anew,
> No gladness lost, no depth of mortal joy;
> Let us go through this new world that is the same.
> For it is given back, but it is known,
> A playing ground and dwelling-house of God
> Who hides himself in bird and beast and man
> Sweetly to find himself again by love,
> By oneness. (719-20)

In the Epilogue there are some key lines and expressions that need to be highlighted to understand the message properly. The first line that everything has changed, but yet everything is the same points towards the transformation that has taken place via supramental spirituality in their bodies and minds. The next few lines signify the bond between Satyavan and Savitri on both the corporeal and the psychic planes, when she says that Satyvan's body is part of Savitri's body and his heart monitors her heartbeat—it just points towards their union via corporeal and spiritual planes. Also, there is a constant reference to the return from a different world—which signifies the descent from the world of the divine. It is a descent not just from the world of the divine, but rather the power of the divine helps Savitri to persuade death to leave and to give immortal life to Satyavan instead. Thus, through her power of the divine, she transforms Satyavan's body.

In this (epic poem) Sri Aurobindo conveys the message that supramental spiritual power has such strength that death can be conquered once this power descends and transforms the body.

Given this consideration, one might think of reading his disciple Satprem's book *The Mind of the Cells* which discusses this aspect of Sri Aurobindo's theory. Chitra Banerjee Divakaruni's *The Mistress of Spices* also deals with this aspect of the transformation of the body to achieve the right state of consciousness. The heroine of Divakaruni's fiction goes through several transformations of her body—the last one allowing her to achieve the perfect relation with her lover. The next few sections discuss this in detail.

Resistance to Jouissance in *The Mistress of Spices*

Chitra Banerjee Divakaruni's heroine Nayantara is transformed into Tilottoma, the mistress of spices by the First Mother, who also acquires a new body through the changing of her name and then falls in love with a man called Raven, who possesses ethereal characteristics. The story matures and culminates when Tillottoma triumphs over all her dilemmas to resign from her role as the mistress of spices and achieves fulfillment through her corporeal and spiritual union with Raven. The story is very complex and as the author of the book *The Postmodernist Fiction* suggests that this type of fiction has many layers much like box of Pandora; *The Mistress of Spices* feels the same way. In this section, and in the following one, I try to untie some of these knots, as it will also help elucidate the theme of my book. First, I want to untie the mystery of her identity as the mistress of spices and how in this role, an unearthly character falls in love with a man with an earthly body and a spiritual mind. The mistress of spices turns into a magical role by her First Mother. Who is this First Mother? This character takes us back to the world of magic, which I discussed earlier as a strategy shared by many writers who create postmodernist and postcolonial fiction.

The First Mother is a symbolic character who owns the island where Nayantara arrives floating as she is rescued from the pirates by snakes. In the book the First Mother (who is also addressed as the Old One by Nayantara) and her relation with the various mistresses of spices is thus narrated:

> When we had passed the ceremony of purification, when we were ready to leave the island and meet our separate destinies, the Old One said, "Daughters it is time for me to give you your

new names. For when you came to this island you left your old names behind, and have remained nameless since.

But let me ask you one last time. Are you certain you wish to become Mistresses? It is not too late to choose an easier life.
Are you ready to give up your young bodies, to take on age and ugliness and unending service? Ready never to step out of the places where you are set down, store or school or healing house? Are you ready never to love any but the spices again?" (42)

What the First Mother asks them to do is to shun the corporeal life altogether; which is similar to what Freud suggests through the tying of the primary process. The First Mother/the Old One is invoking a kind of harsh existence for these girls who were driven by some ill omen of destiny to her island. The life that she invokes will deprive them of many of life's pleasures and of the freedom of the spontaneity of the heart. The Old One tries to impose the sort of mechanical control over their lives that Freudian theory suggests one should follow in order to control one's imagination or primary process. Another interpretation that could be offered is that by asking them to leave their young bodies, and to accept age, ugliness and unending service, she invokes the rigorous lifestyle of the saintly life preached by Buddha and Shankara in the East, and the life of the Christian nuns in the West. Let us also look at the description given about Shampati's fire (a mythical bird) which purifies their bodies and turns each of them into a real mistress of spices. The lure that the First Mother creates regarding the role of Shampati's fire is appalling. Thus speaks Nayantara:

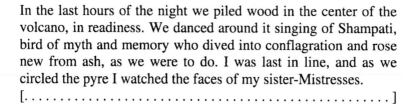

In the last hours of the night we piled wood in the center of the volcano, in readiness. We danced around it singing of Shampati, bird of myth and memory who dived into conflagration and rose new from ash, as we were to do. I was last in line, and as we circled the pyre I watched the faces of my sister-Mistresses.
[. . . . .]

Still it was a hard thing, to confront for the third time in my brief existence the extinguishing of all I knew life to be. (58-60)

The life that is given to the mistress of spices is not an alluring one; it is informed by emptiness and not fulfilling at all. It seems that Shampati's fire stands for the transformation not of ego in the right way, but in a cruel way by stifling one's spontaneous emotions. As I just mentioned earlier, Chitra Banerjee Divakaruni's *The Mistress of Spices* shows the journey—one could hypothesize from Freud to Irigaray and from Irigaray to Sri Aurobindo. It does embody *ānanda* and fulfillment through the proper distribution of energy—and does manifest it through a man-woman relationship—that is, a relationship of complementarity and balance, which is also represented through the Indian Sankhaya philosophical theory of *Puruṣa* and *Prakṛti*, as discussed in the previous chapter as well. The heroine of *The Mistress of Spices*, Nayantara points towards this lack in the First Mother's ritual as she articulates her agony derived from this ritual signifies the "extinguishing of all I knew life to be." So, the ritual of purification, is a ritual of burning everything life stands for—hence, it is a total rejection of life.

The magical role of being a mistress of spices serves as a trope through which different worlds coalesce. The world in Oakland, California in which she sells spices and heals people from different kinds of sufferings; the world that the mistress of spices really represents as well as the world in the island in which she is transformed into the mistress of spices through the ritual of burning and given the name Tilottoma; and finally the world she creates with her lover Raven in which she is newly born by shedding her old self. She heals people as the mistress of spices; but the spices have stifling qualities, which impede her to explore her own desire. While on the one hand she serves the people of Oakland with her medicines concocted of various spices, and while spices sometimes help her, we also come to realize that the spices give her constant warnings not to become involved in any relationship that undermines balance between a man and a woman. She is subjected to warnings that if one becomes involved, or, in other words, if the mistress of spices becomes involved, in any relationship of love, not only she be destroyed, literally, burnt, but, the entire land.

Love in the World of *The Mistress of Spices*

In this section I want to explore and analyze the world of love[4] as created by the mistress of spices in opposition to the world of celibacy offered to her by the First Mother. It is significant to note here the meaning of the name "Tillotoma," as the mistress of spices herself adopts the name to signal her new identity. The First Mother warns her by pointing out that the history of this name is that of the most beautiful *apsara* (dancer in the court of Gods in Hindu mythology) who fell from heaven to earth as punishment for falling in love. But, ironically, choosing this name, the heroine undertakes to face the challenge of life, and not run away from them—in other words, she chooses not to be confined to her ethereal role as the mistress of spices, but, to break the spell and descend willingly down to the corporeal/material plane as well. On the earthly plane, in the grocery store set at Oakland, California, she meets her beloved Raven.

Raven—the hero of *The Mistress of Spices* seems to incorporate a certain kind of magical reality. As his name indicates, it originates from the name of the raven and he relays a story to the mistress of spices about it. He tells her how there is a mystery related to his identity and his forefather's identity. He tells the story of how his mother left her own family, perhaps, for lack of material prosperity and how they were called to her mother's grandfather's deathbed and how his great-grandfather wanted to pass spiritual energy onto him. He wanted to give a bird to him, but, because of his mother's resistance, the bird fled but the plume of the bird dropped on his hand and melted into his palm. Thus, symbolically with the bird's fleeing, only a certain amount of spiritual energy transmitted. Identical to Tillotama's transformation of her body, Raven also has a magical quality in his being. Thus, both characters are imbued with the characteristics of magical realism—which is a common strategy of the authors who negotiate postcoloniality in their works—or more specifically, in the writings of their diasporas.

The relationship of love between Raven and Tilottoma embodies the same sort of ethics of love presented by Irigaray. It also represents in its synthesis of the spirit with the body, or in its union between the spiritual and the material/corporeal planes, a connection with Irigaray and Brennan on the one hand and with Sri

Aurobindo on the other. Thus, it negotiates between different worlds. But, by doing so, it does not undermine what Spivak suggests, "undermines the struggle by simulating an effect of a new third world, by piecing together great legitimizing narratives of cultural and ethnic specificity and continuity, and of national identity—a species of 'retrospective hallucination'"(360). On the contrary, it creates a narrative of fulfillment in which spirit and body, and the celestial and the corporeal merge together. Brennan's book *Exhausting Modernity* addresses this aspect very well. Brennan elucidates the spirit-body synthesis by suggesting that the notion of cosmic connection between beings and their environment existed earlier in Western culture and is in the offing now. In her chapter entitled "Energetics" she asserts that the theory of *energetics* has been revived in modern era, but it had been prevalent before.[5]

Earthly Paradise

Thus, with this theoretical vision as I approach *The Mistress of Spices*, I see these theories embodied extensively in this work. Chitra Banerjee Divakaruni strives to reconstruct some of the ancient Indian philosophical heritage in this work. The metaphor of the earthly paradise embodies the supramental philosophical notion that paradise could be achieved on earth, as I explain it later through discussion of Sri Aurobindo's the *Savitri*. The earthly paradise seems to be the place he envisions, which can occur on earth. Let us look at it through his dream/vision:

> "Somewhere in that thirsty night the dream came.
> I stood on a hill of ashes amid a lake of fire while a searing wind blew over me.
> [. . . . .]
>
> And so I threw myself off the hilltop into the burning lake, and even as I fell I wondered, What if I don't die, what if I continue to burn?
> That was when the raven came.
> I don't know where it came from, but it swooped to catch me in its wings [. . .]. There was a song in my ear, harsh but not bitter, filled with strength, the bird's voice. I realized it was giving me its name. I closed my eyes, drank it down, and my thirst receded.

When I opened them the raven was gone, and I was in the place I told you of. Eucalyptus and pine, California quail, deer [. . .]. A place of wildness and wet, to labor in and grow strong and pure again [. . .]. Then I woke up."

[. . . . .]

"It's a real place," says Raven. "I 'am sure of that. It's the place where my happiness lies. I think that's what the bird came to tell me. To stop wasting my life on trivialities and find it. To go back to the old ways, the ways of the earth before it was spoiled. To the earthly paradise." (267-69)

The place that Raven inscribes as earthly paradise could be construed in different ways. According to ancient Indian philosophy it could be construed as the place where one can achieve fulfillment through transcendence of the ego. Raven suggests that the life in the earthly paradise does not entail any grappling with trivial matters. One can also read in it what both Tagore and Sri Aurobindo have suggested—the attainment of the supramental level of consciousness. Also, one can read Brennan's philosophy here—to retrieve one's connection with God or, as she terms it, the original logic.

The best way to interpret the earthly paradise put forth in Divakaruni's novel is through Sri Aurobindo's philosophical theory of supramental consciousness. According to this philosophical theory, one does not need to escape the confines of earthly life to attain fulfillment. Rather, it can be achieved on earth. This concept of fulfillment on earth is the distinguishing feature of the supramental theory of consciousness, which distinguishes it from Buddhist philosophy or the illusionism of the twelfth century Indian philosopher Shankara who posited that the entire mundane world is an illusion, and that one has to escape from earthly life in order to achieve the Brahman or the absolute. In the chapter called "Reality and the Cosmic Illusion," Sri Aurobindo suggests the fundamental distinction between the philosophy of Shankara and of the *Upaniṣads* is that of supramental consciousness. Shankara suggests that there is "Transcendence which is forever self-existent and immutable and a world which is only phenomenal and temporal" (62). It tells us the fundamental distinction between the philosophy of Shankara and the version by Sri Aurobindo. Sri

Aurobindo further suggests the distinction between him and Shankara in the same chapter: Thus, the lacuna of Shankara's philosophy is the permanent dichotomy between intuition and reason, and this dichotomy Shankara is not sure how to bring the transcendence into the material plane or the terrestrial world. Therefore, if one has to achieve the Absolute, he suggests an escape into the world of Brahman. The two worlds, the world of reason and the world of spirit could not be brought together according to Shankara. That is where Sri Aurobindo triumphs over Shankara philosophically. However, when *The Mistress of Spices* alludes to the "earthly paradise" it *points* towards the plane on which matter and spirit are synthesized. The world that Raven and Tilottoma/Maya create is a world of fulfillment through love. The relation between the lovers in the novel would best be understood through Sri Aurobindo's epic poem the *Savitri* which embodies fulfillment through love as well. Sri Aurobindo discards Shankara's philosophy of escape and insists on the philosophy of ascent and descent; in the *Savitri* he portrays his two-fold philosophy of the ascent and the descent through the love of Satyavan and Savitri

"The Book of Love," canto three of the *Savitri* is crucial to understand the ethics of love through Sri Aurobindo. The story of their love has been mentioned briefly in the beginning of this chapter, but here I want to address it more fully. There are three sections in canto five "Book of Love": The Destined Meeting Place, Satyavan and Satyavan and Savitri. Sri Aurobindo in these three sections develops the theme that the lovers have a divine origin. They are not merely ordinary human beings; but that does not mean they are unearthly figures. They have the potential to usher in their divinity to an earthly plane through their experience of love.[6] With this preamble, I would like to introduce a quote from Book Five canto three, in which Satyavan hails Savitri's divine origin, "For more than earth speaks to me from thy soul/And more than earth surrounds me in thy gaze," (400). But, this is not all. Satyavan does not stop remarking about Savitri's divine origin, but discusses the transformational impact on him— the ethereal power that she possesses transforms Satyvan individually and caters to the transformation of the world. Let us look at another quote from the "Book of Love":

"I sat with the forest sages in their trance:
There poured awaking streams of diamond light,
I glimpsed the presence of the One in all.
But still there lacked the last transcendent power
And Matter still slept empty of its Lord.
The spirit was saved, the body lost and mute
Lived still with Death and ancient Ignorance;
The Inconscient was its base, the Void its fate.
But thou hast come and all will surely change:
I shall feel the World-Mother in thy golden limbs
And hear her wisdom in thy secret voice.
The child of the Void shall be reborn in God.
My Matter shall evade the Inconscient's trance,
My body like my spirit shall be free:
It shall escape from death and ignorance." (405-6)

Satyavan here invokes Savitri through whose divine presence in
his life, he conquers his own body—in other words—his body is
metamorphosed by her spiritual presence. Thus, spirit descends
into the matter through their relation and bond of love. The
promise of greater life and the descent of the supramental
consciousness are ushered in the last few lines of Satyavan's
recitation. Satyavan foresees through his relationship of love, his
body shall be free like his spirit and his psyche will sever any
connection with the inconscience. But, all the miracles will happen
through his psychic/corporeal relation with Savitri. Let us look at
the lovers' encounter. When encountering Savitri, Satyavan
realizes the promise that she bears—the promise of transformation
and earthly paradise. He adores Savitri with his ecstasy, "Descend,
O Happiness, with thy moon-gold-feet, / Enrich earth's floors upon
whose sleep we lie." (408). Notice the oxymoronic adjectives that
Sri Aurobindo uses here to illuminate Savitri's divine and
supramental status, which brings fulfillment on earth itself.
Satyavan suggests that her tread itself awakens and enriches the
earth. Savitri proclaims that she searches for Satyavan and knows
that only he is her supreme soul mate, "I know that thou and only
thou art he," which is then followed by the description of her body
beaming with light:

Her many-hued raiment glistening in the light

Hovered a moment over the wind-stirred grass,
Mixed with a glimmer of her body's ray
Like lovely plumage of a settling bird.
Her gleaming feet upon the green gold sward
Scattered a memory of wandering beams
And lightly pressed the unspoken desire of earth
Cherished in her too brief passing by the soil. (409)

Notice the expression that Savitri invoked the unspoken desire of earth. Many times symbolically her limbs have been described as golden limbs, and there is a glimmer in her body which radiates light. Here, one can see the analogy between Savitri's body and the transformed body of Tilottoma. But, what is more significant to see here for our discussion is that Savitri with her divine body descends to earth and unites with her lover Satyavan who lives with his father King Dyumatsen, who has been banished to the forest. The point is when Savitri meets Satyavan, he feels her aura and glory and the power of transformation, but their love takes place in the forest, on earth, not on an unearthly plane. Satyavan relies on the divine power of Savitri to transform his state of inconscience and make his body free, which she eventually does in the epilogue when Savitri challenges the king of death and brings Satyavan back from the kingdom of death. The assurance is there that the paradise could be brought on earth—the concept of the descent of the spirit in the body predicts the future of the lovers in *The Mistress of Spices.* Hear in Savitri's own words her dream of earthly paradise and prior to that let us encounter the moment when Savitri with her divine status enjoys human bliss through love, "He gathered all Savitri into his clasp. / Around her his embrace became the sign / Of a locked closeness through slow intimate years, / A first sweet summary of delight to come, / One brevity intense of all long life" (410). The divine Savitri experiences human love with her lover Satyavan and pledges to join him in the woods, which is heaven to her:

Her happy voice cried out to Satyavan
"My heart will stay here on this forest verge
And close to this thatched roof while I am far:
Now of more wandering it has no need.
[. . . . .]

A nave of trees enshrined the hermit thatch
The new deep covert of her felicity,
Preferred to heaven her soul's temple and home.
This now remained with her, her heart's constant scene. (412)

For now, Savitri leaves Satyavan to go back to her father's house, but she returns and they get married and through her love bring Satyavan back from the realm of death. It is significant to observe that Savitri strives to establish paradise on earth in a "hermit thatch," which is her "soul's temple and home," and which she chose over heaven.

To create this earthly paradise, both the hero and the heroine of *The Mistress of Spices* undergo several stages of transformation. Raven has already gone through the process of transformation when he chose to meet Tilottoma, after experiencing the premonition through his recurrent dream of an earthly paradise. The dream indicated to him that there is a place called earthly paradise and he could achieve it through the union with Tillotoma. But, this is a union of fulfillment—not just a trivial love affair. The depth of this love affair is articulated by Raven when he tries to create an earthly paradise on his own, but does not succeed fully. Therefore, he becomes convinced that he can only achieve it through his lover Tilottoma. He invokes her to join him, "Will you come with me, Tilo? Will you help me find the earthly paradise?" (270). It is both interesting and significant to observe how Tillotoma accepts the challenge of helping Raven to create the earthly paradise.[7]

Triple Transformation of the Body

In this section I want to focus specifically on Tilo's corporeal transformation. In order to perform that role Tillotoma invokes a special kind of spice called *makaradwaj*, "Make me beautiful, *makaradwaj*, such beauty as on this earth never was. Beauty a hundred times more than he can imagine" (277). Why does Tilo want to achieve that level of perfect beauty? One can read here Irigaray's concept of wonder in the theory of jouissance that helps with ravishing beauty:

I am dazzled by the face looking back at me, young and ageless at once, the fantasy of fantasies come to life, spice power at it fullest. Forehead flawless like a new opened shapla leaf, nose tipped like the til flower. Mouth curved as the bow of Madan, god of love, lips color of—there are no other words for this— crushed red chilies. For kisses that will burn and consume.

It is a face that gives away nothing, a goddess-face free of mortal blemish, distant as an Ajanta painting. Only the eyes are human, frail. In them I see Nayan Tara, I see Bhagyavati, I see the Tilo who was. Wide elated eyes, but also telling me something I did not expect. (297-98)

What we notice here is a pastiche. But, before we start unraveling the meanings, I must say that Chitra Banerjee Divakaruni reconstructs her Indian cultural heritage in this new pastiche of Tillotoma's beauty. She uses the name of the Indian god Madan instead of Cupid, and expressions like *shapla* leaf and *til* flower to depict Tillotoma's beauty. One more crucial point to notice is that Tilottoma invokes not only the spice *makaradwaj* to make her beautiful, she acknowledges all the spices contribute to make her beautiful. So, she has started transforming the spices as well towards the journey of fulfillment. Thus, she prepares her body to create a sense of wonder in Raven. It could also be thought of as Tillotoma exploring her corporeal jouissance which she feels through the multiple sexuality of her body.

As we have seen, Tilottoma reaches the peak of her beauty; she wants to share it with Raven, to invoke a sense of wonder in him. We see them bound in love in which both the bodies and the minds are connected: " 'Tilo,' cries Raven urgently, pulling my hips into him, again, again, bone to bone, till I feel the hot release take us both. Till we are one body and many bodies and no body all at once" (307). Tilottoma dreams about love and earthly paradise and she dreams the same dream regarding earthly paradise as Raven does—a place in nature impervious to chaos, "A land to grow into, to be transformed by. Its winter of chill caves and smoky fires, its waterfalls frozen into soundlessness" (308). Raven dreamt the same dream, "A place of wildness and wet, to labor in and grow strong and pure again. A place with no people to spoil it. Then I woke up" (268). This dream indicates a paradise which is separated from the earth, even though they are searching for an earthly paradise, which they find at the end of the story, and which involves returning to earth and relinquishing paradise. At the above phase, however, they are searching for it, and in their search they ascend to a higher plane of consciousness, just like Satyavan and Savitri (the characters in Sri Aurobindo's the *Savitri*). But, in order to really find the paradise on earth, they must return from paradise with a heightened consciousness. The underlying message is that the perfection they are striving for needs to be found on earth. The return to earth happens in successive stages.

First, Tilottoma's body goes through another transformation; since her transformation of bodily existence to the peak of beauty was attributable to the spices, she promises to come back to her former gnarled body as the mistress of spices. But, in reality, what happened was that her body did not regress to that gnarled state of existence. On the contrary, it assumes a stature, which is not too old, not too young, but, as she felt, just right. This transformation and the subsequent descent to the material plane occur in several phases. The land in which Tilottoma and Raven are lovers—in fact, all of Oakland experiences the transformation of land as well through earthquake. At first glance, it might sound supernatural—but one must remember as well that Divakaruni uses the literary technique of magical realism to enhance her postcolonial ontology. The spices always warned Tilottoma what might occur if she mutates from her existence as the mistress of spices. But, interestingly enough, the spices which warned her constantly about the danger of betraying the spices, that she would be scorched and burned by Shampati's fire, is not valid anymore. Tilottoma almost flees from Raven knowing that Shampati's fire will get Raven as well into trouble if she stays near him, but in reality, she is forgiven by the spices. Thus, she writes to Raven as she persuades him to drive her back to her store at Oakland:

Raven forgive me, the note will say. I do not expect you to understand. Only to believe hat I have no choice. I thank you for all you have given me. I hope I have given you a little too. Our love would never have lasted, for it was based upon fantasy, yours and mine, of what it is to be Indian. To be American. But where I am going—life or death, I do not know which—I will carry its brief aching sweetness. Forever. (310)

At this stage Tilottoma still thinks that their love will not achieve fulfillment, because she did not anticipate the transformation of the spices. She is also skeptical about the materialization of the concept of earthly paradise. Along with this we notice that Divakaruni does not forget to remind her audience about the issue of postcoloniality by articulating through her heroine that the lovers are from different countries—another emphasis on the importance of the world of matter or the material plane.

The last chapter of the book is significant because we see the lovers' dream come true through transformation on different planes as I alluded to in the earlier paragraph. Tillotoma is astounded by the fact that the spices forgave her, as she is by her new body, "I touch again to make sure. Arc of calf, triangle of cheekbone, column of throat. No mistake. This is not a body in youth's first roseglow, but not one in age's last unflowering either" (325). It is quite remarkable to see a transformation of one's body three times, in the span of one life. This triple transformation could be attributed first to what Sri Aurobindo enunciates as the supramental change, which occurs in the body. For the case of Tilottoma it happens because it is the part of the equation—that her body needs to adjust to participate in the process of fulfillment/ ānanda that she achieves with her lover Raven. If she had remained in the gnarled body of Tilottoma—which is even inconsistent with the name Tilottoma—she could not have participated in achieving jouissance or ānanda. So, she has to transform herself physically to become the real Tillotoma—the peak of beauty (as the name signifies, and as it is also referred to in Hindu mythology) to create wonder in her lover Raven's mind. After this phase she needs to return to her ordinary human body— neither the crooked body she had as the mistress of spices, nor, the unearthly ravishingly beautiful body given by the spice makaradwaj is conducive to the concept of jouissance on a material plane. So, she finally settles herself into the body which justifies her earthly existence as a lover. But, it is still involved in the process of achieving fulfillment and, it is achieved through their proper union as shown in this last chapter.

The forcefulness of their coming together leads to an earthquake in California, where the lovers live. When Raven comes to help her overcome the obstacles of the earthquake, he finds her in the newly changed body which is neither the body of an unusually beautiful woman nor that of a crooked one (because corporeal beauty and corporeal jouissance are significant factors conducive to fulfillment). All of Oakland has suffered from the earthquake but Raven finds the "new" Tilottoma in her new body just as she abandons the name of Tilottoma:

> You didn't even look like you, not like when I dropped you off, and not like before either. But I knew. So I got you into the car. Wrapped you up. Hit the road going north [. . .]. We've been moving for about an hour. We had to take some detours—parts of the freeway are pretty bad. But we are almost at the Richmond Bridge. It's the one left undamaged—almost as though it's fate, don't you think, so we can cross it and keep going North, to paradise. (330)

Raven is so committed to reaching their earthly paradise that neither the change in Tilottoma's body, nor the earthquake deters him: he is completely unperturbed and determined to reach their paradise. In the above quote, he says openly that her bodily change does not have any impact on his love for her. She asks him repeatedly about her transformation, but he assures her of his love and the earthly paradise he is striving to reach.

But do the lovers really attain it? The lovers go through another phase of descent. Tilottoma decides to go with Raven on his journey to the earthly paradise and as she tells Raven, "Raven you have made my decision for me" (330). As has been said in Irigaray that lovers can be united even in their breath, it happens to them, "so that his breath is mine and mine his" (332). Also, in the same chapter, Maya or Tilittoma describes their love existing both on the material plane and on the spiritual plane. As Raven rescues her from the rubble, and calls her, she imagines as she puts out her hand towards the sound and touches a wall of fur, "The lining of a sarcophagus, I think, a communal sarcophagus where lovers are burned, their dust left to mingle till world's end. Only, this one is flying through galaxies, swerving to dodge meteor showers that streak us with sudden light" (324). So, we have been exposed to many nuances about their love existing on both planes; but, what is important now is to see their descent to the material plane—their finding an earthly paradise not somewhere in the wilderness, but in Oakland, where the earthquake has taken place. As they start leaving Oakland in search of their earthly paradise, having been touched by the rubble of earthquake and in general by people's suffering, she suddenly withdraws from the trip. She thus exclaims:

> "It wouldn't work, Raven. Even if we found your special place." I take a deep breath, then say it. "Because there is no earthly paradise. Except what we can make back there, in the soot in the rubble in the crisped away flesh. In the guns and needles, the white drug-dust, the young men and women lying down to dream of wealth and power and asking in cells. Yes, in the hate in the fear." (336)

This is a crucial statement, when Tiliottoma tells Raven her significant realization that there is no earthly paradise away from civilization, that is, it is to be found only in the real world. Paradise needs to be brought down on earth. When she suggests there is no earthly paradise, but that paradise needs to be realized in the rubble of the earthquake, she reinforces the value of fulfillment manifest on the earthly plane. Here, Chitra Banerjee Divakaruni's heroine voices a staunch critique of the philosophy of Shankara which believes that *ānanda*/fulfillment is not achievable on earth. Tilottoma reinforces the concept of fulfillment to such an extent that Raven is convinced that his philosophy of earthly paradise is wrong, although the expression "earthly paradise" is correct. Raven confesses, "Then I guess I'll have to come too." It is also significant to see this last encounter. Tilottoma feels first relieved because she had difficulty accepting that she has to live her life without a companion. But, she still has moments of suspense since she is not totally convinced that Raven wants to stay with her to help her achieve an earthly paradise in Oakland, i.e., on the material plane. Let us look at this important encounter between them, "We kiss, a long, long kiss. 'Is this what you meant?' he asks when we pause for breath. 'Is this what we were saying about the earthly paradise?'" I start to speak. Then I see he needs no answer"(337). Thus, there are two underlying messages we can derive from their conversation: an earthly paradise exists on the earthly plane; and, love between a man and a woman which is grounded in both corporeality and spirituality contributes to create an earthly paradise.

There is still one more twist to the descent to the earthly plane. Tilottoma changes her name and takes the name Maya—which is highly significant. The name acquires an additional significance because the name is given by Raven. Furthermore, it was chosen out of a few names that Raven suggested to Tilottoma. As soon as she finds out that Raven desires to join her in Oakland and create a real earthly paradise among people through what they have achieved via love, she wants to change her name. Also, it is significant that Raven did not blindly suggest the name Maya to her, as he seems to be aware of the special meaning of the name, "And doesn't it have an Indian meaning, something special?" (337). Tilottoma answers, "In the old language it can mean many things, illusion, spell, enchantment, the power that keeps this imperfect world going day after day. I need a name like that, I who now have only myself to hold me up" (338). Raven reminds her, "You have me too, don't forget." (338). The entire conversation signifies several things: first of all not just Tilottoma/Maya, but Raven as well is extremely conscious of the evolution of their beings in the journey of fulfillment and therefore Raven suggested the name Maya. Secondly, he reminds her of his presence and the concept of complementarity which is conducive to the concept of *ānanda*/fulfillment. In fact, their relationship could be interpreted as between *Puruṣa* and *Prakṛti*.

In Indian philosophy Maya is another name given to *Prakṛti*. Maya is a very significant word in Indian philosophy. The fundamental ideology behind it as advocated by the *Upaniṣads* is that the entire world is a manifestation of Brahman; but Brahman cannot function without the help of Maya or *Prakṛti*. In the *Swetaswetra Upaniṣad*, it has been said that Brahman—the Absolute functions with the help of the power of the Maya—which means illusion. Thus, the concept of *Puruṣa* (male energy) and *Prakṛti* (female energy) prevailed in the *Upaniṣads* and later it evolved in the Sankhaya philosophy. However, both the Vedanta and Sankhaya philosophy reiterate the belief that the world runs by the power of two different kinds of energy—one is male and one is female. The illusion or *maya* is identical with female energy, which is called *Prakṛti* in Sankhaya philosophy.[8] However, if we analyze Tilottoma's comment that she wants to adopt the name Maya, which means spell, illusion, and enchantment, it becomes quite obvious why Divakaruni uses the name. Chitra Banerjee Divakaruni chooses this name for her heroine deliberately to give the message from Indian philosophy that when Tilottoma finally changes her name to Maya, she undertakes the philosophical task of Maya or *Prakṛti* to help her companion Raven to usher in the earthly paradise, which is not a romantic land somewhere else, but right in Oakland where the land cracked and where people need help. By making her heroine adopt such a name as Maya, Divakaruni alludes to the philosophical task of running the world by the mediation of two energies, *Puruṣa* and *Prakṛti*.

Raven and Maya, at the end of the book, do more than represent symbolically the connection between *Puruṣa* and *Prakṛti*, but it embodies the concept of fulfillment/*ānanda*. With her new name Maya, she has acquired a new identity which completely liberates her from the role of the mistress of spices. As a matter of fact, we see a range of transformation in the end of the novel. The spices forgive her and she is not burned; rather, is exempt from the usual punishment for the violation of the rule of the mistress of spices, falling in love. The spices forgive her for her compunction as they tell her. But, the underlying message is that the spices go through transformation as well. The energy that was suppressed by the creation of the myth of the mistress of spices is finally relieved through the transformation of the character of Nayantara, from Tillotoma to Maya. By being Tillotoma she attains the peak of love and beauty—in other words she experiences her jouissance through love and her beautiful body creates wonder in her lover. But, as Maya, she returns to the terrestrial world, or, brings her jouissance back to the earthly plane. Her body becomes a body that embodies fulfillment in the material plane and her love for Raven helps direct him to create an earthly paradise, which is on earth, and which could be created on earth. Although Raven, like the Brahman and *Puruṣa* of the Indian Hindu philosophy, functions like a Conscious-Force and gives her the idea of earthly paradise, it is eventually Maya who makes it materialize, like *Prakṛti*. As she says, "I need a name like that, I who now have only myself to hold me up" (338). But, then Raven says, "You have me too, don't forget" (338).

Here, Sri Aurobindo's theory of "supramental consciousness" becomes manifest too in their returning to Oakland. The fulfillment is to be realized in the terrestrial world; if one wants to escape, the fulfillment cannot be achieved. Sri Aurobindo's Savitri returns to earth with Satyavan; coming back to the earthly plane is so important that Savitri makes Satyavan conquer death through her spiritual power of "supramental consciousness" and brings him back. In *The Mistress of Spices*, conquering death seems to happen in the span of one incarnation, in which Nayantara without physical death transforms herself from Nayantara[9] to Tilottoma and finally to Maya. Irigaray would be very happy to learn that in the character of Maya we can see an embodiment of her theory of jouissance both corporeally and spiritually, which intersects with the Indian philosophy of *ānanda*.

NOTES

1. The expression "hyper-epic," refers to an epic which transcends the qualities of an ordinary epic. The Mother of Sri Aurobindo Ashram Pondicherry described the *Savitri* as the hyper-epic, as it offers the theory of "supramental consciousness."

2. My reservation is that perpetuating the image of the *Sati* of Hindu mythology, we run the risk of overlooking many other positive aspects of Hindu mythology which cannot only teach women in East (India) in West as well. For example, Chapter 3 "Body in Transcendence: Jouissance and Kali," attempts to deconstruct Lacanian interpretation of women's mind and the body. It thus upholds positive message that one could derive from Hindu mythology. But, I must caution that the chapter in no way attempts to relegate women to the realm of the myth or the imaginary serving to patriarchy. However, let me refer to this specific observation from Spivak's *A Critique of Postcolonial Reason*:

> Figures like the goddess Athena—"fathers' daughters self-professedly uncontaminated by the womb"—are useful for establishing women's ideological self-debasement, which is to

be distinguished from a deconstructive attitude toward the essentialist subject. The story of the mythic Sati, reversing every narrative of the rite, performs a similar function: the living husband avenges the wife's death, a transaction between great male gods fulfills the destruction of the female body and thus inscribes the earth as sacred geography. To see this as proof of the feminism of classical Hinduism or of Indian culture as goddess-centered and therefore feminist is as ideologically contaminated by nativism or reverse ethnocentrism as it was imperialist to erase the image of the luminous fighting Mother Durga and invest the proper noun Sati with no significance other than the ritual burning of the helpless widow as a sacrificial offering who then can be saved. (306)

First, it is too far-fetched to compare the image of goddess Athena to the image of goddess Durga, because, the cultural and the mythical contexts are different. Second, in India women are smart enough not to misconstrue the image of the goddess Durga as the image of the *Sati* forever. During the British rule in India, this catachresis occurred for a long time. But, in the twenty first century Indian women have intellectual capability to differentiate between the image of goddess Durga and the symbol of the *Sati*. We should start redefining some of the positive stories of the Hindu myth in a more positive way.

3. In the other chapter called, "The Sevenfold Chord of Being," in *The Life Divine*, Sri Aurobindo suggests:

The Divine descends from pure existence through the play of Consciousness Force and Bliss and the creative medium of Supermind into cosmic being; we ascend from Matter through a developing life, soul and mind and the illuminating medium of Supermind towards the divine being. The knot of the two, the higher and the lower hemisphere, is where mind and Supermind meet with a veil between them. The rending of the veil is the condition of the divine life in humanity; for by that rending, by the illumining descent of the higher into the nature of the lower being and the forceful ascent of the lower being into the nature of the higher, mind can recover its divine light in the all-comprehending Supermind, the soul realize its divine self in the all-possessing all-blissful Ananda, life repossess its divine power in the omnipotent Conscious-Force and Matter open to its divine liberty as a form of the divine existence. (264-65)

It is significant to note Sri Aurobindo's use of the term veil. In the *Isha Upaniṣad* the reference has been made in one of the *slokas* that the face of truth is covered by a gold disk and one has to rend that veil to reach the truth or the highest level of consciousness—which can happen only through the transcendence of ego. Sri Aurobindo's explication says that through the rending of the veil between the mind and the Supermind the highest form of consciousness descends into the lowest level of consciousness (the Freudian id, or the ego) and then the lower level of mind is coerced into a higher or even the highest level of consciousness of being, and then fulfillment can take place in the form of *ānanda*. Whereas Freud denies such a transformation of consciousness as "benevolent illusion," Sri Aurobindo asserts its materiality.

4. Luce Irigaray in her *Ethics of Sexual Difference*, and most recently in *To be Two* has done a wonderful job in offering her ethics of "sexual difference." Her ethics of "sexual difference," is an ethics of love through which the male-female relationship can be established on a harmonious plane with "irreducible difference in sex." Likewise, Brennan offers her theory of *energetics*. The entire world needs to be connected according to her, through this theory of "energetic," to achieve consciousness through transcending one's ego. In her most recent book, *Exhausting Modernity* which is an abbreviation of her book *History After Lacan*, Brennan discusses this energetic connection, and posits that it informed the West before, and it is appearing again. She further differentiates this energetic connection as different from the cosmic consciousness theory of consciousness of New Age Culture. Offering the critique of New Age Culture she suggests, "While the idea of a connecting force survives, in New Age culture especially, it survives on miserable arguments, and is always assumed to be good." (43)

5. Spinoza contributed to the spirit-body synthesis and most recently in the modern time Walter Benjamin has done so. Brennan writes:

> Spinoza is traditionally regarded in the history of ideas as an aberration. At approximately the same time that Descartes was apparently marshalling mind and body into their classic dualistic distinction, Spinoza was developing the view that 'mind' and 'body' (Spinoza's own terms are 'thought' and 'extension') are the equivalent of twin attributes of One Substance. This One Substance is Deus sive Natura (God or Nature), an energetic force that is mindful, as well as material, and connects being to being, entity to entity and source to force. The shorthand way of

understanding Spinoza is to see him as a pantheist, and despite considerable theological debate, I do not see much wrong with this. What is more interesting is the fact that from the perspective I have outlined, Spinoza is less of an aberration than he is a continuation of the idea of connection. As we have seen, the notion of energetic connection between beings seemed to be the rule rather than the exception in premodern times. A second point of interest concerns the fact that while Spinoza contributed to the Romantic movement in philosophy (after the sixteenth century all connected thinking came to be designated Romantic or irrational), Spinoza himself stressed logic as the greatest good. God is logic, and logic is connection. (47-48)

Brennan's own theory of the original logic is derived from Spinoza, as she has reiterated both in *History After Lacan* and specifically here, in her latest book, that mind and body are attributes of One Substance, which she also defines as God. What is significant for our discussion is that Brennan's theory emphasizes the synthesis between the corporeal and the spiritual and thus in this sense it intersects with the Indian philosophical theory of supramental consciousness which advocates the descent of spirituality into the body. She inscribes Spinoza's concept of One Substance as God or Nature and suggests that this energetic force is both material and mindful, and connects being to being and links everything through this energetic connection. This energetic connection is identical to the Hindu philosophical concept of Brahman which I have explored thoroughly in Chapter 3 of the book.

6. Let me recount here the interpretation of the poet and interpreter of Sri Aurobindo's work, Sri Jagadish Chandra Das' observation on canto five in his book *Lectures on Savitri*:

I shall quote the most memorable expressions from the canto three of this book five of "Book of Love":
So utter the recognition in the deeps. This is a very very important line.
When Satyavan and Savitri met in the forest, their mutual recognition was an utter recognition, and it was a recognition of the deeps within in the outside. We say that we recognize a thing. But the true recognition is a recognition by identity in the inner self of oneness within. This recognition is not a surface recognition or a false recognition camouflaged. In that true way, do we often recognize ourselves in our other selves, though we

loosely say that we recognize each other or a thing in the world
and life and cosmos of the Creator? (79)

Das explicates the fact that both the lovers recognize them from inside;
that their connection is not superficial or just mundane but it involves
their spirit.

7. It is also possible to see their relationship in the light of the Indian
philosophical theory of *Puruṣa* and *Prakṛti* that I discussed in my earlier
chapter on Tagore. In their relationship Raven is waiting for Tillotoma to
execute things; he executes the role of *Puruṣa* and Tillotoma does that of
Prakṛti—goes through many changes to do adjustment with Raven in
order to achieve earthly paradise, which I call fulfillment or *ānanda*. It
seems Tilottoma in playing the role of *Prakṛti* goes through several
vagaries. Because *Prakṛti* or nature has the right to be capricious, she
seems perfectly to play the role. But, *Prakṛti* also has the role of
manifestation of *Puruṣa* or Conscious—Force on earth. Therefore, she
goes through many changes both in her body and in her psyche which are
conducive to the manifestation to usher in fulfillment. The truth is
Puruṣa and *Prakṛti* have to work together harmoniously to obtain
fulfillment.

8. I would like to refer back here to the previous chapter on Tagore, in
which I discuss the relationship between *Puruṣa* and *Prakṛti* in great
detail. However, I must assert here that Maya is identical with *Prakṛti*.
Prakṛti literally means nature and conceptually stands for the female
energy which unlike Western psychoanalysis is rendered as a positive
energy by Indian philosophy/psychoanalysis.

9. When Nayantara was stolen by the bandits, she also had a name called
Bhagayvati. But she did not play a very significant role in that name.

Selected Bibliography

Aurobindo, Sri. *Savitri, a Legend and a Symbol.* Pondicherry, India: Sri Aurobindo International University Center, 1954.

—. *The Life Divine: Book One and Book Two Part One.* Sri Aurobindo Ashram, Pondicherry, India: All India Press, 1973 (8th Indian Printing).

—. *The Future Poetry.* Pondicherry, India. Sri Aurobindo Ashram, 1953.

Banerjee, Sumanta. *Appropriation of a Folk Heroine: Radha in Mediaeval Bengali Vaishnavite Culture.* Shimla: Indian Institute of Advanced Study, 1993.

Berg, Maggi. "Escaping the Cave: Luce Irigaray and her Feminist Critics." *Literature and Ethics.* Ed. Gary Wihl and David Williams. Kingston: McGill-Queen University Press, 1988.

Bhattacharaya, Mihir Kiran. Ed. and Trans. by Sadhakprabar Jagonmohon Tarkalankar. *Mahanirvanatantram* (Vols. 1 & 2). Regent Park, Calcutta: 174/6/1 Netaji Subhas Chandra Basu, 1962.

Bose, Girindrashekhar. "Sattva, Rajah, Tamah." *Pravasi* 30, Part 2 (1) (1930): 1-5.

Braidotti, Rosi. "The Politics of Ontological Difference." *In Between Feminism and Psychoanalysis.* Ed. By Teresa Brennan. London and New York: Routledge, 1989.

Brennan, Teresa, ed. *Between Feminism and Psychoanalysis.* London and New York: Routledge, 1989.

—. The Interpretation of the Flesh: Freud and Femininity. London and New York: Routledge, 1992.

—. *History After Lacan.* London and New York: Routledge, 1993.

—. *Exhausting Modernity, Grounds for a New Economy.* London and New York: Routledge, 2000.

Burns, Christy L. *Gestural Politics, Stereotype and Parody in Joyce.* Albany: State University of New York Press, 2000.

Butler, Judith. "Bodies that Matter." *In Bodies That Matter: On The Discursive Limits of "Sex."* New York: Routledge, 1993.

Chandidas. *Love Songs of Chandidas: The Rebel Poet-Priest of Bengal.* Trans. Deben Bhattacharya. London: George Allen and Unwin Ltd., UNESCO, 1967.

Chanter, Tina. *Ethics of Eros: Irigaray's Rewriting of the Philosophers.* New York, London: Routledge, 1995.

Chatterjee, Partha. *The Nation and Its Fragments: Colonial and Postcolonial Histories.* Princeton, New Jersey: Princeton University Press, 1993.

Cixous, Helene. Catherine Clement. *The Newly Born Woman.* Trans. Betsy Wing. Theory and History of Literature. Vol. 24. Minneapolis: University of Minnesota Press, 1986.

—. Readings: *The Poetics of Blanchot, Joyce, Kafka, Kleist, Lispector, and Tsvetayeva.* Ed. And Trans. Verena Andermatt Conley. Theory and History of Literature. Vol. 77. Minneapolis: University of Minnesota Press, 1991.

Cornell, Drucilla. *The Imaginary Domain: Abortion, Pornography and Sexual Harassment.* New York and London: Routledge, 1995.

Das, Ashmita. "Jouissance and Divinity: Reading Lawrence and Lispector through Irigaray." Diss. Bowling Green State University, 1994.

Das, J. C. *Their Songs and Whispers.* Calcutta, India: The Associated Publishing Co., 1971.

—. *Savitri, A Series of Lectures.* Calcutta, India: Associated Publishing Co., 1972.

—. "One by One I Catch the Star." Trans. Nolini Kanta Gupta. *Light of Life,* Vol. 5, Nolini Kanta Gupta Birth Centenary Edition. Shakespeare Sarani, Calcutta, India: Nolini Kanta Gupta Birth Centenary Celebrations Committee, 1989.

—. "J'attrape les etoiles." Trans. Prithwindra Mukherjee. *Anthologie de la poesie bengalie.* Paris, Noel Blandin, 1991.

Divakaruni, Chitra Banerjee. *The Mistress of Spices.* New York, London, Toronto, Sydney, Auckland: Anchor Books, Doubleday, 1997.

Doniger, Wendy and Sudhir Kakar. Introduction. *Kamasutra: A New, Complete English Translation of the Sanskrit Text.* By

Vatsayayna Mallanga. Oxford, New York: Oxford University Press, 2002. xi-lxviii.

Fitz, Earl E. *Clarice Lispector*. Boston, Massachusetts: G. K. Hall and Company, 1985.

Froula, Christine. *Modernism's Body, Sex, Culture, and Joyce*. New York: Columbia University Press, 1996.

Gallop, Jane. "Quand nos levres s'ecrivent: Irigaray's Body Politic." *Romanic Review* 74.1 (1983): 77-83.

Grosz, Elizabeth. *Jacques Lacan: A Feminist Introduction*. London and New York: Routledge, 1990.

—. *Volatile Bodies: Toward A Corporeal Feminism*. Bloomington: Indiana University Press, 1994.

Gupta, Lina. "Kali, The Saviour." *After Patriarchy: Feminist Transformations of the World Religions*. Ed. Paula M. Cooey, William R. Eakin and Jay B. McDaniel. Maryknoll, New York: Orbis Books, 1991.

Hawley, Stratton John and Donna Marie Wulff, eds. *The Divine Consort: Radha and the Goddesses of India*. Boston: Beacon Press, 1986.

Henry, Paget. *Caliban's Reason, Introducing Afro-Caribbean Philosophy*. New York: Routledge, 2000.

Hutcheon, Linda. "Circling the Downspout of Empire." Ed. Bill Ashcroft, Gareth Griffiths, and Helen Tiffin. *The Postcolonial Studies Reader*. London and New York: Routledge, 1995. 130-35.

Irigaray, Luce. *An Ethics of Sexual difference*. Trans. Carolyn Burke and Gillian C. Gill. Ithaca, New York; Cornell University Press, 1993.

—. *Speculum of the Other Woman*. Trans. Gillian C. Gill. Ithaca, New York: Cornell University Press, 1985.

—. *To Be Two*. Trans. Monique M. Rhodes and Marco F. Cocito-Monoc. New York: Routledge, 2001.

—. *Marine Lover of Friedrich Nietzsche*. Trans. Gillian C. Gill. New York: Columbia University Press, 1991.

—. "Divine Women." Trans. Gillian C. Gill. *Sexes and Genealogies*. New York: Columbia University Press, 1993.

—. *Between East and West, from Singularity to Community*. Trans. Stephen Pluhacek. New York: Columbia University Press, 2002.

Jagadishwarananda, Swami, ed. and trans. *Gita.* Calcutta: The Indian Press, 1985.

Jardine, Alice A. *Gynesis: Configurations of Woman and Modernity.* Ithaca and London: Cornell University Press, 1985.

Joyce, James. *A Portrait of the Artist as a Young Man.* New York: Signet Classic, 1919.

Kakar, Sudhir. *The Inner World: A Psycho-analytic Study of Childhood and Society in India.* Delhi, Oxford, New York: Oxford University Press, 1978.

Kinsley, David. *Tantric Visions of the Divine Feminine: The Ten Mahavidyas.* Berkley, Los Angeles, London: University of California Press, 1997.

Kishwar, Madhu and Ruth Vanita, eds. *In Search of Answers: Indian Women's Voices From Manushi.* Totowa: Biblio Distribution Center, 1984.

Lispector, Clarice. *The Stream of Life.* Trans. Elizabeth Lowe and Earl Fitz. Minneapolis: University of Minnesota Press, 1989.

—. *The Passion According to G. H.* Trans. Ronald W. Sousa. Minneapolis: University of Minnesota Press, 1988.

—. *An Apprenticeship or The Book of Delights.* Trans. Richard A Mazzara and Lorri A. Parris. Austin: University of Texas Press, 1986.

Lyotard, Jean-Francois. *The Postmodern Condition: A Report on Knowledge.* Trans. G. Bennington and Brian Massumi. *Theory and History of Literature,* Vol. 10. Minneapolis: University of Minnesota Press, 1979.

Matisons, Renee Michelle. "Feminist Philosophy of the Body." *The European Journal of Women's Studies,* Vol. 5, 1998.

Miller, Barbara Stoller, ed. and trans. *Love Songs of the Dark Lord: Jayadeva's Gitagovinda.* New York: Columbia University Press, 1977.

Mukherjee, Bharati. *The Middleman and Other Stories.* New York: Ballantine Books, 1988.

Nandy, Ashis. *The Savage Freud and Other Essays on Possible and Retrievable Selves.* Princeton, New Jersey: Princeton University Press, 1995.

Nasreen, Taslima. *Nirbachita Kalam* (Selected Columns). Calcutta: Ananda Publishers Private Limited, 1992.

Panikkar, K. M. Introduction. *Kamasutra*. By Vatsayana. Trans. Sir Richard Burton and F. F. Arbuthnot. Ed. W. G. Archer. Berkley: G. P. Putnam's Sons Inc., 1966. xxi.

Peixoto, Marta. *Passionate Fictions: Gender, Narrative, and Violence in Clarice Lispector.* Minneapolis, London: University of Minnesota Press, 1994.

Prigogine, Ilya, and Isabelle Stengers. *Order out of Chaos: Man's New Dialogue with Nature.* Toronto, New York, London, Sydney: Bantam Books, 1984.

Radhakrishnan, Sarvepalli, and Charles A. Moore, ed. *A Source Book in Indian Philosophy.* Princeton, New Jersey: Princeton University Press, 1957.

Roer, E. *The Twelve Principal Upanishads: Texts in Devanagari; and Translation with Notes in English from the Commentaries of Shankaracharaya and the Gloss of Anandagiri.* Delhi, India: Nag Publishers, 1979.

Rose, Jacqueline and Juliet Mitchell. Ed. and Trans. by Jacqueline Rose. "God and the Jouissance of the Woman." *Feminine Sexuality.* New York, London: W. W. Norton and Pantheon Books, 1985.

Roy, Dilip Kumar. "Sri Aurobindo as an Aesthete." *Sri Aurobindo Mandir Annual.* No. 54 (1995): 92-99.

Satprem. *Sri Aurobindo or The Adventure of Consciousness.* Trans. Tehmi. Pondicherry: Sri Aurobindo Ashram, 1968, 1970.

—. *The Mind of the Cells.* Trans. Jennifer Lou and Michel Danino. Auroville, India: Auroville Press, 1999.

Scholes, Robert, and Richard M. Kain, eds. *The Workshop of Daedalus: James Joyce and the Raw Materials for a Portrait of the Artist as a Young Man.* Evanston, IL.: Prentice-Hall, 1968.

Schor, Naomi. "This Essentialism Which is Not One: Coming to Grips With Irigaray." *Differences: A Journal of Feminist Cultural Studies.* Vol. 1, No. 2 (Summer 1989): 38-58.

—. "French Feminism Is a Universalism." *Differences: A Journal of Feminist Cultural Studies.* 7.1 (Spring 1995): 15-47.

Scott, Joan Wallach. *Gender and the Politics of History.* New York: Columbia University Press, 1988.

Sen, Atulchandra, Sitanath Tattawabhusan and Mahendra Chandra Ghosh, Eds. *Upanishads.* Calcutta: Haraf Prakasani, 1972.

Spivak, Gayatri Chakravorty. *In Other Worlds: Essays in Cultural Politics*. New York and London: Routledge, 1988.

—. *A Critique of Postcolonial Reason, Toward a History of the Vanishing Present.* Cambridge, Massachusetts, London, England: Harvard University Press, 1999.

Tagore, Rabindranath. *The King of the Dark Chamber.* New York: The Macmillan Company, 1916.

—. *Rabindrarachanabali, Song* Vol. 4. Ed. Sri Rabindrakumar Dasgupta, et al. Calcutta: Saraswati, 1987.

Vatsayana. *The Kamasutra.* Trans. Sir Richard Burton and F. F. Arbuthnot. Ed. W. G. Archer. Berkley: G. P. Putnam's Sons Inc., 1966.

Vidyapati. *Love Songs of Vidyapati.* Trans. Deben Bhattacharaya. Ed. W. G. Archer. London: George Allen and Unwin Ltd., UNESCO, 1963.

Whitford, Margaret, ed. *The Irigaray Reader.* Cambridge, Massachusetts: Basil Blackwell Inc., 1991.

—. *Luce Irigaray : Philosophy in the Feminine.* London and New York: Routledge, 1991.

—. "Rereading Irigaray" in *Between Feminism and Psychoanalysis.* Ed. Teresa Brennan. London and New York: Routledge, 1989.

Wulff, Donna Marie. "Radha: Consort and Conqueror of Krishna." *Devi and the Goddesses of India.* Ed. Stratton John Hawley and Donna Marie Wulff. Berkley: University of California Press, 1996.

Index

About the Author

The author is a Visiting Scholar of The Pembroke Center for Study and Research on Women at Brown University. She also teaches writing and literature courses at the University of Massachusetts, Lowell. Prior to that she taught at Bowling Green State University, Bentley College, and Algonquin (Ottawa, Canada) College. She is a scholar in feminist postcolonial theory, psychoanalysis, and twentieth century literature. She presented many papers on Luce Irigaray's theory of jouissance in International conferences in the USA, Canada, and Calcutta, India. Two of her articles on the cross-cultural analysis of Irigaray's theory of jouissance are forthcoming in the *Calcutta University English Department Journal* and in the *South Asian Review* (University of Pittsburgh at Johnstown, PA) in 2003. She obtained her Ph.D. in English literature from Bowling Green State University in 1994. She lives in Lexington, Massachusetts with her family.